CYPRUS

CYPRUS

THE IMPACT OF

DIVERSE NATIONALISM ON A STATE

Halil Ibrahim Salih

The University of Alabama Press
University, Alabama

To
my wife, Sharon
and my son, David Kerim
and daughter, Julie Shermin

Library of Congress Cataloging in Publication Data

Salih, Halil Ibrahim.
    Cyprus, the impact of diverse nationalism on a
State.

        Bibliography: p.
        Includes index.
        1. Cyprus—History.   I.   Title.
DS54.5.S24   956.4'5   76-21743
ISBN 0-8173-5706-8

CONTENTS

ACKNOWLEDGMENTS

It is impossible to list all those who have given me their time, attention, and valuable information to make this book possible. I cannot list all the authors whose books and articles have added to my understanding of the contemporary political affairs of Cyprus and their effects on international institutions.

I am particularly indebted to Dr. Neçdet Ünel, President of the House of Representatives of the Turkish Cypriot Administration, who unhesitatingly gave me his time, comments, and assisted me in every possible way in obtaining primary sources and interviews with all the important Turkish Cypriot leaders. Zafer Ali Zihni, Director of the Turkish Cypriot Information Office in Nicosia, was generous with his assistance in supplying me with information that has been invaluable for my research. I wish to express my gratitude to the following people for granting me interviews as well as extending their warm hospitality: Dr. Fazıl Küçük, former Vice-President of Cyprus; Rauf R. Denktaş, Vice-President of Cyprus and President of the Turkish Cypriot Federal States; Osman Örek, Vice-President and Minister of Defense; Asaf İnhan, Ambassador of Turkey to Cyprus. They made helpful suggestions on both historical and contemporary details. A special thanks goes to Mr. Denktaş for arranging an interview for me with his esteemed colleague Glafkos Clerides, President of the House of Representatives.

Dr. Lyle Williams, Professor of History, and Dr. Carl G. Schrader and Karen S. Perkins, Professors of English, read parts of the manuscript, made constructive criticism, and helped put the book in its final shape. Sally Lunday's technical skill was matched by a fine typing of the manuscript with great speed and enthusiasm. I also acknowledge with gratitude the grants that made possible my visits to Cyprus and the secretarial help that I received from the Brown Memorial Trust, T. J. Brown and C. A. Lupton Foundation, Inc., of Fort Worth at Texas Wesleyan College. I also am indebted to the library staff of Texas Wesleyan College for their willing and tireless assistance in locating documents, periodicals, articles, and books.

All those who helped me make this book possible share in its credit, although any errors of fact and inaccuracies of judgment are mine.

March, 1978   HALIL IBRAHIM SALIH

PREFACE

This study of the complex current Cypriot crisis is intended for the layman as well as the scholar who is perplexed by the Cypriot political issues of recent years. The research material was compiled after many years of investigation into the causes and effects of the Cypriot communal conflict. The sources for this work are personal interviews with leaders of both communities in Cyprus, as well as books dealing with political science and the Cypriot question. My information is based not only on scholarly research but also on social and political contacts with both communities on the island. I was born in Cyprus and am a Turkish Cypriot who is now an American citizen; my background has been an asset as well as a liability because I tend to sympathize more with the Turkish Cypriot cause—family members and friends still live on the island and were affected by the recent events. I was fortunate to have been born in the small town of Kyrenia, which was an integrated community, and I had and still have connections with many Greek Cypriots whose friendship I cherish and value. I have attempted to the utmost of my ability to do justice to the subject by remaining as objective as is humanly possible.

After recent visits to the island of Cyprus, I have reached the conclusion, based on empirical evidence, that the two Cypriot communities cannot co-exist under the constitutional system, as it existed from 1960 to 1963, because of the nationalism of the two ethnic communities and their unwillingness to compromise their legal differences under the governmental structure established under the Zurich and London Agreements of 1959. The two communities seem to have coexisted in harmony and mutual respect as long as the political control remained with a more powerful third force, Great Britain, who administered Cyprus from 1878 to 1960, and the situation did not provide any opportunity to compete for political power. However, as soon as there was a change in the political climate, the veneer of peace and tranquility came under a great stress. The tensions and antagonisms that had remained dormant for so long finally shattered the peace in December, 1963.

The escalation of the civil war between the two ethnic groups was checked by the intervention of Great Britain, Greece, and Turkey at the invitation of the president and vice-president of Cyprus. In 1964 and 1967 Turkey took unilateral military action and carried out air bombardments against the Greek positions that were endangering the Turkish Cypriot enclaves. It was during this time that war between Greece and Turkey was imminent. Fortunately, reason prevailed and the two countries once again resorted to diplomatic talks to work out an amicable solution to the Cypriot crisis. After the coup d'état in 1974, President Makarios was ousted from power and forced to escape to Western Europe. Turkey, justifying its action under the treaty commitments, intervened in Cyprus with a military force to prevent the rebels from declaring the union of Cyprus with Greece. The invasion of Cyprus by Turkey has created a permanent separation of the two ethnic groups and placed them under their own autonomous jurisdictions.

Since 1968, the two ethnic communities of the island, along with Greece and Turkey, have been carrying on private diplomatic talks. The talks collapsed during the war in 1974 but were resumed following the ceasefire. Tension has been eased between the two communities by the talks, but as yet no solution has been forthcoming. The United Nations peace force has been actively keeping the peace on the island, and its role has been significant. It is hoped that the United Nations peace force will continue to be present in the area until a political solution to the islanders' problems is reached.

On Cyprus, there now exists a separate authority for each ethnic community; they have been administering the affairs of the two communities independently since 1964. *Enosis** (union of Cyprus with Greece), as endorsed by the Greek Orthodox Church in union with General Grivas sympathizers (known as EOKA-B) or a unitary system under the Greek Cypriot domination, is vehemently rejected by the Turkish Cypriots. The solution for the Cypriot political dilemma will be either double union (partition of Cyprus between Greece and Turkey) or autonomy for each community in its domestic political affairs while a unified policy is maintained in external matters. It is my conviction that under a new constitution, with representation in government allocated to each of the two ethnic communities in accordance with the proportion of its population on the island, with the consensus of the Greek and Turkish Cypriot leaders, the harmony, peace, and totality of Cyprus can once again be attained.

---

*Enosis will be rendered enosis hereinafter for clarity and simplicity. For the same reason, *enosists* will be rendered enosists.

CYPRUS

CYPRUS

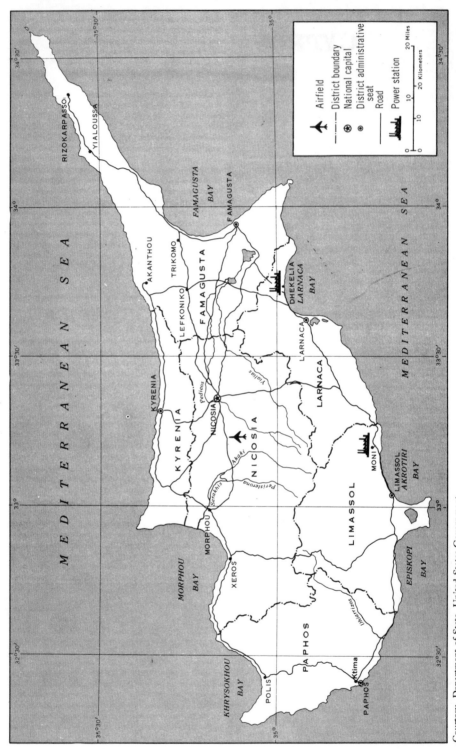

Courtesy, Department of State, United States Government

1 HISTORICAL BACKGROUND

Cyprus is an island located in the northeastern corner of the Mediterranean Sea 40 miles south of Turkey, 60 miles west of Syria and Lebanon, 240 miles north of Egypt, and about 500 miles from the Greek mainland. It is the third largest island in the Mediterranean Sea after Sicily and Sardinia, with an area of 3,572 square miles. It is 140 miles long from east to west and about 40 miles wide from north to south. The total population of the island at the end of 1971 was estimated to be 640,000, of which 78 percent were Greek Cypriots and 18 percent were Turkish Cypriots; the remaining 4 percent belonged to various minority groups.[1]

Greek Cypriots are descendants of the early Greek colonists. The original settlers on Cyprus were the Mycenean Greeks, who migrated during the period of 1400 to 1200 B.C. and introduced the Hellenic culture.[2] They were followed by the Phoenicians, who had come to the island from the coastal regions of Syria, and the Achaean colonists from the Greek mainland. The Greek colonists on the island came from the south coast of Asia Minor and Aegean Islands. Phoenicians settled on Cyprus about 1000 B.C. The first Greek population spoke an Arcado-Dorian dialect of Greek, which later merged with the Hellenic Koine, the present dialect of the island. Today, the Greek language and the Christian Orthodox religion are the major factors that identify the Greek Cypriots with the rest of the Hellenic world.

Turkish Cypriots are Sunni Muslims of the Hanafi sect. The original Turkish Cypriot settlers were principally drawn from the Lâla Mustafa Pasha's soldiers, thirty thousand of whom were given fiefs on the island by Sultan Selim II. Turkish Cypriots have a strong cultural, historical, and nationalistic attachment to Turkey.

Most of the rulers of Cyprus have left their mark on its long and fascinating history. However, this study is primarily concerned with the contemporary political developments during the late nineteenth and the twentieth centuries. The early history of Cyprus will not be discussed, because there is an adequate number of scholarly books on the subject.[3] More justice can be done to the subject matter if we concentrate entirely on the political problems the Cypriots have been facing since the independence of Cyprus on August 16, 1960. Even though this is not a historical study, mention will be made concerning the last three colonizers of the island.

The Venetians appropriated Cyprus from the Lusignan dynasty on February 26, 1489, because of its importance for the trade routes in the eastern

Mediterranean sea. Occupation of Cyprus by the Venetians marks their last expansion in the Levant. Venetian rule was military and oppressive in its restriction on personal liberties of the citizens of Cyprus. The Greek Orthodox Church of Cyprus was under the bondage of the Latin Church until the Ottoman Conquest in 1571. The domination of the Latin Church increased the political unrest of the Greek Cypriots. In addition, the Venetians neglected the development of the island's economy. Under their rule the island fell into rapid decline economically, financially, and culturally. The main objectives of the Venetians were the collection of revenues and the building of stronger fortifications in the major towns against a possible Turkish invasion. The Venetians' prosperity and their maritime trade began to decrease with the discovery of the trade route to India around the Cape of Good Hope. The discovery of gunpowder in the fourteenth century rendered the Venetian castle defenses useless against the new artillery.

When the Ottomans conquered Egypt in 1517 from the Mamluks, Cyprus continued under Venetian rule. The Ottoman sultan wished to be paid tribute by the Venetians as they had done to the Mamluks and the Arabs, so that he might continue supplying Mecca and Medina with revenues. In 1570, the Porte formally demanded the cession of Cyprus from the Venetians in return for commercial privileges, but when the Venetians refused, preparation for war was ordered. Fifth Vezir Lâla Mustafa Paşha led the Ottoman force of 350 galleys, 50,000 men, 2,500 horses, thirty heavy artillery pieces, and fifty small cannons for the conquest of Cyprus. After the occupation of Cyprus in 1571, the administration of the island was linked to the nearby Anatolian districts of Alaiyye and Selifke, as a single province.

The Ottoman sultan, Selim II, conquered Cyprus in order to safeguard his political and territorial interests in the Levant and at the same time to insure his supply of the Cypriot wine. It should also be mentioned that the Ottomans were annoyed by the Venetian harassment of Turkish ships and the use of Cyprus's harbors by the Maltese corsairs who raided and molested the Muslim ships in the Mediterranean. The Maltese were given sanctuary in Cyprus by the Venetians. The Turks administered the island until they were forced to agree to cede it to Great Britain at the Congress of Berlin in 1878, with the understanding that Great Britain would come to Turkey's assistance in case of aggression from Russia.

Great Britain, under Premier Benjamin Disraeli in 1874, was very concerned about the Russian imperialist expansion in the Balkans, as well as the safeguarding of the routes to her empire in Asia. Premier Disraeli wanted to help Abdul Hamid II, the "sick man of Europe," solve the political problems of his empire and at the same time play the role of a balancer to prevent the Russian encroachment in the Middle East and protect the route to India. Unable to cope with the internal political crisis of his empire as well as external pressure of the big powers, and having no other alternative, the sultan concluded a pact with Great Britain on June 4, 1878, known as the Cyprus Convention.[4] Under this convention, Great Britain was to help the sultan defend his empire in Asia against Russian expansion. By July 12, 1878, Great Britain was in full possession of the island, and on July 22, Sir Garnet Wolseley was sworn in as high commissioner and commander-in-chief of Cyprus. The two governments, under the convention, had also agreed that if Russia restored Kars and other conquests made by it in Armenia during the Russo-Turkish war of 1877 to the Ottoman Empire, Cyprus would be evacuated by Great Britain and the convention annulled.[5]

The Greek Cypriots, who composed the majority of the population of Cyprus, welcomed the British rule and expressed their desire for enosis. Ever since Greece had gained its freedom from the Ottomans in 1830, the Greek Cypriots had been eager for Cyprus to become a part of "Mother Hellas." In 1878, the first British high commissioner, Sir Garnet Wolseley, was greeted by the bishop of Citium with the following: "We accept the change of Government inasmuch as we trust that Great Britain will help Cyprus, as it did the Ionian Islands, to be united with Mother Greece, with which it is naturally connected."[6] The Greek Orthodox Church in Cyprus acted as the spokesman for enosis, Panhellenism, or the Megali Idea, which was the Greek dream of reconstructing the Byzantine Empire under the rule of Greece, following the Greek revolt against the Turks in 1821, and the church is still the champion of the Greek Cypriot cause.

The Turkish Cypriots were opposed to the enosists' ideas and informed the British administrators on the island that if Great Britain had any intentions of leaving the island, it should be given back to Turkey. The mufti—the high religious leader or he who gives legal decisions (*fatwâ*)—of Cyprus, Ali Rifki, in the following supplication made the Turkish Cypriot desires known to the British administration: "In case of it being necessary by the illustrious British Government to abandon the Island, we all pray and solicit, in the name of justice that . . . the Island may be restored to our august sovereign, our illustrious Caliph and Monarch, the ever-lasting Ottoman Empire."[7]

The division of the Greek and Turkish Cypriot into separate communities prevented the formation of an institution within which they could lay the foundation of a cohesive national consciousness. The political polarization of Cyprus made any future cooperation in self-government extremely difficult. The British administration did not stress national integration because the development of national loyalties by all Cypriots would have been a threat to its political authority. The outsiders expected the long-entrenched political traditions of the Greek and Turkish Cypriots to be overcome once the island was given its independence. After Cypriot independence—as before—the two communities' elites, instead of emphasizing national integration, encouraged loyalties to Greece and Turkey, which created new problems of integration. The failure of the two communities to integrate, which will probably continue in the immediate future, will force one of the outside powers to absorb Cyprus and its population as part of its territory or the two communities to separate on a permanent basis.

In November, 1914, due to the outbreak of war between Great Britain and Turkey, Cyprus was annexed to the British dominions and the Cyprus Convention of 1878 was annulled. In 1915, Great Britain offered to cede Cyprus to Greece on the condition that Greece would enter the war on the side of Serbia against Bulgaria. Because she was unprepared for war, Greece chose to remain neutral and the offer was retracted.[8] Through the Sykes-Picot Agreement of 1916, France was given a voice in the future of Cyprus. Article 4 of the Franco-British Convention of December 23, 1920, provides: "In virtue of the geographic and strategic position of the island of Cyprus, off the Gulf of Alexandretta, the British Government agree not to open any negotiations for the cession or alienation of the said island of Cyprus without the previous consent of the French Government."[9]

On July 24, 1923, Great Britain officially annexed Cyprus after the signing of the Treaty of Peace at Lausanne. Concerning Cyprus, the treaty stated:

Article 16
Turkey hereby renounces all rights and title whatsoever over or respecting the territories situated outside the frontiers laid down in the present Treaty and the islands other than those over which her sovereignty is recognized by the said Treaty, the future of these territories and islands being settled or to be settled by the parties concerned. The provisions of the present Article do not prejudice any special arrangements arising from neighbourly relations which have been or may be concluded between Turkey and any limitrophe countries.

Article 20
Turkey hereby recognizes the annexation of Cyprus proclaimed by the British Government on the 5th November, 1914.[10]

Cyprus was proclaimed a crown colony on March 10, 1925, and the high commissioner, who was the chief British administrator on the island, was to be called governor. The British government's interest in the island was military, in relation to its operations in the Middle East, especially to protect her oil interest in that area and the Suez Canal.

The British national interest was diametrically opposed to the political aspirations of the Greek Cypriots. Even though Greece had recognized the British sovereignty over Cyprus, the Greek Cypriot agitation for enosis had persisted. When the Labour party took control of the Parliament in 1929, the Greek Cypriot delegation headed by the bishop of Citium was sent to London to renew its plea for enosis. In the message to the colonial secretary in London, the Greek Cypriot pointed out: the "complaint of the Greek people of Cyprus is that . . . they are being kept separated from their Mother country, Greece, with whom sacred and unbreakable ties of blood, religion, language, traditions, and national conscience link them together."[11] The members of the Greek Cypriot delegation in London were disappointed when they were told that they needed fewer political debates and more constructive developments.

The Turkish Cypriots continued to actively oppose enosis and informed London that they wished to stay under British colonial rule or have the island returned to Turkey. The Kemalist government in Ankara was interested in the future of Cyprus, but it was too preoccupied with its own internal economic and political affairs. Ankara was confident of the continued British rule over Cyprus, and it did not wish to jeopardize the Greco-Turkish friendship bonded by the leaders of Greece and Turkey, Eleftherios Venizelos and Gazi Mustafa Kemal Pasha Atatürk.

In October, 1931, an uprising was instigated by the Greek Cypriot Church leaders on behalf of enosis. The Greek Cypriot rioters were successful in reaching the governor's mansion, which they burned down. The demonstration left six dead and about fifty wounded. The leaders of the rioters, Nocodemos, bishop of Citium, and the bishop of Kyrenia, together with some Legislative Council members and other ringleaders, were deported from Cyprus. Thereafter, the British administrators took steps to prevent a repetition of similar incidents; they promoted a decentralized form of government for the island, severely limited civil liberties, and passed laws aimed at curbing the enosis movement.

After World War II, the Greek Cypriots renewed their drive for enosis, but the Labour party in London was in no position to honor their wishes because the island, thanks to its strategic location in the Mediterranean, had played an invaluable role for the army, air force, and navy of Great Britain during the war against the Axis powers. Greece, being in a weak position economically, financially, and militarily and wishing not to antagonize the British, who were helping the Greek people in their struggle for a livelihood and independence, did not endorse the enosis movement. The British government was not only helping Greece economically and militarily, but at the same time it was the sole power trying to contain communist expansion. Great Britain, unable to continue its military and economic assistance to Greece, in February, 1947, asked the United States to aid the Greek people. On March 12, President Truman received from Congress $400 million to help Greece and Turkey preserve their independence from totalitarianism. The willingness of the United States to assist the Greek and Turkish people was based on the American conviction that communism should not be allowed to spread into the eastern Mediterranean. This generous aid allowed Greece and Turkey to develop their economies and defenses, successfully blocking the Soviet encroachment into their territories. In 1951 both nations were admitted to NATO, which strengthened the containment of the communist nations by the Western allies.

At the time of the British withdrawal from Palestine in May, 1948, London, aware of growing Arab nationalist demands for independence in the

Middle East, offered to the Cypriots the Winster Constitution. The Winster Constitution of 1948, which provided more autonomy, was rejected by the Greek Cypriots on the recommendation of the Greek Orthodox Church leaders because the British plan might have closed the enosis question. The church conducted an open plebiscite on January 15, 1950, to let the Greek Cypriots make their opinion known to the world by means of the ballot box. Of the Greek Cypriot community over eighteen years of age, 95.7 percent was declared to have voted for enosis. The enosists' movement was strengthened by the election of Michael Mouskos, the bishop of Citium, as Archbishop Makarios III on October 18. On February 11, 1951, the Greek government took a more active part in the enosis movement by making it an official national policy. In November, 1951, the Greek government raised the Cyprus question in the Trusteeship Committee of the United Nations. The archbishop of Cyprus in a letter to the secretary general of the United Nations, Dag Hammarskjold, on August 10, 1953, wrote: "An open unimpeachable plebiscite was held on January 15, 1950, the result of which was that 95.7 per cent of the Greek inhabitants or 80 percent of the whole population of Cyprus by their vote expressed their determination to be incorporated into the Greek state by the organic union of this island with its Mother-country Greece."[12]

In 1951, Archbishop Makarios III came in contact with Colonel Georgios Grivas, who was then a retired army officer in Athens, and the two men's association culminated in the organization of the guerrilla war against British colonial rule on Cyprus. In 1952, Makarios secured the support of Field Marshal Alexander Papagos, who had won the premiership of Greece in the November elections, to place the issue of enosis before the United Nations. At the United Nations the Cyprus issue was shelved after a persuasive argument by the British representative that it was an internal affair and that it was up to the Parliament in London to determine policy matters. The first official approach by Greece to Great Britain for enosis was made in the fall of 1953 by Prime Minister Papagos during the visit of Foreign Secretary Anthony Eden to Athens. The British refusal to discuss the matter forced Greece to submit the Cyprus question to the United Nations General Assembly in September, 1954. Great Britain refused enosis because London needed Turkey's support of its policies in the Middle East. Former Prime Minister Anthony Eden (Earl of Avon) in his book *Full Circle* wrote: "I regarded our alliance with Turkey as the first consideration in our policies in that part of the World."[13]

In the same book, Eden wrote: "The Cyprus dispute could never be settled until the importance of the Turkish position was understood and accepted. This meant that Enosis must be ruled out as a solution."[14]

The Greek resolution asking for self-determination for Cyprus was once again shelved by the United Nations General Assembly's Political Committee. The failure of political attempts to solve the problem in the world body left the Greek Cypriots with no alternative but to resort to armed warfare.

The Turkish government representatives at the United Nations actively gathered opposition to the Greek resolution and fully cooperated with the British scheme to shelve the Cypriot issue. Turkey was opposed to self-determination because the result would have been enosis. They also emphasized the importance of the island to Turkey:

> Turkey is primarily concerned with the status of this island because of racial, historical, and contractual reasons. . . . such course of action . . . could lead to serious consequences. . . . [In the] "Question of Cyprus," nothing can be deemed to be based on justice and equity unless the cooperation and consent of Turkey is unequivocally obtained; for, otherwise, . . . no decision can be lasting. . . . Cyprus is important for the defense of Southern Turkey and of the Northern Mediterranean in general.[15]

Turkey had always been interested in Cyprus but was not as active as Greece in drawing world attention to it. Ankara was also of the opinion that Great Britain would be resolute in its determination to stay on the island.[16]

The Greek Cypriots, under the leadership of Archbishop Makarios, formed the National Organization of Cypriot Fighters or Ethniki Orgánosis Kipriakoú Agónos (EOKA). The military operation of EOKA was to be under the direction of Colonel Grivas, who was a Cypriot by birth but a Greek citizen, while the supreme leader of the whole operation was Makarios. The Greek government gave its blessing to the guerrilla operation, supplying it with money and weapons. The planning of the organized violence was done in Athens on July 2, 1952, but Grivas as early as July 5, 1951, was paying visits to Cyprus to draw up his plans for the guerrilla operations. When the British became suspicious of the activities of Grivas, he was declared a persona non grata, but he was smuggled back into the island on November 10, 1954. In the summer of 1954, Athens Radio became the mouthpiece of national liberation. Until the capture of a Greek caique on January 25, 1955, by a British patrol boat near Paphos, London did not show too much concern over the rumors that arms were being smuggled into the island. On board this captured caique were arms and ammunition destined for delivery to EOKA. The underground struggle of EOKA, which started on April 1, 1955, was to continue until 1959.

The Turkish Cypriots were opposed to the EOKA operations and joined British law-enforcing operations in attempts to crush the guerrilla movement. At first, the objective of EOKA was to leave the Turkish Cypriots alone and to concentrate on the British; however, when the Turkish Cypriots joined hands with the British in hunting down the guerrillas, they also became targets. The Turkish Cypriots created their own underground organization, known as VOLKAN ("volcano"); and later it changed its name to Türk Müdafaa Teşkilatı ("Turkish Resistance Organization") or TMT. TMT was able to organize a united front against the EOKA forces, but it never did become as organized or as disciplined as the groups under Grivas.

The TMT members did undergo some military training in Turkey, and money and arms were also supplied by the Turkish government. Under the leadership of Dr. Fazıl Küçük, the Cypriot Turkish party was organized all over the island and among the Turkish Cypriots on the mainland. The conflict on the island was no longer between the British colonial government and the Cypriots but had shifted to a confrontation of the two major ethnic groups.

In order to ease the tension on the island and prevent the Cyprus issue from giving rise to an international crisis, Sir Anthony Eden invited Greece and Turkey to a tripartite conference, which opened on August 29, 1955. At the conference, Great Britain offered a constitution for limited self-government, which Greece opposed. The Macmillan constitutional plan denied Greeks self-determination and ruled out the end of British sovereignty in Cyprus. In London, Turkey expressed the opinion that if any change were to be made in respect to the sovereignty of Cyprus, it should be returned to Turkey. Turkey was partial to the proposal for self-government based on proportional representation of the two major ethnic groups on the island if Greece would drop its demand for self-determination. With the breakdown of the London Conference, the violence in Cyprus intensified and the diplomatic relations between Greece and Turkey continued to deteriorate rapidly.

While the diplomats of the three nations were attempting to reach some kind of an agreement pertaining to Cyprus, a bomb exploded at the Turkish consulate in Salonika, Greece, damaging the house in which the founder of the Turkish Republic, Mustafa Kemal Atatürk, was born. This deplorable incident outraged the Turkish citizens and gave the extremist elements in the major cities a reason to rampage in widespread anti-Greek riots, wrecking millions of dollars' worth of goods and property. This emotionalism on the part of the extremists went unchecked by the Turkish government, and during the trials of the deposed President Celal Bayar, Prime Minister Adnan Menderes, and Foreign Minister Fatin R. Zorlu in 1960, they were all accused of abdicating their responsibility.[17]

When no settlement could be reached at the London Conference satisfactory to Greece, the Cyprus issue was taken to the United Nations and a request was made that the Cypriot question be placed on the agenda of the Tenth Session of the General Assembly. The British delegate argued against the Greek action and informed the members of the assembly that Great Britain was diligently trying to reach a political agreement with the interested parties to the Cyprus question. Thus, the British again succeeded in blocking United Nations action on the issue.

With the breakdown of the London talks, Great Britain appointed Field Marshal Sir John Harding, on September 25, 1955, as governor of Cyprus. Governor Harding began talks with Makarios and once again offered self-government, which was rejected. The archbishop in turn presented the governor with his own plans, which were unacceptable. After all means to reach an agreement were exhausted, on November 26 a state of emergency was declared. On December 14 the communist party, Anorthotikon Komma Ergazomenou Laou ("Progressive Party of the Working People"), or AKEL, was outlawed and its leaders arrested. EOKA was also banned and a price was put on the head of Grivas, whose assumed name was Dighenis.

When the political proposals and counterproposals between Harding and Makarios failed to produce an agreement, Makarios, the bishop of Kyrenia, Kyprianos, his secretary, and a priest were exiled on March 9, 1956, to the Seychelles Islands in the Indian Ocean. Makarios was deported after strong evidence of his connection with the terrorist activities of EOKA was uncovered. The Greek Cypriots were enraged by the British action toward their spiritual leader and became more dedicated to the fight for their cause. Harding, hoping to deter the terrorist elements and their sympathizers, announced that he would use all means available to him to bring law and order.

While Governor Harding was given the sword, the authority to use all the military potential of Great Britain to crush the violators of his harsh laws, London was resorting to the pen to formulate a constitution for the Cypriots. On July 12, 1956, Lord Cyril John Radcliffe Radcliffe, a noted jurist, was appointed to formulate a liberal constitution while safeguarding the British base rights on the island. The constitution recognized self-government and the principles of proportional representation for the Greek and Turkish Cypriot communities at all institutional levels. The Greeks rejected the plan because it failed to specify the date for self-determination, while the Turks were favorable to it and considered it a viable basis for negotiation.[18]

King Paul of Greece appointed Constantine Karamanlis in 1956 to the office of prime minister, which was vacant due to the death of Papagos. Along with premiership, Karamanlis inherited the Cyprus puzzle, for which there was no apparent solution. His government pursued the Cyprus affair at the Eleventh Session of General Assembly of the United Nations. Greece once again pressed the world body to support its cause and bring diplomatic pressure on Great Britain to apply the principle of self-determination to Cyprus. To the disappointment of the Greek delegation, the General Assembly by-passed the issue without any strong commitment and adopted a resolution stating that all the interested parties in the Cyprus question should resort to negotiations. On December 19, the British colonial secretary, Lennox-Boyd, and the foreign minister of Greece, Averoff-Tossizza, had both expressed the opinion that the partitioning of Cyprus between Greece and Turkey might be the only remedy. This proposal never materialized. In 1957, the Greek policy changed substantially: Averoff stated his willingness to accept the idea of an independent Cyprus as a solution to the Cypriot crisis and said that enosis was to be pursued within this political context.

Athens brought the Cyprus issue before the General Assembly of the United Nations in 1957 and 1958. In 1957 Greece not only asked for self-determination for Cyprus, but it also accused Great Britain of violating the human rights of the Greek Cypriots. The Political Committee encouraged all member nations concerned with Cyprus to negotiate further, but the resolution was not approved by the General Assembly because it failed to win two-thirds of the vote. In 1958 the Greek delegation acted once again as in previous years, and the reaction of the General Assembly was the same.

The opposing political policies of Greece and Turkey only encouraged the intercommunal strife on Cyprus, which ultimately confronted the motherlands with the question of whether they would resolve the conflict by war or find a compromise enabling the two communities to coexist in the island. As a first step in de-escalating the crisis in Cyprus, Makarios was released from the Seychelles Islands in March, 1957, and taken to Athens. The military rule of Field Marshal Harding was replaced by the civilian rule of Sir Hugh Foot on December 3, 1957. Governor Foot's first objective was to relax the tensions between the Greek and Turkish Cypriots and build confidence in his administration so that it could attain their cooperation in reaching an amicable solution acceptable to the two communities and Great Britain. Governor Foot proposed a plan for five to seven years of Cypriot self-government under the British colonial tutelage, after which period the Cypriots were to determine their political future.[19] The Turkish Cypriots rejected the plan because it did not have enough safeguards against enosis. Thereafter, Ankara, supported by Turkish Cypriots, became adamant in its demands for *Taksim* (partition). On June 19, 1958, Prime Minister Harold Macmillan proposed the Seven-Year Partnership Plan, under which the best interests of all the Cypriots, Greece, Turkey, and Great Britain would be protected. The island was to be ruled jointly by Great Britain, Greece, and Turkey for seven years without altering its international status. At the same time, Great Britain was to retain its bases and installations on the island and with the cooperation of Greece and Turkey was to strengthen peace and security in a vital area. Greece and Makarios rejected the plan as being undemocratic and considered it to be a preparation of Cyprus for partition.[20]

The crisis not only had the symptoms of a possible Cypriot civil war as hostilities increased, but Greco-Turkish relations had deteriorated almost to a point of no return. The relations of the two NATO members alarmed the organization's affiliates and hardened that organization's desire to prevent the further worsening of the situation on its southern flank. Since December, 1956, the NATO secretary general's office had been offering its services to Athens and Ankara for the peaceful settlement of the Cyprus issue. In September, 1958, NATO Secretary General Paul-Henri Spaak took a more active role and encouraged tripartite talks and offered his services for possible negotiations. Spaak submitted to the NATO Council meeting in Paris, on September 24, 1958, a plan that was similar to that of Macmillan, which had been submitted earlier. Due to the procrastination of the Greek government the Spaak proposals achieved no results.

Great Britain, in order not to jeopardize the Greek and Turkish government's rapprochement by the continued critical developments between the two Cypriot communities on the island, indicated its readiness to give up sovereignty over Cyprus. Since all the efforts of the United Nations and NATO had failed, London felt that the only alternative was to settle the Cyprus question through direct negotiations by means of bilateral talks, which started in January, 1959. Greece and Turkey valued their alliances and close military cooperation in NATO as essential for their national interest and security, and both nations wished not to upset this association. Both governments therefore agreed that a fair compromise would be better than war, and they worked out the outlines of such a compromise at Zurich after full consultation with the leaders of the Greek and Turkish Cypriot communities. London gave its blessing to this compromise, and after eighteen months of hard bargaining between the two communities with the help of their motherlands, the future of Cyprus was decided. Its independence would rest on the division of political power between the two Cypriot communities. The Greco-Turkish Agreements were reached at Zurich on February 11, 1959, between the Greek and the Turkish prime ministers, Constantine Karamanlis and Adnan Menderes.

To ratify the agreements reached concerning Cyprus, the representatives of Great Britain, Greece, Turkey, and the leaders of the two communities on Cyprus, Archbishop Makarios and Dr. Küçük, met in London. The three powers concerned about the future of Cyprus decided to give the Cypriots their independence after the settlement of the division of political power between the two ethnic groups, and they endorsed the Zurich Agreement on February 19.[21] The representatives of the participating nations made statements expressing their satisfaction with the settlement. The Zurich-London Agreements provided:

1. One year from the time of signing Cyprus would become an independent republic.
2. The new Republic of Cyprus would have a Greek Cypriot president and a Turkish Cypriot vice-president, each elected for five years from communal rolls, each having veto power over decisions of the House of Representatives concerning foreign affairs, defense, or security.
3. Both enosis and partition would be forever prohibited.
4. Britain would retain sovereignty over two areas containing British military bases.
5. One of the key ministries, Defense, Finance, or Foreign Affairs, would be held by a Turkish Cypriot.
6. The Cypriot civil service and security forces would be composed of 70 percent Greek Cypriots and 30 percent Turkish Cypriots.
7. The 2000-man army would be in the ratio of 60 percent Greek Cypriots to 40 percent Turkish Cypriots.
8. The House of Representatives, to be composed of 70 percent Greek Cypriots and 30 percent Turkish Cypriots chosen by universal suffrage from

communal rolls, would have legislative authority over all matters not reserved to the two communal chambers.

9. Two communal chambers, one for each community, would have the rights
   to impose taxes for the needs of each community and have authority in
   matters of religion, cultural affairs, education, and personal status.
10. Each of the five largest towns would be divided into Greek and Turkish
    municipalities, each of which was to have its own council.
11. A Supreme Constitutional Court composed of one Greek Cypriot, one
    Turkish Cypriot, and a foreign neutral judge, all chosen jointly by the
    president and vice-president, would rule on any conflict of authority that
    might arise between the House of Representatives and the communal
    chambers.
12. Two treaties would be considered as integral parts of the Cyprus
    constitution:
    a A Treaty of Guarantee giving Great Britain, Greece, and Turkey—the
    three protecting powers—the right to take individual or joint action in
    Cyprus to maintain its independence and constitutional integrity.
    b A Treaty of Alliance establishing a Tripartite Headquarters (Cypriot,
    Greek, and Turkish) in Cyprus; Greece was to be allowed to station 950
    men on Cyprus, Turkey 650; the president and vice-president could to-
    gether request either mainland government to increase or reduce these
    contingents.
13. The basic structure of the republic could not be altered or amended.[22]

The Greek Cypriots were not altogether satisfied with the Zurich-London
Agreements, but they decided to accept them, having been left with no other
alternative. The major opposition to the Cypriot independence came from
General Grivas, whose opinion of the agreement was evasive.[23]

One observer, in an article on the Cypriot issue, wrote: "Although certain
articles of the Zurich Agreement must appear in some respects to be inconsistent with the basic principles of national sovereignty, Archbishop Makarios obviously believed that half a loaf was better than none. Perhaps, as
many others feel, he was willing to accept what he could get at the time, to
move forward on that basis, and to regroup and renegotiate at a later, pos-
sibly more favorable time."[24]

The constitutional subdivision of Cyprus into two communities was not
really satisfactory to either (especially to the Greek Cypriots), but it seemed
to be the best alternative. Greece and Turkey have always been interested
in the island because of its location and the ethnic origins of its people. Some
Greek-American political scientists in the United States, such as Dr. Harry
J. Psomiades, are of the opinion that Makarios was under duress from the
Greek government to accept the Zurich and London Agreements. Dr. Psomiades, in an article in *Current History*, wrote:

The Cyprus settlement keenly disappointed the Greek Cypriots. Their aspirations for *enosis* had not been realized and their struggle and sacrifices for
majority rule had gone unrewarded. Anticipating the bitter reaction of the

Cypriots to the final settlement, the Zurich agreements were worked up in secrecy. It was agreed that the proposed constitution would not be subject to a plebiscite, and that the Cypriots would not be permitted to bargain for changes in the constitution that would in any way alter the political rights granted to the Turkish minority.

At the conference table at Lancaster House, Archbishop Makarios was faced with the difficult decision of accepting the Zurich and London agreements in toto and restoring peace to the island, or of rejecting them completely and subjecting his people to more war and more suffering. All the interested powers implored him to sign the agreements and avoid further bloodshed. Britain threatened him with the partition of Cyprus, and Turkey warned that she would walk out of the conference if Makarios tried to tamper with the Zurich constitution. Appeals were made to him from Athens and the Greek royal family to sign. The Greek prime minister shouted at him impatiently, "I give you Cyprus on a plate, and you refuse to take it. It's monstrous," and threatened Makarios with the withdrawal of all support if he rejected the Zurich terms. Only the Cypriots warned him that to accept them would be a betrayal of everything that he himself and the Cypriots had fought to achieve. Under pressure from all sides, Makarios capitulated and the Greek Cypriot delegation voted 27 to 8 in favor.[25]

After the London Agreement was signed, the preparations for independence commenced early in 1959. On February 22, the suspected terrorists were released from the detention camps, and five days later amnesty terms were announced for the EOKA members. On March 1, Makarios was returned to Cyprus from Athens, where he had stayed since his return from exile on March 29, 1957. Makarios, in his return speech to his people, said: "Let us not forget that freedom is not just a privilege and a right, it is also a heavy responsibility and a supreme duty. Let us hold out the honest hand of friendship and cooperation to all. Especially let us cooperate wholeheartedly and sincerely with our friends in the Turkish community."[26] Colonel Grivas, who directed the Greek Cypriot struggle against the British colonial administration for four years, was given a safe conduct to leave the island on March 17, 1959. Athens welcomed Grivas as a hero and raised his retired military rank to lieutenant general.

Since the London Agreement did not satisfy extremist enosists, the weapons of EOKA were partially returned to the government. The Turkish Cypriots, foreseeing future confrontation with their compatriots, began to stockpile arms and ammunition from Turkey, purchasing some others from the British soldiers on the island. In short, there was no cohesive effort on the part of the Cypriot populace, as the 1963 and later crises testify. The major opposition to independence came from Grivas and the bishop of Kyrenia, Kyprianos, who felt that the EOKA struggle had been betrayed by Makarios.[27]

The communist party was for independence but was opposed to the British military bases at Dhekelia and at Akrotiri.

In spite of all the political drawbacks, the plans for independence were drawn. Makarios, as the candidate of the Patriotic Front, won the presidency on December 13, 1959, against a challenger, John Clerides, the candidate of the Democratic Union, by a vote of 144,501 to 71,753. Dr. Fazıl Küçük, who ran unopposed, was elected as the vice-president by the Turkish Cypriots. The elections for the Cypriot parliament took place on July 31, 1960, giving the Patriotic Front thirty of the seats, and the remaining five seats went to the communist party, which had agreed to cooperate with Makarios. The elections for the fifteen Turkish Cypriot seats in parliament took place on August 7 and were won by the National party candidates of Dr. Küçük.

After independence on August 16, 1960, the two Cypriot communities cooperated and collaborated in many areas, but certain important constitutional questions remained unsettled. The Turkish Cypriots were opposed to any important constitutional changes that would infringe on their political rights. The Turkish Cypriots were of the opinion that the Greek Cypriot demand for constitutional changes would in effect make Cypriot independence a Greek independence that would culminate in union with Greece. The two Cypriot communities had cooperated artificially to create a state where there was no national unity to support it, a must for the formation of a lasting and stable community and representative government. The political leaders of the two communities, after the constitutional crisis of the early 1960s, would be the first to admit that they were too amateur in the dynamics of social politics and were unable to form a government that represented the community. Unfortunately, after the formation of a state, the two communal political leaders were unable to unify their efforts to overcome the major obstacles that threatened the chances of success of the Cypriot state. The Cypriot compatriots were unable to achieve: (1) the establishment of a central government over the whole island and its peoples, regardless of their ethnic or religious background; (2) the unification of all aspects of the national economy; (3) the adherence to the political rule to block separatism and ethnic antagonisms; and (4) the creation of the feeling of belongingness, common identity, loyalty and the expansion of the principle of nationhood. When these political objectives did not materialize, the prospects for the success of the Cypriot state were in doubt.

In 1963, President Makarios attempted to amend the Constitution of Cyprus by a method that was contrary to the agreed treaties at Zurich and London. The Turkish Cypriots, as well as the Turkish government in Ankara, were opposed to Makarios' constitutional plans, which are known as the thirteen-point plan. The thirteen-point plan will be analyzed more in depth later in the book. The political differences of the two communities ultimately generated physical hostilities and later civil warfare all over the island. As stated earlier, the Greek Cypriots did not look upon the 1960 London settlement as an end in itself but as a springboard for enosis; the Greek Cypriot leadership drafted a scheme called the Akritas Plan, which was a design for achieving their political ends by resort to armed force. Glaf-kos Clerides, the president of the House of Representatives, said of the plan:

> The Akritas plan was a contingency plan which had been prepared to meet a possible Turkish-Cypriot insurrection in view of information which was reaching us about Turkish-Cypriot secret importation of arms and the creation of armed groups. A similar plan was prepared by the Turkish-Cypriots, before the events of December, 1963, of which we informed the [United Nations] Security Council in 1964. The lesson to be drawn from those two contingency plans is that what we need is a solution free from the divisive provisions of the Zurich Agreements, which would provide the basis for close and sincere co-operation between the Greek and Turkish Cypriots and would be animated by the realization that differences must be resolved by sitting around a conference table and not by preparing for armed conflict.[28]

While the writer was conducting research on the island of Cyprus the Turkish Cypriot leaders expressed to him the conviction that the Greek Cypriots had resorted to armed confrontation with the intention of creating worldwide publicity for the Greek cause, and that the 1960 agreement was not just and had not settled the Cypriot question. They felt that the demand for constitutional changes was a pretext for the planned upsurge of violence.

2 THE ROOTS OF
THE CONSTITUTIONAL
CRISIS

Eighty-two years of British rule came to an end when the Cypriots were given their independence on August 16, 1960. All concerned hoped that the Zurich-London Agreements of 1959 and 1960 between Great Britain, Greece, Turkey, and the two communities of Cyprus would provide the basis for equilibrium and harmony between the Greek and Turkish Cypriot communities and at the same time preserve the national interests of the three outside powers. Some hoped that the agreement reached had finally solved the complex political issues to the satisfaction of all the Cypriots, but others believed that the settlement was precarious.

The Constitution of Cyprus had special safeguards to protect the rights of each community under a republican form of government. The Greek and Turkish Cypriot communities were to be autonomous; the Constitution included several provisions for insuring the fair participation of the estimated 80 percent of the population that was Greek and 18 percent that was Turkish in legislative and governmental functions. Under the Treaty of Guarantee, Greece, Great Britain, Turkey, and Cyprus were to respect the Constitution, independence, and territorial integrity of Cyprus. The Treaty of Alliance guaranteed the state of affairs created by the fundamental articles of the Constitution. The signers of the treaties were to consult among themselves if the treaty was violated, with a view to taking the necessary measures to assure respect for their obligation. The independence of Cyprus on the basis of these treaties was to end permanently the possibility of enosis or *Taksim*. Greece, Great Britain, and Turkey agreed "to prohibit, so far as concerns them, any activity aimed at promoting, directly or indirectly, either union of Cyprus with any other State or partition of the Island."[1] It was on the foundation of this mutual renunciation that the whole structure of the new state was erected.

After the independence of Cyprus had been achieved, the principles that were agreed upon and inserted into the Constitution could not be implemented because of the negative attitudes of the two communities. The major disagreements between the Greek and Turkish Cypriots concerned: (1) the establishment of separate municipalities in five districts as stated in Article 173, section 2; (2) the 70:30 communal ratio in the Public Service according to Article 123; (3) the income tax legislation, Article 78, section 2; (4) the integration of the Cypriot army, Article 129; (5) the separate majority right in the House of Representatives, Article 78; (6) the veto power of the vice-president, Article 50. The Turkish Cypriots were adamant in guarding their constitutional rights in order to prevent the domination of the Cypriot administration by the Greek Cypriots. They also realized that if they deviated from the provisions of the Constitution, the Greeks might take the opportunity to abrogate the agreement.

From 1958 until independence, separate Turkish Cypriot municipalities existed and were recognized as *de jure* by the British colonial administration in Cyprus. The separation of Turkish municipalities was instigated by the political antagonism between the two communities. The Greek and Turkish municipalities functioned under different laws—CAP 240 and 33/1959 respectively. Article 188, section 2, of the 1960 Cypriot Constitution extended the municipalities laws that predated independence for six more months so that the two communities could come up with a compromise acceptable to both sides. When no agreement was forthcoming, the House passed the Municipalities Law No. 10/1961, which extended the provisions of Article 188, section 2, for three additional months. The law was extended repeatedly when no agreement could be reached. The Turkish Cypriots wanted to implement Article 173 as provided in the Constitution. The Greek Cypriots were opposed to separate municipalities because they believed them to be a step toward *Taksim*.[2]

On March 19, 1962, President Makarios stated that the separation of the municipalities was difficult to implement and suggested instead the formation of a united municipal authority in each town based upon proportional representation of Greek and Turkish Cypriot population. On December 31, 1962, the Turkish Cypriots passed a law known as the Turkish Communal Chamber's Turkish Municipal Corporations Law, which legitimized the separate status of the Turkish Cypriot municipalities in the five districts.

On January 2, 1963, the Council of Ministers, under the direction of President Makarios, issued an order that put all the municipalities under The Village Administration and Improvement Law, CAP 243. The law created municipal councils, giving them all the powers and authority and replaced the Municipalities Law No. 10/1961, which expired on December 31, 1962, after having been extended eight times. The Greek Cypriots, by their voting power, controlled the Council of Ministers and pressed for the unification of Greek and Turkish Cypriot municipalities. The law that was supported by the Greek Cypriots would nullify the separate Turkish municipalities that had existed since 1958 and render ineffective Article 173 of the Constitution by giving the municipal services to an appointed body of men.

Since no agreement developed that was acceptable to both communities, the issue of the municipalities was taken to the Supreme Constitutional Court of Cyprus. The court delivered its decision on April 25, 1963, finding both the Greek Cypriot law—The Village Administration and Improvement Law, CAP 243—and the Turkish Cypriot law—Turkish Communal Chamber's Turkish Municipal Corporation Law—unconstitutional.

Each community was steadfast in its stand in respect to the municipalities. While the Greek Cypriots demanded a constitutional amendment to unify the government under majority rule, the Turkish Cypriots insisted on the full implementation of the constitutional provisions. This issue was not solved, and each community continued to have its own separate municipalities.

The Public Service of the republic was to be composed of 70 percent Greek and 30 percent Turkish Cypriots. During the early period of the republic, the Greek and Turkish Cypriot Civil Service Associations worked in close cooperation in applying the 70:30 ratio principle and made recommendations to President Makarios. The associations suggested that if any Greek or Turkish Cypriot was adversely affected by the 70:30 principle, he was to be compensated by the state. President Makarios, who had originally agreed with Vice-President Dr. Küçük to abide by the advice of the associations, considered the scheme too expensive to implement and too complicated to apply.[3]

The Greek Cypriots also argued that the Turkish Cypriots did not have

Vice-President Fazıl Küçük, President Makarios, and U.N. Secretary General Kurt Waldheim at a cocktail party in Nicosia on June 9, 1972.

enough qualified individuals to fill the 30 percent quota to which they were entitled.[4] The Turkish Cypriots claimed that they did have qualified individuals for many positions, but they also admitted that in some instances there were no qualified individuals to fill the posts reserved for them in the higher grades. The Turkish Cypriots, however, argued that this did not justify the Greek Cypriots' abrogating the 70:30 ratio and that the percentage allocated to the Turks could have been honored by assigning them to other positions. More than a hundred cases were pending hearing in the Supreme Constitutional Court before the 1963 crisis.

The personal income tax was collected by the Greek and Turkish Cypriot communal chambers from their individual communities, and in return the chambers provided such services as schools and agricultural cooperatives. Customs duties, property taxes, license fees, road taxes, and excise duties continued to be collected by the Cyprus government. Any issue that might cause a controversy between the communal chambers or the House in regard to the constitutionality of the chambers' right to tax was to be taken before the Supreme Constitutional Court. Any law or decision passed by the Cypriot communal chambers was to be signed by the president or the vice-president before becoming official. Because the income tax collected by the communal chambers was not sufficient to cover their expenses, under section 2, Article 88, of the Constitution, the communal chambers were to be assisted financially by the central government; however, this never occurred. The Greek representatives maintained that the income tax should be under the control of the central government, whereas the Turks opposed the idea and wished to follow the Constitution in order to safeguard their legal rights under the Constitution. They stated, however, that they were willing to change the income tax laws after an experimental period of three years if they proved to be an encumbrance to governmental administration. No agreement or compromise could be reached.

The two communities had different concepts with respect to the formation of an army. The national Cypriot army was to consist of 2,000 men, 60 percent Greek Cypriots and 40 percent Turkish Cypriots. On the advice of the Greek and Turkish military experts, the Turkish Cypriots refused to comply with the Greek Cypriot proposal that all units should be integrated.[5] The Turkish Cypriots made a counterproposal that the Cypriot army be mixed at the battalion level but expressed a desire for separation at the company level because of linguistic and practical religious differences. The Council of Ministers decided in favor of a completely mixed army, which Vice-President Küçük used his constitutional power to veto. The veto was used as a pretext to avoid resolving this disagreement. Osman Örek, the defense minister of Cyprus before the December, 1963, crisis, asserts that when he gave instructions to the Greek Cypriot commanders, they did not comply until approval was given by President Makarios.[6]

As a result of these differences, even though the nucleus of an army was formed, a Cypriot army never materialized. Instead, each of the two communities began organizing a secret army and arming it with weapons smuggled from Greece and Turkey. As stated earlier, the leaders of both communities on the island openly admit that they had men going through military training in Greece and Turkey, and that weapons were smuggled and hidden in planned areas all over the island.

Under the Constitution of 1960, legislative power is vested in the House of Representatives, which is elected for a period of five years and has fifty members, thirty-five Greek Cypriots and fifteen Turkish Cypriots. To alter the membership in the House of Representatives, the approval of a two-thirds majority of each of the two communities was needed in the House. The enactment of certain bills such as the Electoral Law, items relating to municipalities, and taxes required a separate simple majority of the Greek and Turkish Cypriot House members. The Greek Cypriots believed that the Turkish Cypriots were abusing the powers given to them in the House and demanded the abolition of the constitutional provisions requiring separate majorities for enactment of certain laws in the House. The Turkish Cypriots rejected the charges of their counterparts in the House and justified all their procedures.

The vice-president, always a Turkish Cypriot, has the right of final veto on council decisions and on laws or decisions of the House of Representatives concerning foreign affairs, defense, or security. Archbishop Makarios' proposal that the veto powers of the president and the vice-president be abandoned was vehemently opposed by the Turkish Cypriot community.

In the summer of 1963, President Makarios criticized the Treaty of Guarantee and challenged the right of any state to intervene unilaterally in the island. In August, he declared his intention to amend the Constitution, a course of action contrary to the agreement signed in London and to the articles of the Constitution.[7] George Papandreou, who was trying to oust Premier Karamanlis at the November elections of 1963, capitalized on the Cypriot issue and encouraged Makarios to continue with his scheme. Papandreou criticized the Cyprus agreements and promised to fight for enosis if elected. The Center Union party of George Papandreou and Sophocles Venizelos won the election, and, justifiably, the electorate expected the fulfillment of the campaign pledge in respect to Cyprus. Although Papandreou won the election, his party captured only 138 out of 300 seats in the Greek Parliament; therefore, he asked King Paul to declare new elections for February 16, 1964, so that the Center Union party could obtain a greater mandate. King Paul favored the formation of a coalition government instead of new elections, which Papandreou rejected. The new elections took place on February 16, after which Papandreou reclaimed the prime ministership and hoped to deliver to his people the island of Cyprus, as he had promised.

President Makarios, aware of the political instability in the parliaments in Ankara and Athens, on November 30, 1963, presented his proposals in a thirteen-point plan to Vice-President Küçük and to the three guarantor powers—Great Britain, Greece, and Turkey.

1. The right to veto of the president and the vice-president of the Republic to be abandoned.
2. The vice-president of the Republic to deputise for the president of the Republic in case of his temporary absence or incapacity to perform his duties.
3. The Greek president of the House of Representatives and the Turkish vice-president to be elected by the House as a whole and not as at present the president by the Greek members of the House and the Vice-President by the Turkish members of the House.
4. The vice-president of the House of Representatives to deputise for the president of the House in case of his temporary absence or incapacity to perform his duties.
5. The constitutional provisions regarding separate majorities for enactment of certain laws by the House of Representatives to be abolished.
6. Unified municipalities.
7. The administration of justice to be unified.
8. The division of the Security Forces into Police and Gendarmerie to be abolished.
9. The numerical strength of the Security Forces and of the Defense Forces to be determined by a law.
10. The proportion of the participation of Greek and Turkish Cypriots in the composition of the Public Service and the Forces of the Republic to be modified in proportion to the ratio of the population of Greek and Turkish Cypriots.
11. The number of the members of the Public Service Commission to be reduced from ten to five.
12. All decisions of the Public Service Commission to be taken by simple majority.
13. The Greek Communal Chamber to be abolished.[8]

Makarios' proposals to amend the Cyprus Constitution were contrary to the provisions provided in the London Agreement of 1960. The proposal indicated that the Greek Cypriot leadership had decided to attempt to amend the Cyprus Constitution[9] and the treaties unilaterally.[10] Makarios was convinced that it would be to the Greek Cypriot advantage to make a unilateral move and unify the Cyprus government under his leadership, and he expected no major opposition from Ankara and Athens because of their internal political instability.

Makarios was under the illusion that the United Nations would automatically endorse his declaration of enosis, thereby guaranteeing the success of his scheme. Glafkos Clerides, the president of the House of Representatives, now admits that the Greek Cypriot leaders were amateurs in international politics, nearly forcing Greece and Turkey to go to war.[11] From the statements President Makarios made available to the press in recent years, it can be seen that he will never repeat such a political gamble. Makarios stated that a struggle for enosis must be approved by Greece since Athens will pay "the greater price in all kinds of sacrifices." He went on to say: "I can now disclose that I have stated clearly and categorically to Greek Governments from time to time that I would unhesitatingly proclaim Enosis, if I had the consent to this end, that is if Greece were prepared to accept Enosis and share the responsibilities for the repercussions from such a venture."[12]

On December 16, the Turkish government refused to accept the proposals of Makarios. The Turkish Cypriots rejected the whole plan and refuted Makarios' claim that the formation of a unitary state, free of all treaties, would benefit both communities. The Turkish Cypriots discredited the proposal because it was considered an attempt to remove their constitutional safeguards.

Emotionally and politically the setting was ripe for a direct confrontation between the Greek and Turkish Cypriots, which was to lead to wider international repercussions than anticipated.

3 FACTORS CONTRIBUTING TO CYPRIOT DISUNITY

When the Cypriots were given their independence, many observers were apprehensive about the political future of Cyprus. Cyprus was a nation in name only, for it lacked the principle conditions for the development of nationalism. The Greek and Turkish Cypriots were expected to lay aside their traditional animosity, which had been revived during the late 1950s. Since 1964, the two communities have become steadfast in their determination to remain two distinct societies and have shown little desire to have a common government. After the establishment of the Republic of Cyprus, the objective of national self-preservation, the willingness to survive, and the zeal to create a national homogeneity for the preservation of territorial integrity or independence did not become the common interest of the two communities. The political aspirations of the Cypriot leaders were to inspire Cypriots with a love and loyalty to either Greece or Turkey instead of a mutual concern for the unity of their nation and for their own self-preservation as Cypriots.

The elements that separate the two Cypriot communities are the following:

Ethnic origin—Greeks and Turks both belong to the Caucasian race but are of different ethnic backgrounds. The Greek Cypriots identify themselves with the Hellenistic past, and the Turkish Cypriots are direct descendents of the Ottoman Turkish conquerors.

Religion—The Greek Cypriots are followers of the Greek Orthodox Church. The church directs the Greek schools and enhances the Greco-Byzantine tradition. The church preserves and fosters the national sentiment against the Turks. The Turkish Cypriots belong to the Sunni sect of the Muslim religion. Both organized religions support the national policies of Greece and Turkey.[1]

Language—The first Greek settlers on Cyprus spoke an Achaia-Dorian dialect of Greek, which later merged with the Hellenic Koine, the present dialect of the island. The Turkish Cypriots speak Turkish, or as some scholars prefer to call it, Ottoman Turkish. Some members of the two communities have mastered English, Greek, and Turkish and use all three languages extensively. It has also been the policy of some high schools to offer all three languages to their students. After the independence of Cyprus, the official languages of the republic were Greek and Turkish.

Culture—The two communities are greatly influenced by the folkways, customs, and institutions of their respective mother countries, and this in turn perpetuates the ideals of Hellenism and Kemalism on the island. Dwelling together in some areas of the island did cause some Cypriots to assimilate to some extent each other's customs, mores, habits, and other behavior patterns, but for the most part members of the two communities retain their ethnic and cultural separation, and this has been reinforced since 1964.

Allegiance—Each community considered Greece or Turkey as its mother country. The Greek and Turkish Cypriots have more loyalty to these two countries than they do to Cyprus. The Greek and Turkish flags are more in evidence than the flag of Cyprus. The Republic of Cyprus does not even have a national anthem, and the anthems of Greece and Turkey are played instead. The Cyprus government has not undertaken a program to capture the minds of the young Cypriots so that it may lay the foundation for Cypriotism. The sense of Cypriotism would contribute to domestic peace and the establishment of an independent state. The lack of a unified people will frustrate all attempts to create a national homogeneity. The objective of all the Cypriots, regardless of their ethnic background, should be to preserve the territorial integrity and independence of Cyprus, but this will be undermined as long as the ideas of enosis or *Taksim* continue to linger in the minds of the people. The Cyprus Republic can succeed only if both communities are willing to join efforts for the common interest of all the Cypriots, because without this will and commitment all endeavors will be futile. Leaders of both communities should be challenged by this issue and if they are pessimistic in respect to it, then each side should honestly tackle the Cyprus issue and reach an agreement to end the continued misery and frustration of thousands of Cypriots. Because neither enosis or *Taksim* will materialize through the mere passage of time, the two communities should reach an agreement for a common government within which the interest of all the Cypriots will be preserved.

Traditions—Some practices are common to both communities, but the majority of the traditions are identified with one or the other ethnic group. Aside from rare exceptions, the two communities do not intermarry and ostracize those who do.

Literature—Each community is influenced by the books imported from Greece and Turkey, which are widely in use in their schools.[2] During my interview with Glatkos Clerides in the summer of 1972, he expressed an unfavorable opinion of the fact that the majority of Greek and Turkish Cypriot students continue their education at universities in their respective mother countries. He felt that the university courses of Greece and Turkey were too subjective and had a great impact on the national sentiments of the Cypriot graduates. The Cypriot university graduates from Greece and Turkey, when compared with the university graduates from the other countries, had stronger partisan feelings. This emotional commitment to Hellenism and Kemalism undermines all efforts to pursue the idea of Cypriotism.

Unity—There is a lack of striving among the Cypriots to live under one state. There is also physical separation of the Greeks and Turks in some towns and villages, which has been intensified since the communal hostilities in December, 1963. In 1960 Cyprus had 619 villages, out of which 393 were primarily Greek, 120 Turkish, and 106 were mixed.[3]

Equality—Citizens of the two communities are unwilling to recognize their equality as Cypriot citizens. The average Greek and Turk have stereotyped images of one another: Greeks view the Turks as intruders, brutal barbarians, and the Turks view the Greeks as selfish, degenerate cowards. The literature of the two communities illustrates that each considers its race to be superior and more civilized.

Patriotism—The public spirit for the love of Cyprus and Cypriotism is absent. Citizens of the two communities love the island, but their supreme loyalty and allegiance is to their respective fatherlands. The Greek and Turkish Cypriots are too preoccupied with strengthening bonds with Greece and Turkey. Some educators of the two communities are opposed to the promotion of Cypriotism and press for either Hellenism of Cyprus to achieve enosis or Kemalism to attain *Taksim*. Both groups are chauvinistic in their attempts to reach their objectives. The leaders of the two communities are erecting monuments glorifying the heroes of their own people all over the island. Their oratory at national holidays of Greece and Turkey dissipates all hope for Cypriotism.

The absence of the rudiments of nationalism will prevent the formation of Cypriotism. Cypriotism can become a reality if methods to induce nationalism are utilized. The instruments that can be employed are: The two communities can cooperate in the establishment of integrated schools which use literature that is not biased, preferably books that are published in the West. The pageantry that inflames the unhappy memories of the past can be modified, and the development of Cypriot ritualism can be encouraged. The news media, such as the press, radio, and television, can be directed to use more discretion in reporting. At present, most of the news reports are biased or unsubstantiated. Slogans for self-preservation and independence can be substituted for those of enosis and *Taksim*. A new design for a Cypriot flag and an anthem could create a new attitude toward Cypriotism. The shrines and monuments that glorify the heroes of Greece and Turkey could be subdued and at the same time erected in less prominant spots to avoid antagonism. The uniform of the armed forces, which is a highly visible symbol of the state, could be redesigned to the liking of both communities so that Cypriots will be proud of it. Such measures as these might cause a negative reaction from many people, and the writer will be the first to admit that they would be very difficult to put into practice. But without a radical scheme Cypriotism will never become a reality. The polarization of the two communities will continue, along with distrust, and each will resort to schemes to out-manuever the other.

The principles of self-determination and national liberation were the political philosophy of President Wilson in 1918. He crystallized these two ideas in the Fourteen Points and the Four Principles during the peace talks in Europe after World War I. Wilson was the proponent of the idea that the people should be given the right to set their own destiny. Wilson's conception of self-determination derived from American democratic and national ideals. According to the Wilsonian ideals, the application of self-determination, popular sovereignty, was to be the basis for world peace. The people, who are conscious of themselves as members of a community or a nation, are endowed with the right of determining their own state and the assertion of national sovereignty. The principle of national self-determination gives the people of each nation the right to constitute an independent state. In a democracy, the people of a nation are the supreme authority, and they have the right to form their own constitution. By means of a plebiscite the formal expression of the will of the people can be obtained.

The principle of self-determination is an attribute of nations and not of each small community such as those found on the island of Cyprus. The demand by the Greek Cypriots for self-determination does not justify an unconditional right to political independence. Self-determination is not an absolute right for each fragment within a community; if it were, individual rights would be denied in support of the principle that might is right. If Greek Cypriots were to exercise self-determination, Turkish Cypriots and Ankara would have to sacrifice power, the strategic military value of the island,[4] and their sense of national interest and pride. One would be profoundly mistaken to assume that the Turkish Cypriots and Ankara would sacrifice so much in order that the larger Greek Cypriot community could exercise self-determination. Since self-determination is not an absolute right for any one community on the island, it, therefore, can be confined to utopia. President Wilson himself did not envisage such a broad application of the principle that would include small communities such as those on Cyprus.

According to the Greek Cypriots, the Turkish Cypriots, representing only 30 percent of the population, have seriously complicated the achievement of self-determination. However, the Greek Cypriots' claim to the right of self-determination is not sufficient justification for disregarding the rights of the minority. Self-determination would represent an evasion of, not a solution to, the Cypriot question. The Cypriot population is not homogeneous but consists, rather, of communally conscious citizens. Since the Cypriots at present are unassimilable, there is no common allegiance to the Cyprus state, which presents a danger for the survival of a single state. The idea of self-determination is good in theory, but it must be modified with regard to reality. In attempting to protect the sacredness of the Greek Cypriot majority rights, one cannot justify overriding the interest of the Turkish Cypriot minority. The mere existence as a majority does not constitute a right to decide the future of the island of Cyprus by violating the right of the minority. Self-determination is not absolute; it is relative to the size and interest of the group. If the principle of self-determination is going to be utilized, the combined consent of the interest groups will need to be involved if an amicable solution to the Cyprus issue is to be reached. The principle of concurrent majority will permit each group to have the right to protect its own interest.

The principles of democracy can operate best where a homogeneous society exists; the presence of strong cultural pluralism hinders the functioning of democratic institutions. Democracy, similar to the system practiced in the Western states today, involves the active participation of the citizens in political life. Democracy was first developed in ancient Greece in the sixth and fifth centuries B.C. *Democracy* is a Greek word, which translates *demos*, "the people," and *Kratia*, "authority," but its principles of liberty and equality did not apply to all the citizens of Athens. The Athenians recognized the inequality of men, possessing slaves and assigning lower status to foreigners. Therefore, one should not equate the modern Western democratic ideology with that of Athens. Nor are the modern concepts of democratic principles being practiced in Cyprus, Greece, or Turkey, because none of these countries are fully implementing these principles in governing their citizens. When the Greeks in Greece were disillusioned with democracy, they replaced it many times with the expedient of a military coup d' état, the latest one being on November 25, 1973. Dictatorship is more efficient in solving domestic problems and, therefore, is attractive to people in the midst of crisis.

The Turkish Cypriots, aware of past events, were too cautious to be lured by the proposition that modern Western democracy would work in Cyprus without certain modifications. The Turkish Cypriots are adamant in their insistence that protective clauses should be inserted in any future Cypriot constitution so that Turks can be guaranteed that their freedoms will not be violated or that they will not be relegated to the position of second-class citizens. They wish to have a representative democratic system in which their people will fully participate in government. Because of Turkish Cypriots' protectionist tendencies, they refuse to allow the majority to seize the government, under a pretext of majority rule, and expedite the means of enosis.[5] President Makarios' consistent statements about enosis, such as the one quoted below, reinforce Turkish Cypriots' fears. "Enosis, as a national aspiration, will never be uprooted from the hearts of the people of Cyprus. The Greek Cypriots are always in favour of Enosis even if it does not seem feasible."[6] A reasonable equilibrium must be maintained between the two communities if the principles of democracy are to survive. A representative form of the democratic system can succeed in Cyprus if the two communities' elected officials participate in all the governing bodies. Exclusion by the Greek Cypriots of the Turkish Cypriots' political right to participate in the government cannot be justified under a democratic system.

The two communities could peacefully coexist under a constitution that recognizes both communities' vested interests. An independent Cyprus should not serve as a means to an end for either side. No constitution will ever succeed as long as there is no will to coexist, to have common ends and common objectives. Cypriotism may be the ultimate remedy for the success of any future state on the island. The extremists who refuse to deviate from the cause of enosis or *Taksim* are obstacles in the endeavor to find peace.

The Turkish Cypriot community feels that it must protect its interests —the memories of past events are too fresh.[7] Every Cypriot's equal rights and liberties should be acknowledged regardless of his identity with one of the ethnic groups. Every state should be governed by its people, whose inalienable rights—life, liberty, equality, and justice for all—should not be infringed. These principles can become a reality under a Western democratic ideology, but such an ideology is still alien to Cyprus. Most Cypriots are not well acquainted with the principles of Western democracy. It also should be emphasized that even a Westerner has difficulty in applying or comprehending the demands of true democratic principles. Clearly, it is not a foregone conclusion that a representative of the Greek Cypriot community, any more than a member of another community, will either execute laws based on the principles of democracy or honor a constitution on the basis of its heritage of democracy.[8]

Greece and Turkey have been promoting their own national interest,[9] which has become evident to both communities in Cyprus. There is a trend toward political awakening by the intelligentsia in both communities, who wish to reach a consensus amicable to all Cypriots. Since December, 1963, the sufferers have obviously been the Cypriots themselves and not the mainland Greeks and Turks. Honest, realistic, and objective attempts to resolve the constitutional differences can be made, and the Cypriots can once again live in peace and harmony. However, the extremist individuals who are empowered to make decisions and policies have to be neutralized; reason must prevail if the trust and cooperation necessary for the successful restoration of a state are to become permanent. Otherwise, the island will be plunged once again into civil war. Peace can be achieved through a bicommunal compromise and guaranteed exclusion of enosis and *Taksim*. In the event of the dissolution of the state of Cyprus, a just and equitable solution to the Cypriot dilemma might be double enosis.[10]

4 THE CONFLICT AND THE ROLE OF INTERNATIONAL INSTITUTIONS

Outbreaks of violence between the Greek and Turkish Cypriot communities took place even before the escalation of the hostilities on December 21, 1963. In the Paphos district, on May 3, 1963, these skirmishes were brought under control, but both sides continued to stockpile arms and to organize their underground units around the island. An explosion on December 3, in Nicosia, which damaged the statue of EOKA hero Marcos Drakos, heightened the tensions between the two communities. There was no substantial evidence to indict Turkish Cypriots for the incident, but the enosists unhesitatingly accused them of being the culprits. The intense intercommunal fighting was ignited on December 21, when two Turkish Cypriots were accidently killed by a Greek Cypriot police officer.

The appeal for peace and reason by President Makarios and Vice-President Küçük went unheeded, and both sides armed for an offensive undertaking. All communications media, since they are located in the Greek Cypriot sectors of the island, were denied to the Turkish Cypriots. The Greek and Turkish nationals left their barracks in Nicosia and took an active part in the fighting between the two communities.[1] The commander of the Turkish contingent justified his action as being necessary for the safety of his troops, since their barracks were located in the Greek Cypriot sector of Nicosia.

Turkish Cypriot leaders stated during interviews with this writer that the commander of the Turkish national regulars refused to allow his troops to join the irregular Turkish Cypriot forces in their fight against the Greek Cypriots. The Turkish commander declined to order his troops to take an active part in the hostilities and instead waited for instructions from Ankara. The Turkish Cypriots expressed their contempt for the Turkish commander's caution and gave him credit for the Greek Cypriot victories in the early period of the fighting. The Turkish Cypriot plea for arms and ammunition also went unheeded by the Turkish commander, forcing them to rely on their rusted guns and damp ammunition, which had been hurriedly excavated for the fighting. Many of the Turkish Cypriots who participated in the civil war claim that most of their ammunition would not function; the dampness had corroded the primer, causing the primer composition to become inert, and the rounds failed to fire. However, during the latter part of the fighting, the Turkish regulars not only joined the Turkish Cypriots at arms but also supplied them with a variety of weapons and ammunition. The Turkish Cypriots were also able to acquire weapons and ammunition, at high prices, from the British soldiers and later from the United Nations forces who were stationed on the island. These weapons were smuggled to the Turkish Cypriots in the Red Cross ambulances and other vehicles.[2] The members of other ethnic groups profited by spying for either the Greek or Turkish Cypriots, and some of them were even able to smuggle arms and other essential items to the Turkish sectors.

Due to the escalation of the fighting on the island, Turkey felt compelled under the treaty obligation to make a move; therefore, on December 25, 1963, it sent two jet fighters over the island while its naval units put on a show of force close to Cyprus's shores. The Greek government took similar action, believing a Turkish invasion of the island to be imminent. Both the Greek and Turkish governments, however, in an attempt to avert the necessity of intervening, pleaded for political support, especially from the members of NATO. Primary consideration was the ending of bloodshed between the two communities.

The Cypriot civil war, which was precipitated by President Makarios' attempt to change the Constitution unilaterally, led to the involvement of other nations interested in preserving the peace, which was in the best national interest of all parties concerned. The Cyprus problem was no longer a domestic issue between the two major ethnic communities, but an international affair.

Great Britain took the initiative toward restoration of the peace and assumed the mediator role in late December, 1963, with the consent of the Cypriot, Greek, and Turkish governments. The purpose of the British involvement in the dispute was to prevent war between Greece and Turkey and at the same time to preserve British strategic interest in the island and the Middle East. On December 25 the leaders of both communities consented to the British assumption of command over a tripartite force for keeping the peace, to be composed of British, Greek, and Turkish contingents stationed on Cyprus. A Political Committee was organized consisting of British, Greek, and Turkish ambassadors and representatives from both communities. The responsibility of the committee was to give recommendations to the commander of the tripartite force relating to peace.

In search of an amicable political settlement to the strife on Cyprus, British Commonwealth Secretary Duncan Sandys went to Cyprus on December 28, 1963, and succeeded in easing the tension and bringing about the smooth functioning of the peace-keeping force. Sandys also encouraged all the interested parties in the Cypriot conflict to attend a conference in London to be held on January 15, 1964. The Greek Cypriots insisted on the revision of the Zurich-London Agreements, and the Turkish Cypriots proposed the physical separation of the two communities into two distinct provinces. The conference ended in failure because of the intransigent political demands by the leaders of both communities.

In February, 1964, George Papandreou formed a new Greek government in Athens and took over the powers of the state from Ioannis Paraskevopoulos, who had headed the caretaker cabinet. Since December, 1963, Turkey had been making threats of invasion against Cyprus in order to protect the Turkish Cypriots from the Greek Cypriot attacks all over the island. The new Greek prime minister notified the United Nations, Great Britain, the United States, and Turkey that he would order Greek forces into Cyprus in the event of a Turkish invasion. Papandreou also called for the revision of the 1960 treaties and voiced support for the enosists. The British peace-keeping operation was criticized for orienting its operations toward the cause of the Turkish Cypriots, bringing about a *de facto* partition of the island, and Turkey became more firm in its determination to support the constitutional and treaty rights of the Turkish Cypriots.

When the British peace-keeping operation in the island came under criticism from both Cypriot communities, Great Britain proposed on January 24, 1964, that NATO members take over the peace-keeping operation in Cyprus. The United States, which was reluctant to become involved in the Cypriot dispute, because of the possibility of antagonizing its Greek and Turkish allies, proposed a three-month limit on the NATO operation. Greece and Turkey accepted the NATO plan, but President Makarios rejected it. Makarios was apprehensive about a NATO solution because of the importance of Turkey in the organization, believing that the Turks would be the main benefactors. He demanded that the international peace-keeping force come under the jurisdiction of the United Nations Security Council. The NATO plan was stillborn because of President Makarios's refusal to accept it.[3]

The United States government was actively seeking a peaceful solution to the Cypriot issue that would be acceptable to all parties concerned. On February 7, 1964, Secretary of State Dean Rusk at a press conference stated that the United States was willing to participate in a peace-keeping operation with other NATO partners.[4] On February 9, George W. Ball, the United States under-secretary of state, was sent to London to work out an acceptable compromise for the establishment of a peace-keeping force from NATO members as well as from nonaligned states. The United Nations Security Council was to have some authority but not control of the activities of the force. The mission of Ball and the policy of the United States government, as the Department of State clarified, was " . . . that it has no preconceptions or preference as to the shape or form of final solutions that might be developed for the Cyprus problem. . . . The United States must emphasize that it does have a major interest in the maintenance of peace in the eastern Mediterranean—an interest which it fortunately shares with many other nations. It will do whatever it can to assure that objective.[5]

Ball's three days of talks with President Makarios fell short of achieving any conclusive results. Makarios stubbornly resisted all arguments and assurances that the NATO members' objective was to maintain the status quo of the Cyprus Republic. Despite all the pressures on Makarios, Ball's mission was a failure. The Cypriot president was unwilling to compromise or accept any settlement that indicated that NATO had overriding supranational interests above those of the Greek Cypriots. Although both Greece and Turkey had accepted the American proposal, President Makarios rejected it.

President Makarios again demanded that the international peace-keeping operation be under the supervision and control of the United Nations Security Council, since he feared that any NATO settlement would be in favor of the Turks. Makarios was under the illusion that the United Nations involvement would enable him to unilaterally suspend the 1960 treaties permanently and prevent any settlement by the NATO members that would favor partitioning Cyprus. The NATO members were primarily interested in preventing hostilities between the mainland Greeks and Turks, and cooperated within the alliance to solve the Cypriot controversy.[6] The NATO supreme commander in Europe, General Lyman L. Lemnitzer, visited the Greek and Turkish capitals, warning the two governments of the fatal consequences to the alliance in case of war between the two nation-states.

Ankara deplored the negative attitude of president Makarios in respect to the American proposal for an international force to keep the peace in Cyprus. The prime minister of Turkey, İsmet İnönü, proposed the creation of a federal government on Cyprus. Papandreou opposed the idea of a federal state because it would have been an acquiescence to the permanent partitioning of Cyprus. In February, 1964, in a speech to the Greek people, Papandreou said: " . . . for the sake of democracy and peace in Cyprus and to preserve our alliance with our neighbor Turkey, it is imperative to revise these treaties in conformity with the principles of international justice."[7] The unyielding policies of Ankara and Athens concerning Cyprus intensified the tension between the two communities on the island.

When the American effort failed to generate a Cypriot settlement, the United States government became more distressed, because a military confrontation between Greece and Turkey would weaken the eastern flank of NATO and negate the alliance's defense strategy in Europe against the Soviet bloc.

The United States decision-makers had been under the impression that they could achieve quick results in Cyprus because of American-Cypriot good will and the United States' economic and financial generosity to the republic. Following the independence of Cyprus, American foreign aid to the island, by June 30, 1963, had reached $20 million. President Makarios, on the invitation of President Kennedy, had visited the United States in June, 1962, and Vice-President Lyndon B. Johnson had paid a courtesy visit to

Cyprus in the latter part of that year. In 1963 Cyprus had purchased more than two million dollars' worth of wheat under the Food for Peace Agreement and had been allowed to pay for it in local currency. Other American loans had been extended to Cyprus by the United States Agency for International Development, to permit Cypriots' purchase of American industrial machinery. Also twenty-three Peace Corps volunteers had been sent to assist in the improvement of agricultural techniques and education in the rural areas of the island. The United States, in return for its generosity, desired a *modus vivendi* between the two communities.

The United States also was concerned about the widening appeal of the communist party, AKEL (Anorthotikón Kómma Ergazoménon Laoú), and Cypriot support of that party. One aim of the communist party was to turn public opinion against Great Britain and the United States. AKEL was opposed to the sovereign base areas and to the presence on Cypriot soil of British bombers armed with nuclear weapons.[8] The American objective was to find a solution to the Cyprus question within the framework of the Western alliance, thus avoiding the exploitation of the crisis by the communists. President Johnson, in a telegram sent to President Makarios and Vice-President Küçük in December, 1963, indicated his displeasure over the fighting between the two communities. "I will not presume to judge the root causes, or rights or wrongs as between Cypriots of the two communities. This is, in any case, inappropriate when innocent human lives are at stake. I hope that tomorrow will find all Cypriots living at peace with one another and with the three nations which have special treaty responsibility for the security of Cyprus."[9] In a letter to President Cemal Gürsel of Turkey, dated December 26, 1963, President Johnson stated that the United States was ready "to support any and all actions proposed by the three guarantor powers which offer any reasonable hope of assisting in a peaceful solution."[10] The purpose of the letter to Ankara was to tone down Turkish threats of invading Cyprus to protect Turkey's national interests and those of the Turkish Cypriots.

The Soviet Union, along with its East European satellites, enjoyed cordial diplomatic relations with the Republic of Cyprus. AKEL, which had polled 40 percent of the Greek Cypriot electoral vote in 1960, was instrumental in arranging economic and commercial agreements between Cyprus and the Soviet bloc. The communist party of Cyprus (Kommonistikon Komma Kyprou) was founded in 1926 by Haralambos Vatiliotis, and on April 14, 1941, AKEL was founded under the leadership of Ploutis Servas. However, it was not until 1944 that AKEL was declared to be the official communist party of Cyprus. The membership in AKEL in 1967 was estimated to be approximately 14,000, which is "probably the largest non-ruling communist party in the world today."[11] AKEL is the oldest and one of the best-coordinated and efficiently operated political parties in Cyprus. It controls seven-eighths of the trade unions. AKEL's propaganda rhetoric reaches the Cypriots through its daily paper *Haravghi* (Dawn), the weekly *Neoi Kairoi* (New Times), its journal *Politiki Epitheorisis* (Political Survey), the labor weekly *Ergatiko Vima* (Workers' Forum), the weekly for the youth front *Neolaia* (Youth), the afternoon paper *Democratia* (Republic), and two monthlies *Nea Epochi* (New Epoch) and *Neos Democratis* (New Democrat). AKEL policy is opposed both to enosis and *Taksim*. It supports Cypriot independence and the nonaligned foreign policy of President Makarios. The Turkish Cypriots associate AKEL with the Greek Cypriots, although some members of the Turkish Cypriot community are communist sympathizers; however, since 1964, communist party activities have been outlawed in the Turkish sectors of Cyprus. Conversely in the Greek sectors of Cyprus, communist party members hold major offices in city municipalities and have elected members seated in parliament.

The Soviet intent in the Middle East has been to extend its sphere of influence and weaken the southeastern flank of the NATO alliance; therefore, the Kremlin concurred with the demands of Makarios that any international peace-keeping force should come under the authority of the United Nations Security Council and warned all nations against interference in the internal affairs of the republic. The Soviet objective was to undermine the cohesion of NATO and expand its sphere of influence in the eastern Mediterranean.

Among the Arab countries, Egypt supported the Greek Cypriot cause most actively. Nasser sought the removal of the British from their military bases on Cyprus,[12] one of the last remnants of British power in the Middle East. The Arabs were of the opinion that the British military presence on Cyprus was tacit support for the Israeli cause and a threat to Arab national security.

When the disputant parties could not agree on a compromise in respect to the structure and operation of the international peace force, Great Britain requested on February 15, 1964, that the United Nations Security Council meet to consider the Cyprus crisis. On the same day, Zenon Rossides, the Cyprus ambassador to the United States and the United Nations made a similar request. In January, 1964, Secretary General U Thant had appointed Lieutenant General Prem Singh Gyani of India as his personal representative to observe and report on the Cyprus situation. Although the British government initiated the request for United Nations involvement in keeping the peace in Cyprus, it also emphasized that such an operation would not infringe on the existing treaty rights. The British representative stated that the creation of a United Nations peace force "would not affect any of the existing treaty rights and obligations of the British, Greek and Turkish Governments relating to the Republic of Cyprus, including the obligations in respect of the independence and territorial integrity of the Republic of Cyprus."[13]

The American government supported the British concern and made it clear that it considered the Treaty of Guarantee to be an organic part of the constitutional structure of the Republic of Cyprus. The United States ambassador to the United Nations, Adlai Stevenson, in a Security Council meeting, expressed the following opinion:

> I think we all know that the Treaty of Guarantee forms an integral part of the organic arrangements that created the Republic of Cyprus. In fact, it is so-called a basic article of the Constitution of Cyprus. . . . This Treaty or any international treaty cannot be abrogated, cannot be nullified, cannot be modified either in fact or in effect by the Security Council of the United Nations.[14]

Greece and the Greek Cypriots were disappointed by the appearance of a pro-Turkish policy of the United States, and in a letter to Washington, Papandreou expressed his regret. The foreign minister of Cyprus, Spyros Kyprianou, accused Turkey of planning a unilateral invasion of the island, and of being the provocateur of the internal tension between the two communities. He urged the Security Council to protect the independence of the Republic of Cyprus against the imminent Turkish aggression. Kyprianou also attacked the Treaty of Guarantee and the Treaty of Alliance, expressing the opinion that the two treaties were imposed on Cyprus and thus should be considered nullified. Rauf Denktaş, the chairman of the Turkish Communal Chamber in Cyprus, rejected the allegation and the charges of the Greek Cypriot representatives. In a letter to the Security Council he wrote: "Greek Cypriot insistence on recognition of the integrity and sovereignty of Cyprus by the Security Council is a trick for finding the untenable excuse to argue that the Treaty of Guarantee is non-effective with the intention of getting a free license to continue the massacre of the Turks under the umbrella of the United Nations."[15] At the invitation of the Security Council, on February 28, Denktaş addressed the council, after overcoming the Soviet delegate's opposition. He reasserted the argument that Makarios aspired to obtain a Security Council resolution that would nullify the treaties and ease the way to enosis. Denktaş also stated the willingness of the Turkish Cypriots to live under the Cypriot Constitution and amend it by legal means. Rossides accused the Turkish Cypriots of being "rebels" who were under the guidance of Ankara. The Greek representative gave the Greek Cypriots full support during the debates in the Security Council. For appearing before the Security Council, Makarios charged that Denktaş had committed a "criminal offense," and he was refused an entry permit to return to Cyprus.[16]

The Soviet representative, Fedorenko, exploited the Cypriot crisis for propaganda purposes. He charged the NATO members with a meditated aggression against the independence of Cyprus. The Soviet representative in principle was reiterating the rhetoric of Nikita Khrushchev, the chairman of the Council of Ministers of the Supreme Soviet and the first secretary general of the communist party. Khrushchev, in a note to the United Nations, wrote that

> certain Powers, flouting the principles of the United Nations Charter and the accepted standards of international law, are at present attempting to impose on the people and Government of Cyprus a solution of those powers' own choosing to problems which affect only the Cypriot people; at the same time they would have it believed that only foreign bayonets can bring Cyprus a solution of these internal problems. . . . Although various alternative "solutions" are being discussed, such as the dispatching of NATO troops or troops from individual NATO countries to Cyprus, the purpose of all these alternative plans is basically the same; the *de facto* occupation by NATO armed forces of the Republic of Cyprus which is pursuing a policy of non-alignment with military blocs. In other words, what we are witnessing is crude encroachment on the sovereignty, independence and freedom of the Republic of Cyprus, and an attempt to bring this small neutral state under NATO military control.[17]

When the debate in the Security Council was concluded, the decision was reached not to condone the unilateral change of the agreement or of the Cypriot Constitution. On March 2, 1964, Bolivia, Brazil, the Ivory Coast, Morocco, and Norway submitted jointly a draft resolution to the Security Council. Two days later the resolution of the five members was unanimously adopted.

The Security Council

> Noting that the present situation with regard to Cyprus is likely to threaten international peace and security and may further deteriorate unless additional measures are properly taken to maintain peace and to seek out a durable solution,
>
> Considering the positions taken by the parties in relation to the Treaties signed at Nicosia on 16 August 1960,
>
> Having in mind the relevant positions of the Charter of the United Nations and its Article 2, paragraph 4, which reads: "All members shall refrain in their international relations from the threat or use of force against the territorial integrity or political independence of any State, or in any other manner inconsistent with the Purposes of the United Nations,"
>
> 1. Calls upon all Member States, in conformity with their obligations under the Charter of the United Nations, to refrain from any action or threat of action likely to worsen the situation in the sovereign Republic of Cyprus, or to endanger international peace;
>
> 2. Asks the Government of Cyprus, which has the responsibility for the maintenance and restoration of law and order, to take all additional measures necessary to stop violence and bloodshed in Cyprus;

3. Calls upon the communities in Cyprus and their leaders to act with the utmost restraint;

4. Recommends the creation, with the consent of the Government of Cyprus, of a United Nations peace-keeping force in Cyprus. The composition and size of the force shall be established by the Secretary-General in consultation with the Governments of Cyprus, Greece, Turkey and the United Kingdom. The commander of the force shall be appointed by the Secretary-General and report to him. The Secretary-General, who shall keep the Governments providing the force fully informed, shall report periodically to the Security Council on its operation;

5. Recommends that the function of the force should be, in the interest of preserving international peace and security, to use its best efforts to prevent a recurrence of fighting and, as necessary, to contribute to the maintenance and restoration of law and order and a return to normal conditions;

6. Recommends that the stationing of the force shall be for a period of three months, all costs pertaining to it being met, in a manner to be agreed upon by them, by the Governments providing the contingents and by the Government of Cyprus. The Secretary-General may also accept voluntary contributions for that purpose;

7. Recommends further that the Secretary-General designate, in agreement with the Government of Cyprus and the Governments of Greece, Turkey and the United Kingdom, a mediator, who shall use his best endeavors with the representatives of the communities and also with the aforesaid four Governments, for the purpose of promoting a peaceful solution and an agreed settlement of the problem confronting Cyprus, in accordance with the Charter of the United Nations, having in mind the well-being of the people of Cyprus as a whole and preservation of international peace and security. The mediator shall report periodically to the Secretary-General on his efforts;

8. Requests the Secretary-General to provide from funds of the United Nations, as appropriate, for the remuneration and expenses of the mediator and his staff.[18]

The resolution was approved by the eleven members on the Security Council, but Czechoslovakia, France, and the Soviet Union abstained. The three powers objected to paragraph 4 because it delegated too much authority to the secretary-general. However, all the members finally did vote for the final resolution on March 4, 1964, despite their reservations.[19]

Cyprus, Greece, and Turkey consented to the creation of the United Nations Peace-Keeping Force in Cyprus (UNFICYP), according to the resolution adopted by the Security Council. The resolution was interpreted by each of the communities on Cyprus as vindicating their respective political positions. Since they were in control of the Cyprus government, the Greek

Cypriots were satisfied with the resolution because it bestowed upon them the responsibility to restore and maintain law and order. The Turkish Cypriots on the other hand considered the resolution an official rejection of the Greek Cypriots' attempt to unilaterally abrogate the Treaty of Guarantee.

On March 4, 1964, the day the United Nations resolution was adopted, a violent confrontation took place between the two communities at Ktima, Paphos. Despite the pleas for a ceasefire from outside powers, the hostilities between the Cypriots continued. On March 13, Ankara sent a note to President Makarios warning him to desist from his military actions against the Turkish Cypriots, who were in the minority in the town and who had inferior weapons, or face the possibility of its intervention to safeguard the Turkish Cypriots. The Permanent Council of NATO called for an emergency session, on March 14, to bring about peace on Cyprus, but the members were unable to reach a positive decision. The prime minister of Greece, George Papandreou, responded to the Turkish threats by warning Turkey that his government would go to the assistance of the Greek Cypriots in case of a Turkish invasion from Iskenderun. The port of Iskenderun, which is adjacent to Syria, is a major Turkish flotilla center for the Mediterranean, and since late 1963 Ankara has strengthened its military position in this area. The naval fleet stationed in this area could be utilized to launch an invasion of Cyprus.

The big powers, spectators to the verbal threats being hurled between Ankara and Athens, continued to try to avert the crisis. Once again the United Nations came to the rescue when Bolivia, Brazil, the Ivory Coast, Morocco, and Norway initiated a new draft resolution that was adopted unanimously by the Security Council. The resolution was supported by the five permanent members of the Security Council.

The Security Council

Having heard the statements of the representatives of the Republic of Cyprus, Greece and Turkey,

Reaffirms its resolution of 4 March 1964 (S/5575),

Being deeply concerned over developments in the area,

Noting the progress reported by the Secretary-General in regard to the establishment of a United Nations peace-keeping force in Cyprus,

Noting the assurance from the Secretary-General that the United Nations Peace-keeping Force in Cyprus envisaged in the Council's resolution of 4 March 1964 (S/5575) is about to be established, and that advance elements of that Force are already en route to Cyprus,

1. Reaffirms its call upon all Member States, in conformity with their obligations under the Charter of the United Nations, to refrain from any action or threat of action likely to worsen the situation in the sovereign Republic of Cyprus, or to endanger international peace;

2. Requests the Secretary-General to press on with his efforts to implement the Security Council resolution of 4 March 1964 and requests Member States to cooperate with the Secretary-General to that end.[20]

The speedy United Nations action soothed the jingoist attitudes of the Greek and Turkish decision-makers, and President Makarios' brinkmanship policy on the island decelerated.

By March 27, the UNFICYP became operational under Lieutenant General Gyani. The operation was to last three months, but later it was expanded to a six-month period, which has been regularly renewed. General Gyani was in command of the 6,369-man peace-keeping force. Great Britain, which had kept the peace in the island since December, 1963, put 3,500 of its troops at United Nations disposal. Other nations that contributed troops were Austria, Canada, Finland, Ireland, and Sweden. The major portion of the expense for the operation of the UNFICYP came from the voluntary contributions of the United States and Great Britain. The other contributors were Cyprus, Greece, Turkey, and West Germany. The three month's operation of the UNFICYP cost about six million dollars. Some nations failed to contribute troops to the UNFICYP because they did not wish to see their troops engage in combat in a Greco-Turkish military confrontation.

The Finnish ambassador to Sweden and former premier of Finland, Sakari S. Tuomioja, was appointed by U Thant on March 24, 1964, as the United Nations mediator in Cyprus. The Finnish diplomat was the second choice, the first being José Rolz-Bennet of Guatemala, deputy chief of the secretary general's cabinet, whose appointment Turkey opposed. To complicate the political problems Tuomioja was facing, Makarios unilaterally abrogated the Treaty of Alliance on April 2, the very day the United Nations mediator arrived in Nicosia.[21] The foreign minister of Turkey, Feridun C. Erkin, challenged the action of Makarios: "Turkey refuses to accept such an illegal abrogation. There is no provision in the Treaty for its unilateral cancellation or abrogation. . . ."[22]

On May 11, 1964, Dr. Galo Plaza Lasso, former president of Ecuador, was appointed by U Thant to be his special representative to conduct negotiations to facilitate the resumption of normal life on the island. He was to undertake direct negotiations with the representatives of the two communities on the island. His function was to cover only nonmilitary matters, and he would be accountable directly to the secretary general. Dr. Plaza was to perform his duties without infringing on the duties of the commander of the UNFICYP or those of the United Nations mediator.

President Makarios erroneously believed that through the United Nations machinery on the island he would be able to suppress the Turkish Cypriot "rebellion" and provide a defensive shield against a potential Turkish invasion from Iskenderun. Makarios presented Dr. Plaza, upon his arrival in Cyprus, with a long list of directives that he was expected to pursue to restore normality. Clearly, Makarios believed that the United Nations was to be his pawn to force the Turkish Cypriots into submission. Contrary to the wishes of President Makarios, the United Nations officials conducted their task under the direction of the secretary general.

When the United Nations administrators persisted in conducting their functions impartially, the Greek Cypriots became critical and obstructive. The Turkish Cypriots also hampered United Nations operations, and they were instrumental in bringing about the replacement of General Gyani by General Kedendera Thimayya, also of India, on July 6, 1964. General Gyani was accused of showing partiality in his peace-keeping task, but the opposition to his presence gathered force when he hampered the Turkish Cypriot plan to construct an airstrip near the Turkish village of Krini at the foot of the Kyrenia mountain range. At times, both communities obstructed the smooth functioning of United Nations operations. In his reports, U Thant continued to clarify the mission of the UNFICYP. He stated that the

> UNFICYP cannot act as an instrument of the Government in helping it to extend its authority by force over the Turkish Cypriot community in the area now under its control. On the other hand, it cannot assume responsibility for restoring the constitutional position which existed prior to the outbreak of hostilities in 1963 and early 1964, nor to contribute to the consolidation of the present stalemate in the island. Both of these courses would basically affect settlement of the country's problems, a matter which is the province of the Mediator and not of UNFICYP.[23]

The secretary general's objective was to conduct all the functions of the United Nations on the island so that peace might be restored. On April 29, 1964, U Thant issued his plan for Cyprus, which dealt with the following points:

1. Freedom of movement on all roads and within the towns.
2. Evacuation and removal of all fortified positions, beginning in Nicosia.
3. Reintegration of Turkish Cypriots into their normal positions in the police and other government services.
4. Disarming of all civilians except in the regular police and gendarmerie, with control maintained over extremists on both sides.
5. Arrangement for a general amnesty.
6. Restoration of the normal functioning of the judiciary.[24]

Since both communities were dissatisfied with the peace plan, they declined to adhere to it; it was therefore ineffectual.

At the end of April, 1964, the Greek Cypriots launched an attack against the Turkish Cypriot stronghold of Saint Hilarion Castle, which overlooks the town of Kyrenia. The castle had been occupied by the Turkish Cypriots during the early months of 1964. Not only is it located in a strategic position the castle is also a threat to Kyrenia in case of all-out hostilities. It should also be mentioned that the Kyrenia range, which is in the vicinity of Saint Hilarion Castle, had become the military stronghold of the Turkish Cypriot irregulars because it gave them control of Kyrenia Pass, which is the major link to the capital. This pass was guarded by the Turkish regular and Turkish Cypriot irregular garrisons. The Greek Cypriot military objective was to seize the area, which would have demoralized the Turkish Cypriots and at the same time would have given the Greek Cypriots complete control of the strategic peaks of the Kyrenia range.

The Greek Cypriot attack was condemned by U Thant, which cost Makarios much of the world's sympathy. Athens was displeased with the attack because Makarios had proceeded without consulting the Greek government, and he was urged to stop. In order to prevent further deterioration of the Greco-Turkish relations over Cyprus, the NATO secretary general, Dr. Dirk Stikker, emphasized that both nations should extend their full support to the United Nations mediator and once again expressed the fear that their quarrel endangered the West's eastern defense posture.

Due to the intransigent Greek diplomacy in respect to the Cyprus crisis, Ankara resorted to a reprisal against the Greek citizens living in Turkey. Ankara eagerly exploited the Cyprus crisis, and despite the Greek government's protest, the Turks became more bellicose. The Greco-Turkish treaty of 1930 was abrogated, abolishing the special status rights given to thousands of Greek nationals living in Turkey. The ten thousand Greek nationals were either deported to Greece or were pressured to relinquish their business affairs in Turkey and go to Greece. The fifty thousand Greeks who were Turkish citizens were not pressured to leave Turkey. On April 6, 1964, Ankara suspended an agreement with Athens that permitted the citizens of each country to visit the other for three months without a visa. The limit of Turkish territorial waters was extended from six to twelve miles, forcing the Greek fishermen to stay away from their usual fishing grounds. The domestic activities of the Greek Orthodox Patriarchate in Istanbul were restricted and two bishops were expelled after being accused of activities detrimental to the Turkish state. Greek charges that Ankara had violated the Lausanne Treaty of 1923 were unheeded by the Turkish government. As a sovereign nation-state, Turkey felt that the control of citizens within its territory or its decision to eject aliens came under its sole jurisdiction. The political and economic reprisals on the part of both states were at times mutual, but the Turkish government's reprisal against the Greek citizens was the least justifiable and the least productive of a significant result.

The pugnacious attitude of the enosists encouraged President Makarios to continue his brinkmanship diplomacy at home and abroad toward Turkish Cypriots. In a major move to enhance its preparedness, the army instituted a plan to reorganize with special emphasis on its enlargement and improvement. President Makarios' intention was to strengthen the Greek military position, which was essential to an effective policy and a deterrent that could be employed if he failed to achieve his political objectives diplomatically. At this time, Makarios announced that the military build-up was for the territorial and administrative preservation of the Republic of Cyprus. He apparently believed that military strength would maximize the Greek Cypriot security and give him the leverage to bargain from a position of strength. Warnings that his actions might inflame the local grievances between the two communities did not deter him. The improvement of the Greek Cypriot military force rendered the role of the UNFICYP exceedingly difficult. In early June, 1964, Makarios introduced military conscription and succeeded in inducing General Grivas to return to Cyprus from retirement in Athens. Grivas was commissioned to organize and train 25,000 Greek Cypriots for the Cyprus National Guard. He came to Cyprus followed by 5,000 soldiers from Greece, in addition to 3,000 tons of military supplies. He took over the command of the National Guard from Lieutenant General George Karayannis, who was a Greek from mainland Greece, on August 15, 1964. After his retirement, General Karayannis was sent back to Greece. It is the conjecture of some Cypriots, that the replacement of General Karayannis by General Grivas was brought about so that the latter could command the Greek Cypriot forces and act as a restraining factor so that the militarist elements could be prevented from precipitating a confrontation with the Turks without the endorsement of Athens. In respect to the presence of Grivas on Cyprus, *The Economist* wrote: "the General has not come back at this juncture simply to do a good turn to the United Nations or the United States. His primary motive is undoubtedly to ensure that there is no weakening within Greek, or Greek Cypriot counsels, and that enosis, his life's dream, is at last realized."[25] President Makarios was also authorized by the Cypriot parliament to purchase heavy armaments from countries friendly to its cause. The Soviet Union and its satellites, along with Egypt, filled the orders of Makarios and continued to furnish his armed forces with sophisticated weapons and ammunitions. Greece, in addition to her 950 soldiers, as was agreed upon in the Treaty of Alliance, smuggled 5,000 men into the island. It should be stated that President Makarios, during this period, was not holding to the international rule of *pacta sunt servanda*, and under the *clausula rebus sic stantibus* had already unilaterally abrogated the Treaty of Alliance, an action that Great Britain and Turkey refused to recognize.[26]

The militarism, the unilateral abrogation of the treaties, the abduction of Turkish Cypriots in all parts of the island, and the economic blockade of the Turkish-held areas increased the frustration and anger of the Turkish government. The economic blockade imposed upon the Turkish Cypriot sectors included items necessary to subsistence, such as food and water. Electricity, motor fuel, construction material for buildings, such as steel, cement, and many other important items, were also unavailable. The Turkish Red Crescent from the mainland, with the permission of Makarios, extended medical supplies, clothing, and food to the Turkish Cypriots, who had become refugees as a result of the communal battles. Most of the refugees were evicted from their homes or villages by the Greek Cypriot militants and sought refuge in the Turkish enclaves. Some Greek Cypriots also became victims and were forced to flee their homes and find new accommodations in the Greek Cypriot sectors.

In the spring of 1964, there was speculation that the Turks were preparing an invasion of Cyprus. On June 5, President Johnson, in a sharp letter to Premier İsmet İnönü, wrote that NATO agreements did not allow member states to wage war on each other; furthermore, he cautioned Turkey of the possible consequences of potential direct Soviet involvement in the conflict between Turkey and Greece.

> I hope you will understand that your NATO allies have not had a chance to consider whether they have an obligation to protect Turkey against the Soviet Union if Turkey takes a step which results in Soviet intervention without the full consent and understanding of its NATO Allies. . . . I wish also, Mr. Prime Minister, to call your attention to the bilateral agreement between the United States and Turkey in the field of military assistance. Under Article IV of the Agreement with Turkey of July 1947, your government is required to obtain United States consent for the use of military assistance for purposes other than those for which such assistance was furnished. Your government has on several occasions acknowledged to the United States that you fully understand this condition. I must tell you in all candor that the United States cannot agree to the use of any United States supplied military equipment for a Turkish intervention in Cyprus under present circumstances.[27]

Turkey's plan to intervene in Cyprus was abandoned because of President Johnson's letter, which was in diplomatic language too severe—more or less an ultimatum—to be used toward a staunch ally.[28] The incident caused Turkey to reevaluate its foreign policy and concentrate more on its national interest. The letter not only intimidated the Turks, but it was interpreted as the American abandonment of Turkey in favor of Greece. Turks believed that the friend they depended on had joined hands with the enemy against them.

It is the theory of some Turks, both in Turkey and Cyprus, that if Turkey had intervened forcibly in the island, the ends would have justified the means. The Turks attest that Washington had always been kept informed of the intentions of Ankara toward Cyprus.[29] By the use of force, Makarios would have been pressured to reach a settlement. Greece (650 miles from Cyprus), being conscious of Turkey's closer position to Cyprus (40 miles distant) and the greater strength of its armed forces, would not have gambled on war with Turkey.[30] The Soviets, although they warned Turkey against an invasion of Cyprus, would have been deterred by the United States and Great Britain from becoming involved in the island's conflict. Furthermore, the Soviet Union would not have embroiled itself in a conflict in which its national interest was minimal. The determined objective of Turkey would have been condemned at first by the Western powers and the Soviets, but after a short time the outcome might have justified the intervention. To the disappointment of the Turks, the United States prevented this course of action.

To ease the tension between the two allies of the United States, Under-Secretary of State George Ball was sent as the president's special envoy to Athens and Ankara. The United States had an unflagging concern in the Cyprus affair and reminded the two opponents that peace in the area depended heavily on their diplomatic cooperation. The United States was deeply concerned that the Greek and Turkish hostilities would escalate the danger of war and allow the Soviet Union the opportunity to exploit their enmity. Greece and Turkey were informed that the policy they were embarked upon would be to the detriment of the security of the NATO alliance. The two antagonists were also reminded that the United States had spent over ten billion dollars in its attempts to develop both countries economically and militarily so that they could uphold their sovereignty and independence and prevent the encroachment of communism. Senator J. William Fulbright, chairman of the Senate Foreign Relations Committee, during his visit to Greece and Turkey in May, 1964, on a fact-finding mission, had also dealt with the same issue. During this visit, Fulbright expounded a suggestion that the Turkish Cypriots be transferred from Cyprus to Asia Minor, which Turkey rejected.

To further promote and stabilize better understanding between Greece, Turkey, and the United States, President Johnson invited the leaders of both countries to come to Washington, D.C., for a full discussion of the Cyprus issue. The purpose of this meeting was to give President Johnson the opportunity to influence the policy decisions of both leaders while preserving the national interest of the United States. Secretary of State Dean Rusk had stated that war between Greece and Turkey was "unthinkable."

In an attempt to further clarify the Turkish government's position in respect to Cyprus, Prime Minister Ismet İnönü visited Washington on June 22 and 23, 1964. After two days of talks, a communique was issued stressing the "present binding effects of existing treaties."[31] The White House talks had encouraged the Turkish leader to avoid a military solution to the Cyprus problem and, instead, to resort to bilateral diplomatic talks with Greece. The United States reaffirmed its support of the 1959 agreements, which was a reiteration of its previous stand.

When the premier of Greece, George Papandreou, met President Johnson for talks on June 25, he expressed the Greeks' disappointment over the Johnson-İnönü communique. No new developments emerged from these talks, but it gave the chiefs of the three states an opportunity to clarify their governments' positions and moderate their policy in respect to Cyprus.

The United States, in order to initiate the bilateral talks, proposed to U Thant in late June, 1964, that the Greek and Turkish delegates meet at the president's Camp David retreat under the chairmanship of Dean Acheson. U Thant suggested that Geneva would be a more conducive location for the talks, under the chairmanship of Sakari Tuomioja. Ankara agreed to the bilateral talks, but Athens rejected the proposal. Premier Papandreou wished to avoid talks that would reaffirm the binding pacts on the Republic of Cyprus and pressed forward the application of the principle of self-determination. President Johnson's forceful message to Papandreou urged Greece to send delegates to Geneva or face the likelihood of a war with Turkey, in which event Washington would do nothing. Having no choice in the matter, Greece reluctantly agreed to participate in the talks and sent its representative to Geneva. The emissaries of the two states were to meet along with the United Nations mediator Tuomioja and President Johnson's special envoy, Dean Acheson, who was to offer his "counsel."

The American government's interest was to find a solution to this dangerous situation that would be satisfactory to both of its allies since the continued rivalry between the two NATO members could seriously damage United States interests in the eastern part of the Mediterranean. Makarios was angered by the American diplomatic involvement in the Cyprus dispute and by his exclusion from the Geneva meeting; he charged that the United States was trying to "impose" a settlement.

In July, 1964, Dean Acheson, former secretary of state of the United States, attended the Geneva talks at the request of President Johnson; he was to assist in finding a solution to the Cyprus issue by trying to establish contact between the Turkish and Greek governments. The first development to emerge from these talks between Acheson and the other delegates was a statement he submitted toward the middle of July in which he outlined his views concerning the solution of the Cyprus question. The Turkish and Greek delegates accepted the proposals as the basis for negotiations, which resumed on July 20. Acheson's proposed plans were:

1. Cyprus to be given a choice between independence and enosis.
2. On the Carpas Peninsula (in Famagusta District) a territory was to be given to Turkey over which it would have sovereignty and which would be regarded as an indivisible part of Turkey. The exact boundaries of this territory were to be determined after further negotiations. On this territory, Turkey was to have the right to station as large a military force as it deemed necessary and thus it would have adequate power to safeguard the Turkish Cypriots' and its own security. On this territory, the Turkish Cypriots were to settle, and at the same time, in case of intercommunal civil war, it was to serve as a place of refuge for the Turks living in areas on the island that were under Greek administration.
3. The Turkish Cypriots who continued to live in areas that were to be governed by Greeks were to have the right of "local self-administration." Un-

der this system, the Turkish Cypriots were to collect the local taxes, decide local expenditures, be in command of the local police force, administer their judicial system, and were also to exercise powers related to local administration. The "local self-administration" was not to assume the character of a state within a state, but was to be answerable to the central political authority under the Greeks, and was to be established in two or three areas of Cyprus where the Turkish Cypriots were in the majority.

4. A central Turkish Cypriot administration was to be established for the protection of the rights of the Turkish Cypriots living in other parts of the island. Operating outside the two or three self-governing Turkish areas, this system was to administer the affairs of the Turkish quarters in towns and the affairs of all Turkish Cypriot villages or villages where the Turkish Cypriots were in the majority.

5. The Turkish Cypriots residing in areas under the Greek administration were to be citizens of that government and were to enjoy the minority rights.

6. An international commissioner was to be appointed either by the United Nations or by the International Court of Justice to observe whether or not the Turkish Cypriots' communal and individual rights were being respected. The international commissioner was to be authorized to hold hearings in case of complaints, to conduct investigations, and to advise the central government of any injustices that should be corrected. It was also suggested that the international commissioner be given the right to enforce the payment of damages or compensation, subject to the right of appeal by the other side. If the *de facto* authority concerned refused to comply with the advice or the decision of the commissioner, the injured party was to have the right to appeal to the International Court of Justice, or, with the consent of both parties, the issue could be appealed to NATO.

7. The Greek government also stated willingness to give to Turkey the Isle of Meis, to further strengthen the Turkish security in the Mediterranean.

In early August the Greek government refused to accept the "Acheson Plan." Upon the rejection of the plan, which in principle was to be used as a basis for discussion, Turkey informed Acheson that it would revert to its firm and explicit stand for partition of Cyprus as had been proposed by the Turkish delegation when the negotiations started on July 8. It was during this period that the Greek government made its own proposals:

1. Greece offered to lease to Turkey an area of thirty-two square kilometers on Cape Greco (in Famagusta District) for twenty-five to thirty years to be used solely as an air and naval base.

2. The Turkish Cypriots' minority rights were to be recognized, similar to the rights of the Turks living in Western Thrace. The Turkish Cypriot community members were to have the legal right of submitting their complaints directly to an international authority.

3. Turkey was to lease an area fifty square kilometers in size on the Carpas Peninsula for fifty years.

The Turkish government rejected the Greek plan and considered it separate from the plan it had accepted as a basis for the talks. It was the opinion of the Turkish representatives at Geneva that compliance with such a proposal would in effect be an endorsement for union of Cyprus with Greece, which Ankara strongly opposed.

On August 20, Acheson submitted to the representatives of the two governments a new proposal, hoping for reconciliation and an amicable settlement, which would be in the best national interest of the two parties. The new proposals of Acheson were:

1. Cyprus was to be given a choice between independence and enosis.
2. Turkey was to have the right of maintaining for fifty years a military base on the Carpas Peninsula, in an area on the east of a line starting two miles west of Komi Kebir and running in a north-south direction. In addition, Turkey was to have free use of the Famagusta Harbor.
3. The Greek government was to give strong guarantees to the Turkish Cypriot community regarding the accepted human and minority rights, including those stipulated by the Treaty of Lausanne and the European Human Rights Charter.
4. Cyprus was to be divided into eight districts and the administrators of two of those districts always were to be Turkish Cypriots. An appreciable number of the officials of the districts were also to be Turkish Cypriots. In areas where the Turkish Cypriots were in the majority, a mixed Greek-Turkish Cypriot police force was to be stationed.
5. To the office of the governor general in Nicosia a senior Turkish Cypriot official was to be designated with a sufficient number of bureau officials under his authority. The Turkish Cypriot administrator's official function was to observe and safeguard the rights and welfare of the Turkish Cypriots. Complaints could be submitted by him to the governor general, the Athens government, and, if necessary, to the international commissioner.
6. With the consent of the Greek and Turkish governments, the United Nations or any other international authority would be allowed to station a high commissioner in Cyprus. The task of this individual would be to supervise and insure respect for the rights of the Turkish Cypriots. He would submit all violations to the Greek authorities, and if a satisfactory solution was not reached, then he would submit them to an international administrative authority.
7. A separate civil law was to be established governing the Turkish Cypriots' civil rights, and cases connected with this were first to be tried by the Turkish judges.

Turkey objected to the two proposals and made a counterproposal: that it should be given a territory over which it would have full sovereignty, to be an integral part of the Turkish mainland. The renting of a base was strongly rejected by Turkey. On August 31, as a result of the rejection of Acheson's proposal both by Greece and Turkey, the United States government had decided to adjourn its efforts in Geneva as a mediator and to recall Acheson for consultations.

Ankara stated its willingness to accept the plan as a basis for negotiation. The Turkish government was not favorably disposed toward the idea of leasing bases on Cyprus, which might be transferred, but wished to have a guaranteed presence on the island.[32] While Acheson's proposal recognized the union of Cyprus with Greece, it also provided for Turkey:

> . . . a military presence unhampered by the need for tripartite consent at every turn. A sequestered base for ground, air and sea forces not only could be a defense for Cyprus but prevent its being used hostilely against Turkey, could defend the sea approaches to the south Turkish seaports, and be a constant reminder on the island of Turkish presence and interest.[33]

The Greeks rejected certain parts of the proposals, claiming that it was a partition plan and a betrayal of Greek and Cypriot interests. President Makarios was not pleased with Acheson's plans. He made derogatory remarks and declared that he would seek self-determination with the backing of the nonaligned nations at the United Nations. Acheson considered Makarios to be "a political priest with considerable gifts of demagogy and ruthlessness."[34] Despite Turkey's willingness to pursue the talks on the Acheson proposals, Greece could not proceed with the talks without Makarios' approval. In Acheson's words, "The Archbishop did not go out of his way to be helpful. He threw a monkey wrench into the machinery."[35]

When Makarios could not get his way in Geneva through the representative of Athens, he tightened the noose on the Turkish Cypriots. He restricted the activities of the Red Crescent and prevented it from distributing food and medicine to the beleaguered Turkish Cypriot enclaves on the island. Furthermore, he enlarged the list of items banned from sale to the Turkish Cypriots and justified this action by asserting that they were destined for military use. The basis for his justification was debatable; if it had not been for the intervention of the UNFICYP, the Greek Cypriots would have cut off even the water supply, which was under their control in most parts of the island.

The Turkish Cypriot village of Kokkina was the only one having access to the sea. The Greek Cypriots claimed that they had evidence that the Turkish submarines were bringing men and military supplies to the Turkish Cypriots. It is a fact, although it cannot be documented, that many Turkish Cypriots studying in Turkey were clandestinely smuggled into the village along with weapons and munitions. Some of these were transferred to other Turkish villages by bribing some of the forces of the UNFICYP. For the Turkish Cypriots this fishing village was an important link to the sea through which they could replenish their war supplies. Makarios, wishing to plug the flow of arms to the Turkish Cypriots, decided to give the Turkish enclave a decisive blow once and for all.

Under the orders of Makarios, UNFICYP's freedom of movement was restricted and it was refused access to certain areas so that it could not hinder his ploy against the Turkish Cypriot enclaves. By restricting the actions of the UNFICYP, the Greek Cypriot military force was able to surround the Kokkina-Mansoura area for an attack. The protest of the secretary general went unheeded by Makarios, and on August 6, 1964, the Greek Cypriots attacked the Turkish Cypriot enclave at Kokkina. The objective of the Greek Cypriot military force, under the leadership of General Grivas, was to obliterate the outnumbered Turkish Cypriots in a coordinated land-sea attack, utilizing gunboats for the sea-borne action. In a three-day drive, the Turkish Cypriot villages of Ayios Theodoros, Mansoura, and Alevga fell to the stronger Greek Cypriot forces, which were armed with T-34 Russian tanks and other mobile armored vehicles, the skeletons of which can still be seen in the area. Ankara was left with two alternatives: either permit the subjugation and devastation of the Turkish Cypriots in the region, or retaliate by bombarding the Greek Cypriot positions. The UNFICYP succeeded in evacuating women and children from the area but was ineffective in its attempts to block the two warring communities.

Due to the inability of the UNFICYP to check the Greek Cypriot military offensive against the Turkish Cypriot enclaves and the Security Council's impotence to bring about diplomatic pressure on the Greek and Cyprus governments, Ankara warned Makarios of a possible retaliation if he did not restrain the attacks. The archbishop doubted the Turkish resolution to act and was confident that pressure from the major powers would intimidate Ankara. Turkey sent jets over Cyprus as a show of force, which Makarios considered to be a bluff. When the Greek Cypriots' attacks persisted and their artillary barrage continued, Turkey retaliated by sending thirty Turkish fighter-bombers to bombard the Greek Cypriot positions near the Tylleria Promontory area and to silence the gunboats that had been shelling the village of Kokkino from the sea. When the Greek Cypriot offensive did not stop, sixty-four Turkish jets bombarded the Greek Cypriot positions on August 9, causing high casualties and paralyzing their mobile units. The second wave of air bombardment was so decisive that the Greek Cypriot war machine had received a major setback. Makarios had underestimated the reaction of Ankara to his rash action.

The Greek government presented a verbal ultimatum to Ankara and warned that if the attacks did not cease within thirty-six hours, it would "assist Cyprus with its air force and with every military means at its disposal."[36] Premier Papandreou was enraged with Makarios for not checking with Athens before launching the offensive military action against the Turkish Cypriots and demanded that Makarios stop all military operations. Athens, as well as the members of the Western world, was critical of Makarios' adventurous undertaking. However, Greece was partially responsible for the affair because it had supplied Makarios with men, arms, and moral support.

The hostilities on all fronts ceased when the secretary general appealed to the adversaries to halt all their military operations. At the United Nations, the representatives of Cyprus, Greece, and Turkey accused one another of aggression, while trying to pin the blame on each other for provoking the hostilities. Orhan Eralp, the Turkish ambassador to the United Nations, defended the Turkish air strikes as "a legitimate police action in accordance with the right of self-defense."[37] The United Nations Security Council, on August 9, passed the following resolution:

The Security Council

Concerned at the serious deterioration of the situation in Cyprus,
Reaffirming the resolutions of the Security Council on this issue dated 4 March, 13 March and 20 June, 1964,
Anticipating the submission of the Secretary General's report on the situation,

1. Reaffirms the appeal of the President of the Council just addressed to the Governments of Turkey and Cyprus as follows: "The Security Council has authorized me to make an urgent appeal to the Government of Turkey to cease instantly the bombardment and the use of military force of any kind against Cyprus, and to the Government of Cyprus to order the armed forces under its control to cease fire immediately";

2. Calls for an immediate cease-fire by all concerned;

3. Calls upon all concerned to cooperate fully with the United Nations commander in the restoration of peace and security; and

4. Calls on all states to refrain from any action that might exacerbate the situation or contribute to the broadening of hostilities.[38]

The objective of President Makarios was to nibble away one by one the Turkish Cypriot enclaves and occupy them by the use of force. The objective was important to Makarios, and he paid the highest price—war. Makarios' naive thinking on international politics simplified issues and ignored the conditions or risk under which decisions are made. The retaliatory strikes by the Turkish air force were a response to the escalated military pressures on the Turkish Cypriots. After this costly venture, Makarios was careful to avoid similar crises. Thereafter, the Turkish air force was a deterrence to the repetition of similar developments. For a time, Turkish aerial reconnaissance was continued until the status quo ante bellum was restored in the area.

Galo Plaza Lasso, who had succeeded Ambassador Sakari Tuomioja following his death on September 9, 1964, submitted a report on his activities to Secretary General U Thant on March 26, 1965. This report covered his activities in Cyprus from September 28, 1964, until March 28, 1965, and dealt with the causes of the constitutional crisis and the two communal political postures. The mission of Plaza achieved no progress toward a settlement because the positions of the principal parties remained unchanged. Against the objections of Turkey, Plaza went beyond his mandate as outlined by the Security Council and offered his own solution to replace the Zurich and London Agreements. He proposed the following:

1. A "fully independent" state that would undertake to remain independent and to refrain from any action leading to union with any other state.
2. The demilitarization of Cyprus, as a contribution to the peace and security of the region. The two British sovereign base areas, since those areas lie outside the territory of the Republic, do not form part of the present dispute.
3. There should be no geographical separation of the communities, but there must be practicable and effective safeguards for the security and the rights of all the citizens of Cyprus, as well as the legitimate rights of the Turkish-Cypriots as a community.
4. The United Nations should act as the guarantor of the terms of the settlement, and any complaint of violation or difficulty in implementation of the agreement be brought immediately before it.
5. A meeting or series of meetings to take place in the first instance between representatives of the two principal parties who belong to Cyprus: the Greek-Cypriot and Turkish-Cypriot communities.
6. The terms of a settlement should be referred to the people of Cyprus directly, and they should be asked to accept or reject it as a single package, and not in its various parts.[39]

Galo Plaza Lasso's report was more favorably received by the Greeks than by the Turks, who objected to his continued role as a mediator. Plaza was critical of the 1960 Constitution and the Treaties of Alliance and Guarantee, considering them to be unworkable and a major hindrance to the smooth functioning of a sovereign government. He also ruled out the ideas for enosis, *Taksim*, and federation proposals that had been proposed by the Turks. For the eventual settlement of the dispute, he stressed the need for talks between the Greek and Turkish Cypriots. In order to guarantee the safety of the Turkish Cypriots, he suggested that a United Nations commissioner be appointed to Cyprus. Archbishop Makarios supported the suggestion of self-determination, as mentioned in the report; however the Turkish Cypriots viewed this as a means by which Greek Cypriots could attain enosis.

Due to the Turkish government's opposition to the report and to his continued role as mediator, Plaza resigned his post.[40] Ankara, while rejecting the United Nations mediator's report, proposed direct bilateral talks between Greece and Turkey. Despite the opposition from Makarios, Greece and

Turkey began such talks in May, 1965, at the meeting of the NATO foreign ministers in London. The talks between the two nations continued until July, 1965, but because of a domestic political crisis in Greece, the talks became paralyzed.

Prime Minister Papandreou's liberal policy toward the far-left organizations in Greece raised fear among the Greek people of possible civil war. Papandreou justified his liberalization policy as an effort to restore full democratic rule. The Greek communist party, called the United Democratic Left (EDA), was permitted to pursue its activities freely. The National Radical Union party (ERE) exaggerated the expansion and danger of the communist party and advocated stringent control by the government. The communist party, in order to secure and preserve its given liberties, along with the Center Union party (EK) of Papandreou, encouraged the prime minister to purge the leading army officers to prevent a coup. Papandreou decided to assume the duties of the Defense Ministry and asked King Constantine to dismiss Defense Minister Petros Garoufalias, which the king refused to do. Papandreou sought the dismissal of the defense minister because he had refused to purge the army as instructed by Papandreou. Andreas Papandreou, who was a deputy minister in his father's government, was linked to the left-wing secret society for army officers known as Aspida ("shield"). A year later, Andreas, who no longer held a post in the government, was indicted by a Greek court-martial for having been the leader of Aspida, whose intention was to stage a coup d'état, with the help of left-wing army officers.[41] He had openly advocated the abolition of the monarchy, the revision of the Greek foreign policy away from NATO alignment, and stronger control over the military.[42] The king, being informed of the illegal activities of Andreas Papandreou, was acting cautiously so that he would not antagonize the army.

When Prime Minister Papandreou was unable to get King Constantine to dismiss the defense minister, he tendered his resignation on July 15, 1965. Papandreou was replaced by the president of the Parliament, Athanasiades-Novas, and he in turn was succeeded on September 17, 1965, by Stefanos Stefanopoulos. The latter had been foreign minister in the Karamanlis administration. The government of Stefanopoulos was weakened when the National Radical Union party withdrew its support on December 20, 1966. The king then accepted the resignation of the prime minister, appointing a caretaker government under Ioannis Paraskevopoulos, governor of the National Bank of Greece. The interim government stayed in office until March, 1967. After the resignation of Paraskevopoulos, the king was unable to form a coalition government, throwing Greece into further political turmoil and instability. On April 3, 1967, Panayotis Kanellopoulos formed a new interim government, but the domestic political crisis among the parties continued until the Greek military took over on April 21, 1967. For the enosists, the political bickering on the mainland was deadly to the Greek cause on Cyprus.

However, they were jubilant when the military took control of the government in Athens; filled with high hopes, they established a Pan-Cypriot United Front (PEM) to promote the idea of enosis. They had been critical of the previous Greek regimes for mishandling the Cypriot issue.

Despite the parliamentary crisis in Greece, Athens continued to support Makarios and cooperate in his pursuit for self-determination and enosis. During this period, a feud also developed between President Makarios and General Grivas, who was in command of the 11,000-man Greek Cypriot National Guard, over the issue of enosis. Makarios, who was opposed to the scheme of "instant enosis" as demanded by Grivas, wished to replace him in command of the National Guard with a Greek Cypriot leader whom he could trust. Makarios distrusted Grivas because the latter might choose to liquidate him or limit his power with the support of the loyal National Guardsmen. Makarios also had taken to heart the charges Andreas Papandreou made in July, 1965, that a group of Greek army officers had plotted to overthrow him.[43] In late March, 1966, Makarios accused Grivas and Stefanopoulos of a plot to assassinate him after a coup set for March 25 or April 1, 1966. Makarios claimed to have uncovered the plot against himself in a letter from Grivas to Prime Minister Stefanopoulos.[44] Grivas repudiated the charge by stating that if he had plans to kill Makarios, he would not be writing letters about it. It was becoming apparent that President Makarios was substituting independence for enosis for the time being. Athens, wishing to have control over the political as well as military affairs in Cyprus, refused to remove General Grivas from his command.

In May, 1966, through his special envoy in Cyprus, Dr. Carlos A. Bernardes of Brazil, U Thant put forward a provisional settlement for the Cypriot conflict. Dr. Bernardes was sent to Ankara and Athens for consultations with the two governments on the plan. The proposals U Thant's plan put forward were as follows:

1. Cyprus would have an independent regime, guaranteed by Great Britain, France, the United States, and the USSR.
2. The 1959 London and Zurich treaties would be suspended for three to five years, after which negotiations would begin for a permanent solution.
3. The Security Council was to guarantee the rights and well-being of the Turkish Cypriot minority in Cyprus, and the council would receive reports periodically on the situation from a United Nations observer in Nicosia.
4. Greek and Turkish contingents stationed on the island were to be evacuated.[45]

The Greek government rejected the plan on the grounds that it would create additional problems, but Turkey and the great powers expressed favorable opinions. Turkey, responding to a Greek initiative, agreed to direct negotiations between the representatives of the two countries. The Greco-

Turkish talks took place in Brussels, on June 9, 1966, under the auspices of NATO. President Makarios gave his blessing to the talks on the condition that the objective of Greece would be enosis.[46] The talks broke down before any new settlement could be reached.

Since the beginning of the political unrest in Cyprus, the Soviet Union has exploited the crisis to the detriment of its own national interest. The Soviet government, in conjunction with the communist party in Cyprus, endorsed President Makarios' demands for self-determination. Moscow was in favor of Cypriot independence and also supplied Makarios with arms via Egypt. Following the 1964 Soviet-Turkish rapprochement, Soviet policy changed and the two governments expressed common interest in the independence of Cyprus and the recognition of the legal rights of the two communities. The Soviet Union rejected enosis for fear that the Cypriot communist party would be repressed by individuals, such as General Grivas, who vehemently opposed the organization. The Soviet Union's goals in respect to the Cyprus crisis were to:

1. Avoid war between Greece and Turkey;
2. Avoid a great power confrontation;
3. Encourage Cyprus to remain an independent state under the two Cypriot communities' control;
4. Induce Turkey to adopt a nonaligned policy;
5. Intensify dissension in NATO;
6. Eliminate the two British bases and the United States intelligence radio stations on Cyprus.[47]

The representative of the Soviet Union in the Security Council, Nikolai T. Fedorenko, made the following statement with respect to the independence of Cyprus and the two Cypriot communities: "the Soviet Union is decisively in support of the independence, sovereignty and territorial integrity of the Republic of Cyprus, against foreign intervention in the internal affairs of this country. . . . The legitimate rights of the Greek and Turkish communities on the island should be observed."[48] The Soviet position was further complicated when the foreign minister, Andrei A. Gromyko, was quoted in the government newspaper *Izvestia* on January 21, 1965, as having said that the "Greek and Turkish Cypriots might decide to choose a federal form of government." Greece and Makarios were unwilling to consider any suggestions for partition or federation.

The Soviets were opposed to the Greek military coup of April 21, 1967, and castigated the junta as "reactionary officers" for making "undisguised inflammatory statements in order to create a pretext for open interference in the internal affairs of Cyprus."[49] The Soviet propaganda was tempered later, but the Soviets continue to oppose any plans of Athens to "liquidate the independence and territorial integrity of the State of Cyprus through so-called enosis."[50]

The Kremlin presently continues to supply Makarios with arms and other material without creating intolerable strains on its relations with Turkey. The Soviet interest is not to control Makarios or widen the Cypriot conflict but to strengthen its relations with its two neighbors while undermining the United States' strategic and diplomatic interests in the area. Due to the impartial policy of the United States with respect to Cyprus, and the Soviet propaganda strategem, the United States' influence in Greece and Turkey has been undermined. Since the Soviet-Turkish rapprochment, the policies of the United States and the Soviet Union are essentially the same: neither is taking sides in the Cypriot affair. The Soviet Union has been successful where the United States has failed because it presents itself and its policies to the two countries on a pragmatic basis, admitting its motives rather than assuming a moral tone. While not freely acknowledging their national interests and objectives, the Soviets and the Americans bring economic pressures to bear on both governments.

In August, 1967, the Deputy Prime Minister George Papadopoulos visited Makarios in Nicosia in an attempt to reach an agreement before the Greco-Turkish bilateral talks. The two leaders were united in their convictions that enosis would be achieved.

Athens's continuing insistence that enosis should be brought about and Turkey's adamant opposition to it made it difficult to believe that either would be willing to compromise. On September 9, 1967, the prime ministers of Greece and Turkey, Constantine Collias and Süleyman Demirel, met at Kesan, a small Turkish town near the border. On September 10, both men met again at Alexandroupolis, Greece. At the talks, Turkey advanced the idea of double enosis, or partition of Cyprus between the Greek and Turkish Cypriot communities. The talks ended without conclusive results. The joint communique issued at the conclusion of the talks stated:

> The two Premiers expressed in detail their points of view on the Cyprus question and underlined the major importance that public opinion in both countries attaches to this issue. They acknowledged the fact that the resumption of good and cordial relations between their two countries depended in the first instance on an equitable solution of this problem. They agreed therefore to continue, through the appropriate channels, the exploration of possibilities for a *rapprochement* of their viewpoints on this issue. . . . They have also acknowledged the need to take appropriate measures to avert the increase of tension in Cyprus and protect as well as facilitate efforts aimed at devising a peaceful and concerted solution.[51]

After the talks, Prime Minister Demirel, at a press conference, reiterated the Turkish government's policy: the existing treaties would be respected and that enosis would never be permitted. This opinion was again stressed by the prime minister to the Athens newspaper *Acropolis* on July 29, 1970. Demirel stated that "enosis was quite unthinkable . . . the Turkish and Greek Cypriots should accomplish a peaceful co-existence in the island." Turkish Foreign Minister İhsan Sabri Çağlayangil, in his address to the Turkish Senate in Ankara on February 4, emphasized that defects in the Cyprus Constitution could be overcome through negotiations with the Greeks. He also stated that he was against any plan "to create a Greek Cypriot State in Cyprus, and to persuade the Turkish community to be content with human rights, or administrative facilities, under the pretence of giving them community rights, when this is neither compatible with justice and equity, nor will it ever be."[52] The inflexible diplomacy of the two countries persisted, allowing no room for compromise.

The Greco-Turkish rapprochement had raised premature hopes of both communities for peace and a settlement. On November 15, 1967, the heavily armed National Guard, under the command of General Grivas, attacked the Turkish Cypriot enclaves in Ayios Theodoros and Kophinou, killing twenty-seven and wounding eight. The action against the two villages was launched when the Turkish Cypriot villagers refused to permit the Greek Cypriot police patrol through their village. The intention of Makarios was to reassert his government's authority and disarm the Turkish Cypriots.[53] Under the order of Grivas, the UNFICYP troops in the area, which was a British detachment, were forcibly disarmed.

Ankara was enraged with the attack against the Turkish Cypriots and pledged that it would come to their assistance. The Turkish Parliament authorized the government of Prime Minister Demirel "to go to war with Greece itself if necessary should the Cyprus situation deteriorate further." The president of Turkey, Cevdet Sunay, in a letter informed the leaders of the major powers that Turkey had decided "to solve the Cyprus problem once and for all, from the roots upward." The Turkish determination to act was strengthened when the major cities were blacked out and antiaircraft batteries were placed around them. While Turkish air-reconnaissance flights took place over the island, the Turkish army and navy were mobilized for the invasion of Cyprus. The Greek ambassador to Ankara was presented with a diplomatic note containing five demands.

1. The immediate recall from Cyprus of General Grivas.
2. Withdrawal from the island of an estimated 12,000 Greek regulars illegally infiltrated into Cyprus.
3. Compensation for the Turkish Cypriot victims in Ayios Theodoros and Kophinou.
4. A relaxation of the restrictions on Turkish Cypriots.
5. Effective guarantees against any further assaults on Turkish Cypriot communities.[54]

The secretary general appealed to all parties involved to restrain their forces for the preservation of peace and urged Greece and Turkey to withdraw those forces in excess of their respective contingents in Cyprus. NATO dispatched Secretary General Manlio Brosio to the area to mediate the crisis. U Thant sent José Rolz-Bennet of Guatemala, who was under-secretary for special political affairs, as his special representative to Athens and Ankara. President Johnson dispatched former United States Deputy Defense Secretary Cyrus R. Vance as his emissary to Greece and Turkey and asked the parties in the conflict "to refrain from any episodes which might culminate in war."

The United States' political reaction to the Turkish invasion threats was not as strong diplomatically as the sharp response of 1964, perhaps because the White House did not wish to further strain its relations with the Turkish government. The United States persuaded Greece to pressure President Makarios to terminate his brinkmanship policy against the Turkish Cypriots because the United States was unwilling to continue deterring the Turks from invading the island. Athens, under the pressure of the United States and the Turkish threat of invasion, restrained Greek Cypriot military actions against the Turkish Cypriots.

A military confrontation between Greece and Turkey was averted thanks to the successful mediation of Cyrus R. Vance, NATO Secretary-General Manlio Brosio, José Rolz-Bennet of the United Nations Secretariat, U Thant's personal representative, and the willingness of the foreign ministers of Greece and Turkey, Panayotis Pipinelis and İhsan S. Çağlayangil, to come to an amicable agreement. The important points of the agreement reached were:

1. The demobilization of the Turkish armed forces that had been poised for war.
2. The gradual withdrawal of the Greek and Turkish troops in Cyprus in excess of the 950-man Greek contingent and 650-man Turkish contingent as permitted by the 1960 Treaty of Alliance.[55]
3. Compensation for the Turkish Cypriot victims in Ayios Theodoros and Kophinou.
4. The expansion of the size and powers of the UNFICYP.
5. The dismantling of the 20,000-member Greek Cypriot National Guard.
6. The recall of General Grivas to Athens.

The agreement between Greece and Turkey was concluded because of the diplomatic skill and the even-handed approach to the crisis of envoy Vance and his associates. The Cyprus problem remained unsolved, but war was averted in the eastern Mediterranean between the two NATO allies. President Makarios was delighted by Athens's withdrawal, on November 19, 1967, and the final retirement in Greece of his archrival Grivas. However, he objected to the disbanding of the Cypriot National Guard and expansion of the UNFICYP's size and role. These two provisions of the Greek and Turkish agreement were opposed by Makarios and were successfully thwarted.

Since the Turkish Cypriots had not had any representation in the Cyprus Parliament since December, 1963, and an early Cypriot settlement was not in sight, they decided to organize a Turkish Cypriot Provisional Administration. On December 29, 1967, the Turkish Cypriot leadership declared that the Turkish Cypriot Provisional Administration was set up in order to direct Turkish Cypriot affairs until all the provisions of the 1960 Constitution had been restored once more.⁵⁶ Greece was strongly opposed to this development because it believed that the Turkish Cypriots, who had the support of Ankara, were seeking a *fait accompli* of a divided Cyprus. The Turkish government assured Athens that this measure did not in any way aim at a political objective and that the provisional administration would *ipso facto* come to an end as soon as the provisions of the Constitution of the Republic of Cyprus were fully implemented once again. One of the primary objectives for the provisional arrangement was to make possible the administration of communal affairs through a central authority and eliminate the confusion, overlapping, and misunderstandings that had existed in the previous year.⁵⁷ Makarios protested the action, declaring it to be "flagrantly unlawful," but brinkmanship diplomacy had been overruled, and instead, he adopted a policy of political realism. He once again stated his adamant opposition to a federation, which was a Turkish proposition, and declared his determination to establish a unitary system under which the Turkish Cypriots would be given minority rights without a major role in government, to which they were entitled under the Constitution.

Due to the recognition of a *modus vivendi* by the two communities, a presidential election was held on February 25, 1968, the first since independence. The archbishop, by polling 96.45 percent, was reelected president of Cyprus for a five-year term. The landslide for Makarios was considered a vote of confidence in his ability to carry out the affairs of Cyprus in time of crisis. His opponent was Dr. Takis Evdhokas, a psychiatrist, who was backed by the extremist enosist organization. Of the 229,488 votes, Dr. Evdhokas received 8,577.

President Makarios moderated his stand on enosis, despite the pressure and demands of the enosists, and began pushing forward the principle of self-determination and independence for Cyprus. With adoption of a new political approach for the future of Cyprus, the intercommunal talks started on April 17, 1968; the hope was that a settlement agreeable to all the interested parties could be reached. Makarios' change of heart concerning the cause of enosis had increased the support for his archenemy Grivas. Makarios' change of policy with respect to the future of Cyprus was partly due to policy dictates of the Revolutionary Government in Athens. Greece's objective was to reach a Cyprus settlement that would be acceptable to Turkey, since it wished to avoid antagonizing Ankara, militarily or diplomatically. Makarios, from time to time, had been irritated by the dictation of policy by Athens, but he also was aware that without the backing of the Greek government, the Greek Cypriots would be unable to stand, either diplomatically or militarily, against the Turks. The continuing failure to find a solution has frustrated both communities, but the enosists are far more restless and are agitated by Grivas for the "holy cause" of enosis.

The rapprochement between the two communities caused Makarios to lift all restrictions, on March 7, 1968, relative to movement of persons and goods in and out of the Turkish Cypriot enclaves.[58] The Turkish Cypriots were gratified by Makarios' gesture of goodwill, but they did not reciprocate by allowing free movement of the Greek Cypriots through their enclaves. The Turkish Cypriot leadership believes that "unrestricted movement of Greek Cypriots through Turkish Cypriot-controlled areas is a matter closely linked to the security of their community and to other aspects of the Cyprus problem, which do not allow independent treatment."[59] The Turkish Cypriots are of the opinion that "giving Greek Cypriots unrestricted access to certain highways lead to the establishment of Government authority over those areas."[60] Some Greek Cypriots are permitted to travel through the Turkish Cypriot enclaves with a special pass during the day, but they are expected to recognize the jurisdiction of Turkish Cypriot authority. An agreement was reached between the two communities and UNFICYP to permit the use of the Nicosia-Kyrenia road under the protection of a United Nations convoy, which passes through twice daily—in the morning and in the evening. The intransigent Turkish Cypriot attitude caused inconveniences to the Greek Cypriots, but because of security considerations the restrictions have not been lifted despite all the efforts of the United Nations command on Cyprus.

Archbishop Makarios is under continuous pressure from the church and the enosists not to deviate from the cause of enosis or accept any political settlement that is not consistent with their plan. In the international political arena, Makarios deemphasized the idea of enosis in 1964 and instead roused support for the abolition of the international treaties, attempting to gain support for the recognition of the sovereignty and independence of Cyprus. According to the Turkish Cypriot leaders, Makarios will revive the idea of enosis when circumstances favor such a course of action. Some enosists have also accused him of jeopardizing the cause of enosis and have lost faith in his leadership. It was just such disillusionment that motivated an assassination plot against Makarios.

On March 8, 1970, the helicopter carrying Makarios to Makhaeras Monastery to officiate at a memorial service for a prominent EOKA member, Grigorios Afksentiue, was fired upon when it took off from the courtyard of the archbishopric, which is located within the walled city of Nicosia. The gunfire came from the roof of the Pancyprian Gymnasium building across the street. The helicopter pilot, army major Zaharias Papadoyiannis, was wounded critically in the abdomen but was able to land the helicopter safely. The president was uninjured.[61] In the evening, Makarios addressed the

Greek Cypriots saying, "If the bullets did not strike my body, they struck and wounded my soul."[62] On March 12, at the Orange Festival in Famagusta, Makarios told his audience: "They have assassinated me, but I have not died, and here I am unharmed among you, among the Cypriot people. . . . I do not know whether another attempt will be made on my life; but if violent death snatches me away from you, I leave only one precept: remain loyal to our history and Greek traditions; faithful to God and Greece. . . . "[63] According to some newspaper reports, if the assassination plot against Makarios had been successful, it would have been followed by other killings.

The assassination plot, though it was committed by Greek Cypriots, led to considerable tension among Greek and Turkish Cypriots alike, but it eased in April. On April 15, Makarios stated that he had reason to believe that Polykarpos Yorgadjis had connections with the assassination plot against his life. Makarios also admitted that foreign sources had warned him about a conspiracy against his life upon his return to Cyprus after his visit to East Africa.[64]

On March 5, Bizim Radyo (Our Radio), which broadcasts in Turkish from Leipzig, East Germany, criticized the National Front and the enosists and announced that "there are also rumors that President Makarios will be assassinated and that the administration will be taken over by fascist elements attached to the Athens junta."[65] However, Makarios acquitted the outlawed National Front of any responsibility or of having any connections with the conspiracy against his life.[66] The leader of that organization was believed to be Michalakis Rossides of Morphou, and the operation of the group had gone underground. These clandestine activities continued, and twenty-one of its members were charged with an armed raid on the Limassol central police station on May 23, 1970.[67]

Polykarpos Yorgadjis' house was the only house searched immediately after the assassination attempt on Makarios' life. The former had served as interim minister of labor in 1959 and had become minister of interior in 1960, then in 1963 he assumed the office of minister of defense, from which he resigned in November, 1968. It was claimed that he was forced to resign by President Makarios because of pressure from Athens. He was accused of being involved in the unsuccessful attempt on August 13, 1968, to assassinate Prime Minister George Papadopoulos of Greece.[68]

On March 12, Yorgadjis was fined £160 ($384) by the Nicosia District Court for possessing two Smith and Wesson revolvers and fifteen rounds of ammunition without a permit. The accused claimed that the two revolvers were gifts from President Makarios on the latter's return from his visit to the United States.[69] The next day, Yorgadjis was prevented from leaving Cyprus for Lebanon by air. The Beirut-bound plane was on the runway preparing for takeoff at the Nicosia airport when the pilot was ordered to return to the apron before the terminal building. The security officers boarded the plane and asked Yorgadjis to disembark. He challenged the government action of banning his exit from the island as being an "illegal and unconstitutional act." When he was escorted off the plane, he warned: "Anything can happen now. To Makarios, people are like lemons: When they are squeezed dry, he throws them away." He was alarmed by the accusations of his masterminding the plot against Makarios and wished to exit Cyprus for his safety.

When Yorgadjis learned that he was suspected of being one of the conspirators who tried to kill President Makarios, he made the following statement: "Immediately after the murderous attempt against the life of Archbishop Makarios I became the target of several and sundry slanderous rumours. . . . I decided to leave temporarily my country, . . . believing that through my withdrawal I could also help those in authority to turn at last their attention in the right direction."[70] The same day, he resigned from his post in the Unified party, of which he was cofounder and organizing secretary. Yorgadjis desperately attempted to prove his innocence but unfortunately failed. On March 15, 1970, he left his home at 8 P.M. following an anonymous telephone call that promised him vital information in respect to the assassination plot against Makarios. At 10 P.M. his body was found, riddled by bullets, in a car on a side track off the road between Mia Milea and Kythrea, near Nicosia. The assassins are still at large. Tragic circumstances and death struck down the man who had served well the Greek Cypriots and President Makarios.

Following the death of Yorgadjis, the Greek Cypriot police investigations resulted in the arrest of four Greek Cypriots on March 13. They were charged with conspiracy to assassinate President Makarios and overthrow his government. Yorgadjis was linked with the conspirators. On November 19, the Nicosia District Court sentenced them to twenty-two years of imprisonment.[71]

This episode created tension in the island, but the Turkish Cypriots were not accused of being connected with the assassination plot against President Makarios. The Turkish Cypriots were gratified that the plot against Makarios had failed because his death and a change of administration could have caused the resumption of the hostilities between the two communities. In case of Makarios' death, there was the possibility of his replacement by a hard-line enosist who could have destroyed the *modus vivendi* and would have undermined the accomplishments achieved through the cooperation of the two communities. Regardless of the political differences between Makarios and the Turkish Cypriot leaders, his leadership and administration is credited with the detente between the two communities. Fortunately, the plot was thwarted without straining the peaceful atmosphere between the two communities.

The administration of Makarios, in order to legitimize its authority in the island at a time when harmony between the two communities prevailed in Cyprus, called for parliamentary elections. The elections were held on July 5, 1970, with no single Greek Cypriot party gaining a majority of seats in the House. The total vote cast was 200,141, which represented 25 percent abstention; however, more people participated in the elections than in the July, 1960, elections. For the thirty-five House seats there were 135 candidates. The Unified party, under the leadership of Glafkos Clerides, now the speaker of the House, won fifteen seats. Its party platform was opposed to enosis and was in favor of the continued independence of Cyprus. Clerides expressed the opinion that the best solution for Cyprus was enosis, but due to the Turkish Cypriots' opposition, another feasible alternative had to be agreed on. The Unified party is considered to be right-wing moderate and holds the largest number of the seats in the House of Representatives. The communist party, under the leadership of Ezekias Papaiannou, won nine seats, a gain of four seats; AKEL previously had five seats, which had been granted it under an arrangement with Makarios and the now defunct Patriotic Front. Headed by Dr. Odysseas Ioannides, the Progressive Front captured seven seats, and the two smaller parties, the Democratic Center Union and Independents, captured two each. The National Democratic party under the leadership of Dr. Takis Evdhokas, who had opposed Makarios in the presidential elections of 1968, was unable to obtain House representation for his party. Dr. Evdhokas' party platform demanded enosis and was very critical of Makarios' domestic and foreign policy.

The Cyprus parliament continued to be completely dominated by the Greek Cypriot representatives. The Greek Cypriots not only amended the Cyprus Constitution unilaterally, but they also changed the oath taken by the thirty-five members of the House of Representatives. The affirmation under the original Constitution was: "I do solemnly affirm faith to, and respect for, the Constitution and the laws made there-under, [and] the preservation of the independence and the territorial integrity of the Republic." An important section of the oath previously taken was deleted, and that taken by the newly elected Greek Cypriot parliamentary members on July 16, 1970, was as follows: "I do solemnly affirm faith to and respect for the laws of the Cyprus Republic and the conscientious fulfillment of my duties."[72]

Several pertinent points may be considered: (1) Does the new oath fail to recognize the Constitution as binding upon members' actions as representatives? (2) Was the change actually an expression of their unwillingness to commit themselves to uphold the independence of the island? (3) Is the republic as originally declared in 1960 still in existence? (4) Do members of the House consider themselves a caretaker government until a permanent solution to the crisis is reached? The Cyprus parliament is functioning without Turkish Cypriot representation, which can legally be considered as *de facto*, and parliamentary members refuse to recognize the elections held by the Turkish Cypriots on July 7, 1970, for the Provisional Cyprus Turkish Administration. Makarios refused to recognize the Turkish elections because they were not conducted under his governmental supervision. Both communities consider their elections as legal and their governments as *de jure*. The three minority religious groups, Armenians, Maronites, and Catholics, are permitted to attend the meetings of the House, but they cannot vote and are not allowed to speak or make suggestions pertinent to a bill unless invited to participate and make a motion. Dr. Ihsan Ali, a medical doctor, was appointed on May 30, 1970, as a special advisor to President Makarios on Turkish Cypriot affairs. Dr. Ali has been living in the Greek Cypriot sector since 1964 and has no Turkish Cypriot support or following. The Turkish Cypriot community considers him to be a traitor and a crony of the Greek Cypriots.

His absence from the island did not prevent Grivas from voicing his political convictions and criticism of President Makarios for mishandling the enosis affair. In order to keep Grivas in touch with the former EOKA fighters, an association was formed in all the districts on the island under the banner of Pancyprian United Front of Fighters (PEMA). Strongly anticommunist, it pledged itself to neutralize the communist movement on Cyprus. Grivas and his sympathizers were antagonized by Makarios' rapprochement with the communist party on the island, and for his pursuance of a foreign policy that was favorable to the Soviet Union. On April 4, 1971, Grivas, at a rally held in Athens to mark EOKA's sixteenth anniversary, told the crowd that a change of government was needed in Cyprus to achieve enosis. He blamed Makarios for undermining all efforts to attain the union of Cyprus with Greece.[73] Makarios refuted this accusation and reiterated his support of the union of Cyprus with Greece.[74]

Grivas disappeared from his Athens residence on August 28, 1971. He was reported to have slipped out of Greece disguised as a Greek Orthodox priest and to have entered Cyprus clandestinely with several of his EOKA subordinates.[75] An aide to President Makarios stated that they would have an idea of what Grivas was planning when he surfaced in public, and if he was in the island to work "peacefully" for enosis, he would be encouraged.[76] Individuals named as aides to Grivas were: retired Greek colonels Antonious Lekkas, Antonious Mexis, Constantine Karydas, and Ioannis Lades. President Makarios condemned the group as being illegal and warned that measures would be taken to crush them.[77] From the leaflets that appeared in Cyprus on October 26, 1971, it was evident that General Grivas had come to lead the enosists' struggle. The leaflets, bearing the signature of Dighenis, a fictitious name used by Grivas taken from a legendary Byzantine hero, stated the following:

> We came back to Cyprus to continue and consummate the struggle for the fulfillment of the age long aspiration to the Union of Cyprus with Greece, and to hand-over to the judgment of history and of the nation the unworthy leadership and the men who are unworthy of even bearing the name of Greeks. . . . We shall bring Greece to Cyprus, and we shall not allow anyone to humiliate Greece and cut off Cyprus from the national trunk.[78]

Since February, 1972, Grivas's group has been raiding Makarios' arms depots to get weapons and has occasionally clashed with the security forces. An aide to President Makarios also charged that Israel was supplying Grivas with arms, which Makarios refused to verify. However, Makarios does doubt the loyalty of some of the mainland Greek army officers serving in the Cyprus National Guard.[79]

In March, 1972, President Makarios and General Grivas had a secret meeting so that the two men might unify their efforts in strengthening the Cyprus internal front. Makarios admitted later that at the secret session with Grivas he had disagreed with Grivas on many points but "never questioned his patriotism or the purity of the motives of his actions and manifestations."[80] According to the December 1, 1971, issue of *Cyprus Mail*, Grivas had come to Cyprus to prevent a new solution serving Turkey's interest. His purpose was to attain enosis, which was unacceptable to the Turks. Attempts by Makarios to reach a compromise with Grivas were futile,[81] and in another leaflet dated February 4, 1973, the latter declared that he would "fight with courage and determination for enosis and only enosis."[82]

Athens was trying its utmost to reach an amicable political solution over Cyprus with Turkey, but President Makarios refused any proposal that recognized Turkish Cypriot rights on the island. The Greek government had been pressuring Makarios to give more autonomy to the Turkish Cypriots, which he adamantly refused to do. In a letter to President Makarios dated June 18, 1971, Greek Premier George Papadopoulos wrote:

Our proposals . . . are the outcome of detailed study and mature thinking by the Greek Government alone. We examined the present situation and all likely prospects, and we unhesitatingly concluded that:

1. The existence of some sort of coordinator is indispensable to the smooth operation of the local administration authorities.
2. The presence of a Turkish Cypriot minister in the Ministerial Council, who would be responsible on questions of local administration as a whole, does not weaken the state; on the contrary it lends support to it.
3. This unique concession—for the Turkish Cypriot side is not asking for any other substantial concessions—is richly compensated for by the proposals made thus far by Denktas, proposals that among other things satisfy almost all your 13 points and allow unhindered operation of the state machine.
4. Under the circumstances an agreement would clearly be in the interest of the Greek Cypriot people.
5. As regards the consolidation of the jurisdiction of the local administration, the need for such consolidation is obvious to any objective judge. In addition to the important advantages that an agreement on the agreed bases would produce, such a settlement would first insure the dissolution of the present partitionist regime, and second, it would forestall another certain crisis whose extent and unfavorable consequences are unforeseeable. . . . I do not

claim that our proposals would be definitely accepted by the Turkish side, but they would render our case internationally unassailable.[83]

It is theorized by some scholars that Athens, with the support of General Grivas and the three senior bishops of the Greek Orthodox Church—the bishop of Citium, Anthimos, the bishop of Paphos, Yennadios, and the bishop of Kyrenia, Kyprianos—had been pressuring Makarios to comply with its demands or step down as president of Cyprus. In March, 1972, the three senior bishops, with the support of the Greek Orthodox Church in Greece, invoked a canon law forbidding bishops of the church to hold ecclesiastical and state posts simultaneously. The canon law had been unused for approximately one hundred years. Why had it not been invoked in 1960 to prevent Makarios from accepting the Cyprus presidency? Were the bishops encouraged by Athens to force Archbishop Makarios to resign from his political office? The supporters of Makarios, including priests, rallied around him, in opposition to the bishops. Pro-Makarios newspapers described the Holy Synod decision as "A shame; a national betrayal."[84]

The three bishops demanded that Makarios relinquish his temporal duties and devote himself to the church and ethnarchy duties. In a letter to the three bishops, Makarios stated that "the abolition of the Cyprus state is conceivable only through the Union of Cyprus with Greece." The bishops, not being satisfied with the reply of the archbishop to their demands, reiterated their threats in a letter to Makarios, dated June 1, 1972, stating the following:

> . . . in full awareness of the responsibilities we incur for a situation most harmful to the Church, we address ourselves once again to Your Beatitude and we demand that you abandon forthwith and without delay the post of President of the Republic, which is incompatible with the archiepiscopal status and confine yourself to your clerical and ethnarchic duties. . . . In case you should continue to stand in confrontation to the Holy Rules, we would inform you with utmost regret that we are compelled to impose on you the sanctions provided by the Holy Rules and the Charter of the Church.[85]

The bishops threatened to "defrock" Archbishop Makarios if he refused to comply with their demands.

Archbishop Makarios rejected the renewed demand of the bishops to resign as the president of Cyprus, and on June 10. His reply was as follows:[86]

Dear Brethren in Christ,

I have received a letter dated June 1, 1972, bearing your signatures, in which I am called upon to abandon "immediately and without fail" the office of the President of the Republic.

In reply, I inform you that the critical circumstances make it imperative for me to continue to offer my services to the people from the post of President entrusted to me by them.

My conscience as a Greek and Archbishop, and also my Ethnarchic mission, do not permit me to abandon the people, who are in great peril and look to me. Such abandonment and desertion of the people would be regarded as treachery on my part. With the wolves swooping down, the shepherd does not desert the sheep and flee.

This is what I have to say, and leave the rest to God. May our Lord keep you in good health.

> Your willing brother in Christ.
> *Makarios,*
> *Archbishop of Cyprus*

Archbishop Makarios' refusal to resign from his temporal office, which was charged as being contrary to the church rules, forced the three senior bishops to bring indictments on February 21, 1973. Makarios was asked to appear before their synod to respond to the charges or face being defrocked. The action of the three bishops was rejected by the archbishop, who responded that any decision taken would be "null and void ab initio" and refused to respond to their summons.[87] The response of the bishops was to defrock the archbishop on the grounds presented in their statement: " . . . the Holy Synod, mindful of the prestige of the Church which has fallen in many respects into anarchy and distress because of the Archbishop's church offence, and having shown long patience, has decided with much regret to defrock the Archbishop from church and clerical office and his return to the lay class." Makarios bitterly attacked the synod and described their act as an "attempt of spiritual assassination" and in a statement he declared the following:

The so called decision to defrock me, taken by the three bishops in a conventicle held at Limassol, is void ab initio and of no value whatsoever. I cannot conceal, however, my deepest regret in that the three bishops, acting on instigation and with an utter disregard of the difficult circumstances now prevailing in Cyprus, have shown lack of episcopal conscience and national responsibility and have attempted today my spiritual assassination. I pray to God that they may be forgiven, for they know not what they do. . . . The decision of the three bishops is causing to the Church of Cyprus a serious wound and is scandalizing the ecclesiastical flock for which, on account of their inefficiency, they do not care less, and which they ought not to despise and hurt. The act of the three bishops, having shown unacceptable behavior of dark medieval mentality, amounts, amongst others, to an utter contempt of the people and flock. . . . With full conscience of my responsibilities as Primate of the Church of Cyprus and of my obligations as national leader I have no other alternative than to take all steps necessary in the circumstances for the protection of the people against sabotage from within and for safeguarding the prestige of the Church, the bishops and shepherds of which must be acceptable and respected by their flock and not objectionable and undesirable.[88]

On July 14, the three bishops were defrocked by the sixteen-member major synod of Middle East Orthodox prelates, which were called into session by Archbishop Makarios. The synod by a unanimous vote ruled invalid the bishops' defrocking decision of Makarios.

Opposition to President Makarios had been supported by the enosist press,[89] EOKA-B, the underground organization whose leader was speculated to be Grivas, and ESEA (Coordinating Committee of the Enosis Struggle), headed by former Chief Justice G. Vassiliades. *Patris*, in support of the three bishops, on May 15, 1972, stated that the enosists would not take part in a cabinet under President Makarios. Furthermore, it stated: "We can undertake state responsibilities only under two conditions: Makarios should quit the Presidency and withdraw to his ecclesiastical duties, restoring the Ethnarchy to its traditional role and the 'feasible' policies should be replaced by self-determination and enosis." Makarios refuses to be intimidated and continues to rule as the head of a sovereign state without complying with the wishes of the enosists and an outside power. However, how long could he ignore Athens and refuse to listen to the dictator of Greece, Brigadier General Dimitri Ioannides?[90] The Greek government might consider the liquidation of Makarios as expedient in order to come to an agreement with the Turks.

President Makarios did carry out a broad reshuffling of the cabinet and formed a government of "national unity," as was demanded by Athens, but was able to block the attempts of Greece to dominate and dictate all policies. Attempts by Grivas and his supporters to disrupt the presidential elections on February 18, 1973, were a failure. Grivas refused to challenge Makarios for the presidency, because of assured defeat at the polls. Makarios was proclaimed president of the Republic of Cyprus for another five years since no opposition candidate was nominated by February 8, which was the legal deadline to file. This obviated the need to hold presidential elections scheduled for February 18. Makarios charged that the aim of Grivas was "to prevent the presidential elections, and to create a chaotic situation so that . . . I might be removed from office." Makarios is unwilling to crush the Grivas underground by force because it might lead to fratricidal strife.[91] After his proclamation as president, Makarios promised to continue his nonaligned foreign policy and his support for intercommunal talks until an amicable compromise could be reached. He also emphasized that the Greek culture and ideals "will always inspire our thinking and our conscience. . . . If factors and situations beyond our control do not make enosis possible, this does not mean we shall cease to be Greeks."[92]

The campaign of the pro-Grivas forces was to raid police stations and government offices all over the island in order to seize arms and radio equipment for the coming offensive against the administration of President Makarios. EOKA-B forces kidnapped Christos Vakis, minister of justice of Cyprus, on July 27, 1973, and for his release Grivas demanded, in the leaflet distributed on July 27, the following: (1) political freedom for enosis supporters; (2) genuine elections for the Cyprus presidency; (3) a choice by Makarios between his ecclesiastical office and politics; and (4) amnesty and reinstatement for political detainees and dismissed policemen and civil servants. President Makarios dismissed about seventy-five Greek Cypriot policemen and a number of civil servants after the kidnapping of Christos Vakis. On August 3, President Makarios refused to discuss the demands made by Grivas because they were tantamount to political blackmail. The refusal of Makarios to adhere to the demands of Grivas escalated the bombing of the government buildings.

A major plot against President Makarios' life and government, which was uncovered in the early part of August, was headed by Grivas and carried the code name of "Operation Apollo." The plot was discovered after the arrest of former army major Stavros Stavrou, second in command to Grivas, in a Limassol hideout. The Apollo plan called for the assassination of President Makarios, coordinated attacks against police stations, government ministries, the Cyprus telecommunications, broadcasting electricity buildings, and Nicosia International Airport. The coup d'état was to be accomplished in such a manner as to avoid antagonizing the Turkish Cypriots so that Turkey's military intervention might be avoided. When Operation Apollo failed, Athens accused Grivas of masterminding the plot against Makarios and offered him an honorable return to Greece.

Publicly, Athens supported the regime of Makarios and his desire to maintain the independence of Cyprus, but the junta in Athens had tried to maneuver him out of office, with the help of the Greek officers on Cyprus who headed the Cypriot National Guard. Greece considered Makarios an obstacle to its attempts to reach an agreement with Turkey. Before the overthrow of the Papadopolos regime by a junta led by Brigadier General Dimitri Ioannides on November 25, 1973, Greek Prime Minister Spiros Markezinis, a distinguished historian and a minister in Greek governments that preceded the April, 1967, military takeover, indicated that he was in favor of an "imposed" Athens-Ankara solution to Cyprus that would bypass the intercommunal talks. Athens was in favor of Makarios' resignation from state politics and wished that he continue as head of the Greek Orthodox Church on Cyprus. Furthermore, the junta in Athens was displeased with Makarios for permitting the island to be a haven for dissident Greek activity against them. The enosists also expressed the opinion that President Makarios wished to have his close friend King Constantine of Greece, who was deposed on June 1, 1973, when Greece was declared a republic, and former Greek prime minister Constantine Karamanlis come to Cyprus from 'Western Europe and set up a "Greek government in exile." However, Makarios is a political realist who is aware of the potential importance of the Greek junta in any confrontation with Turkey.

After the death of General Grivas on January 27, 1974, President Makarios tried to capitalize on the events and bring an end to the terrorist campaign against his administration. He proclaimed an amnesty for all imprisoned Grivas sympathizers, and in response required EOKA-B underground activities to cease. The plan of Makarios was to undermine the cohesiveness of EOKA-B; retired Greek army major George Karousas accepted the offer of President Makarios and ordered his followers to hand in their arms to the loyal forces of the Cyprus government. Major Karousas was recalled to Athens without any explanation. EOKA-B was reactivated with the help of 650 army officers from Greece who were attached to the Greek Cypriot National Guard, including National Guard Chief of Staff Paul Papadakis and Colonel George Kophinas, KYP (Greek central intelligence agency) chief in Nicosia. After the stockpiles of arms at Yeriskipou National Guard Camp near Paphos were stolen by EOKA-B members, President Makarios suspected a conspiracy against his regime and asked Athens to recall General Papadakis and Colonel Kophinas as well as the 650 Greek army officers from Cyprus. President Makarios also charged that he had documentary evidence that Athens was involved in a plot to assassinate him, with the aid of EOKA-B guerrilla organization, and terminate Cyprus independence. The poor political relations with Athens forced President Makarios into a very precarious position.

During his regime President Makarios has been able to preserve the status quo between the two ethnic communities and for that the United States and the Soviet Union regard his government as the best representative body to reach a settlement with the Turks. The Soviet Union and the United States have both applied diplomatic pressures on Athens to restrain its pro-enosis Greek army officers serving on Cyprus. However, the United States, which has no admiration for the military dictatorship in Greece, has been very cautious not to exert excessive diplomatic pressure on Athens because it wants to protect the United States Sixth Fleet base at Piraeus, which the junta has allowed the fleet to make its home port. Because Washington considers the naval base at Piraeus strategically imperative to the NATO alliance in the eastern Mediterranean, it will avoid jeopardizing the accord. The Soviet Union and the Cyprus communist party (AKEL) gave full support to the regime of Makarios because of its change of policy from enosis to independence for Cyprus. The control of Cyprus by President Makarios was tolerable to Turkey as long as the independence of the island and the treaties were left intact and the Turkish Cypriots had the liberty to administer their communal affairs until an amicable agreement was reached between the two ethnic communities.

In 1972, during the writing of this book, I felt that the coming five years of Makarios' presidency would be his hardest. What action would Athens take if the conflict between the Greek Cypriots could not be controlled? If the guerrilla warfare endangered the Turkish Cypriots, there was the possibility that Turkey might intervene militarily. Greece's major objective was to prevent any major crisis between itself and Turkey. Athens was unwilling to confront Turkey during a period of domestic unrest and hostility of the Greek people toward its dictatorial government. Furthermore, Cyprus, which is 650 miles from the Greek mainland, is not important for Greece's national security and national interest. Therefore, Greece would probably avoid a confrontation with Turkey, since war would be contrary to its progress, stability, and future development.

It is the hypothesis of some Cypriots that Grivas was the political instrument of Athens on Cyprus and that he would have been called back to Greece after he was successful in overthrowing President Makarios with his underground forces on the island. Makarios has abandoned the idea of enosis, to which Grivas and EOKA-B members are committed. Makarios is the main obstacle to a compromise involving partition, federation, or any settlement that will provide for a Turkish Cypriot role in a Cypriot government. After the death of Grivas, the Turks hoped for an intercommunity settlement, since the Greek Cypriot leaders had emphasized during the earlier talks that while he was campaigning for enosis President Makarios was barred from reaching any reconciliation for a permanent Cyprus independence. Ankara contends that the Turkish Cypriots should be self-contained under a federal system, but Makarios wishes them to be subject to checks and balances of a central government. President Makarios made the following statement in opposition to the idea of a state: "A federal solution is not possible for Cyprus unless we are prepared to move the population from one part of the island to another as a prerequisite. We see no real reason or necessity for a federal state."[93] The Turkish Cypriot leaders are not in agreement with Makarios' views on a federal solution, and since December, 1963, due to the intercommunal strife, thousands of their people have been living as refugees or for security reasons have settled in their enclaves or in the predominantly Turkish Cypriot sections of a village or city. Therefore, the Turkish Cypriots hold the view that a federal solution is practical and possible and that the population of each community can be brought together without major inconveniences or hardships on either party. It should also be pointed out that both communities have expropriated land and property without giving any compensation to the respective owners. Furthermore, each community is governed by the laws of its own government, and a state within a state has been in operation since 1964.

Athens might have to neutralize the enosis movement while coercing Makarios to comply with its demands so that it could conduct intensive diplomatic conferences with Turkey until a solution to the Cypriot crisis is reached. Greece is convinced that Turkey will never tolerate enosis or a complete Greek Cypriot domination of the island's government, but Makarios refuses to agree. Greece and Turkey hope that the intercommunal talks, which have been in progress since 1968 with intermittent breaks, will achieve a solution of the Cypriot crisis. In early June, 1971, the under-secretary of state for foreign affairs of Greece, Xanthopoulos-Palamas, and the foreign minister of Turkey, Osman Olcay, held a meeting in Lisbon during which they discussed the question of Cyprus. The two diplomats "emphasized the need for a speedy solution to the Cyprus question and expressed the hope that the intercommunal talks would be continued at a quicker tempo and in a constructive spirit."[94] It is the opinion of some Greek Cypriots that Xanthopoulos-Palamas was opposed to the intransigent diplomacy pursued by Makarios and was agreeable to double enosis or partition of the island. In a press statement Xanthopoulos-Palamas said that "if the intercommunal talks failed to produce a solution, Greece and Turkey would begin consultation for the further handling of the issue." The Turkish representative was in accord with the Greek diplomat and went on to say that "there was a need to fix a time-limit for solving the Cyprus problem since the intercommunal talks could not drag on indefinitely. . . . Turkey was not seeking the partition of Cyprus provided the status of Cyprus was not changed fundamentally and the partnership of the two communities was maintained, as defined in the 1960 treaties."[95]

The last meeting between the foreign ministers of Greece and Turkey pertaining to Cyprus took place during the NATO ministerial conference in Copenhagen in June, 1973. Greece and Turkey cannot afford war if they are to protect themselves against Soviet expansionist policy in the Mediterranean region. Makarios' main foreign support consists of the Soviet Union, Eastern Europe, and some of the Arab and nonaligned states. Makarios, by aligning himself with the non-Western powers, has further weakened his relations with Athens.

Greece has exerted increased political pressure on President Makarios, attempting to convince him to restrain his associates from criticizing Athens and to stop massing armaments on Cyprus. Turkey was the first to become aware of the secret shipments of Czechoslovak arms to Makarios' Greek forces on Cyprus. After Athens was informed of the weapons shipments, on February 10, 1972, it asked Makarios to surrender the arms to the Greek-officered Cyprus National Guard or to the United Nations Peace Force. Ankara felt that the imported arms were to be used against the Turkish Cypriots, though pro-Makarios sources claimed that they were intended to block a military takeover of Cyprus by the enosists. On March 14, Makarios agreed to place the arms under United Nations control, but he rejected at first the other two demands of Greece: (1) that Athens be the guiding center for all Greeks including the Cypriot Greeks; (2) that a government of "national union" more favorable to the policies of the Greek government be formed. Makarios reluctantly dismissed anti-Athens Cypriot cabinet ministers whom he had defended earlier, his reason being that it was "impractical and unworkable to have a cabinet containing men loyal to Greece because their views might differ substantially." His underlying objective was to surround himself with supporters of his policies. Makarios has become more willing to recognize Athens as the guiding center for all Greeks while trying to persuade Athens to pursue a policy more in line with his political strategems.

All the parties in the Cypriot dispute agree that Cyprus's national interest must be considered. Both communities on the island, as well as Greece and Turkey, have become convinced that armed conflict diminishes the possibility of a settlement and at the same time weakens their security against the forces of communism. It is hoped that all the parties will resort to reason and not force and be flexible in their negotiations so that they may reach a compromise. The extremist elements of both communities must be neutralized in order to prevent them from shattering the painfully attained tranquility so that the intercommunal talks may progress until peace for all the Cypriots is achieved.

5 THE TURKISH CYPRIOT ADMINISTRATION

Due to the communal hostilities that had begun on December 23, 1963, the Turkish Cypriots were physically unable to go to their places of employment for about five days, until a ceasefire agreement was reached on December 28. The Greek Cypriots whose jobs were located in the Turkish Cypriot sector failed to report to work for fear of being shot, and they were reassigned to positions in their sectors. Since most of the governmental offices are in the Greek Cypriot sectors of Cyprus, it was very dangerous for any Turkish Cypriot to attempt to report to his place of employment for fear of being killed by the Greek Cypriot extremists. It is the conviction of some Turkish Cypriots that the Greek Cypriot objective was to eliminate their positions in the Cypriot administration. When the Turkish Cypriots did not report to work, the Greek Cypriot hierarchy in the civil service refused to allow them to reclaim their jobs, arguing that the issue should be decided after the political settlement. Hence, the Turkish Cypriots had to tend to their official business and functions of their own sectors in makeshift offices. The Greek Cypriot side, having removed all the Turkish Cypriots from the administration, put itself outside the Constitution, insisting the move was an "act of necessity." From the time the Turkish Cypriot civil servants lost their jobs in the Makarios administration, they have depended heavily on the $20 million they receive annually from Turkey.[1]

Since the Turkish Cypriots were denied their jobs by the Greek Cypriot administrative officials, they consider the present government of Cyprus as unconstitutional and as being representative only of the Greek Cypriot community. President Makarios considers his administration's actions as legal and binding on all the Cypriots and that therefore the Turkish Cypriots must accept the legality of the laws enacted during their "absence" when they return to their subservient role. The Turkish Cypriots do not acknowledge the administration of Makarios as the lawfully constituted authority in Cyprus. The Turkish Cypriots have been considered rebels by their Greek countrymen, and they have clustered in their individual enclaves in order to defend themselves in the event of further hostilities. The constitutional government, in which the Turkish Cypriots formally agreed to participate, no longer exists in their opinion. Since December of 1963, the constitutional rights guaranteed by the Cyprus constitution have been obliterated. The Turkish Cypriots have been inflexible in their demand that the Constitution be upheld, while the Greek Cypriots have been eager to make changes in pursuance of their own social, economic, and political interests.

Since the outburst of the civil war, the pressure on the Turkish Cypriots politically, economically, and militarily has resulted in exceedingly poor conditions in the Turkish Cypriot enclaves, which are quite evident to any casual observer.[2] Some Greek Cypriot businesses were also victims of circumstances and suffered heavy losses. However, the Greek Cypriots have benefited economically from the polarization of the two communities because the entire export and import business is under their control.[3] Everything the Turkish community uses must come through the Greek Cypriots, who control all the harbors and the airport.[4] In addition, large numbers of Turkish Cypriots lost their homes and all their possessions during the conflict, when Greek Cypriot extremists looted and burned Turkish areas. Most of Cyprus's 20,000 Turkish Cypriot refugees have subsequently been housed in buildings built near the village of Orta Keuy, which is near Nicosia.

On December 28, 1967, the Turkish Cypriots established the Turkish Cypriot Provisional Administration[5] to direct the affairs of their community until all the provisions of the 1960 Constitution of the Republic of Cyprus were once again applied. The formation of the provisional administration filled the vacuum left by the absence of public services since 1963. The newly created administration was to be a central authority for directing the affairs of the Turkish Cypriots. The Turkish Cypriot leadership was assisted by Zeki Kuneralp, secretary general of the Turkish Foreign Ministry, and Professor Suat Bilge, the chief legal advisor of the same ministry.

The measures adopted by the Turkish Cypriot leadership were in no way to be considered a plan to foster the partition of Cyprus or to create a separate Turkish state on the island. President Makarios considered it "flagrantly unlawful" and proclaimed that "any action deriving from the so-called 'administration' is entirely null and devoid of any legal effect."[6]

The Turkish Cypriot members of the House of Representatives and members of the Turkish Cypriot Communal Chamber jointly constitute the Turkish Cypriot Legislative Assembly. In July, 1970, both approved the election of Rauf Raif Denktaş as the president of the Turkish Cypriot Communal Chamber and Dr. Neçdet Ünel as the vice-president of the House of Representatives. Denktaş was elected by the voters of the Nicosia district as a member of the communal chamber and later, by secret ballot, was chosen by the fifteen members of the Turkish Cypriot Communal Chamber as its president.

On July 5, 1970, the fifteen members of the House of Representatives and the members of the communal chamber were elected to office for a period of five years by the Turkish Cypriots. Eighty percent, or 54,000 of the Turkish Cypriot electorate, who were twenty-five years of age and older participated in the elections.[7] President Makarios considered the Turkish Cypriot elections illegal, invalid, and refused to acknowledge the results. In respect to the elections, Dr. Küçük made the following statement: "our elections were held within the framework of 1960 Constitution, and in accordance with an agreement reached between Mr. Denktaş and Mr. Clerides. The results of our elections are as legal and valid as those of the Greek Cypriot elections."[8] Furthermore, he stated that for the past seven years, the Turkish Cypriot administration had extended its control over all the Turkish Cypriots on the island. Turkish Cypriots in all parts of the island had participated in electing their administrative leaders democratically.[9]

The eight members of the Executive Council of the Provisional Turkish Administration are appointed by the vice-president of the republic. He may appoint any qualified person from within governmental or civilian circles to serve on the Executive Council, but his choice must be approved by the Turkish Cypriot Legislative Assembly. The vice-president of the Republic of Cyprus shall be the president of the Executive Council, and the president of the Turkish Cypriot Communal Chamber shall be the vice-president of the same.

The vice-president of the Republic of Cyprus from August 16, 1960, to February 28, 1973, Dr. Küçük, headed the Executive Council. President Makarios holds the opinion that Dr. Küçük decided to abstain from taking part in the Cyprus administration and therefore had ceased to be the vice-president of the republic. In 1965 the Cyprus Parliament enacted a law extending the terms of office of President Makarios and the Greek Cypriot members of the House of Representatives, but the law did not extend the terms of office of the vice-president and the Turkish Cypriot members. The Makarios government justified its action under Article 2, section 7 of the Cyprus Constitution. Dr. Küçük's contention was that he had always been the legal representative of his people, and he would remain in that position, with the consent of the Turkish Cypriot electorate, until the restoration of a *de jure* Cyprus government. The person next in line of succession to the vice-presidency is Dr. Neçdet Ünel, vice-president of the House of Representatives. Dr. Unel was elected to the House by the electorate of the Nicosia district, and in turn the House and Turkish Cypriot Communal Chamber members jointly elected him the vice-president of the Turkish Cypriot Legislative Assembly.

Due to lack of support and criticism of Vice-President Küçük by prominent leaders of the Turkish Cypriots, primarily because of his health and age, it was decided to hold elections for that office. Dr. Küçük agreed to his retirement and wished to be replaced by a younger man who could continue to uphold the Turkish Cypriot interests he had championed since the period of British colonial administration.

On February 9, 1973, Rauf R. Denktaş's candidacy for the vice-presidency of the Republic of Cyprus was supported by the Federation of Turkish Cypriot Trade Unions and the Executive Council of the Turkish Cypriot Administration. Ahmet Midhat Berberoğlu, the candidate of the Turkish Cypriot

Republican party, was the only challenger to Denktaş. The date for polling was set for February 18. On February 16, Denktaş was officially declared the vice-president of the Republic of Cyprus for a term of five years, when the candidacy for that office by Midhat Berberoğlu was withdrawn. Denktaş assumed the office of the vice-president of Cyprus, thereby also becoming the president of the Executive Council of the Turkish Cypriot Administration. In conjunction with the offices mentioned earlier, Denktaş continues to be the president of the Turkish Cypriot Communal Chamber.[10] The change of leadership is not expected to bring about a major political shift in the Turkish Cypriot administration because, in effect, the major spokesman for the Turks in the latter part of the 1960s has been Denktaş. He has been the spokesman for the Turkish Cypriots domestically as well as externally, besides being the participant in the intercommunal talks.

The Greek Cypriot press was critical of the Turkish Cypriot elections, charging that Midhat Berberoğlu was put under house arrest and was denied candidacy in the elections. The allegations were unfounded and have been refuted by Berberoğlu himself.[11] The Makarios government's steadfast refusal to recognize the office of the vice-presidency has not deterred the representatives of foreign governments and the United Nations officials from acknowledging the official change. It is accepted by all concerned in the Cyprus affair that any intercommunal agreements must have the endorsement of the Turkish Cypriot administrators under the leadership of Denktaş. On February 21, 1973, Denktaş, in respect to the intercommunal talks, stated: "the Turkish Cypriot side was following a policy aligned with the Turkish Government. Cyprus was a national issue and the Turkish Cypriot Administration and the Turkish Government were following a common policy."[12]

The Executive Council is composed of the following officers: (1) minister of defense;[13] (2) minister of justice and interior; (3) minister of agriculture and natural resources; (4) minister of health services and social affairs; (5) minister of education, culture and teaching; (6) minister of works and communication; (7) minister of cooperatives, labor and rehabilitation; and (8) minister of finance and economic affairs.

With the establishment of a provisional administration, the Turkish Cypriot leaders were able to establish law and order in their community and to look after the welfare of their people. Certain activities of the Turkish Cypriot Administration not recognized by the government of President Makarios are: (1) registration and possession of firearms in Turkish Cypriot sectors; (2) running the community lottery; (3) licensing of Turkish Cypriot-owned vehicles that operate exclusively in the Turkish Cypriot-controlled areas; (4) issuance of building permits; (5) licensing of cigarette sales; (6) judicial proceedings; (7) postal services; and (8) control of water supplies. Disregarding President Makarios' legal opinions, the Turkish Cypriot Administration continues to conduct and legislate the legal affairs of its citizens. Furthermore.

the Turkish Cypriot leaders defend their activities as being necessary because the Cyprus government refuses to provide certain services to their community. The formation of this administration does not in any way aim at a political objective and the administration will *ipso facto* come to an end as soon as the provisions of the Constitution of the Republic of Cyprus are fully implemented once again.

Former Vice-President Küçük proposed the following solution to the Cypriot issue:

> . . . a suitable solution for the Cyprus problem would be a system of administration based on partnership that took into consideration the existence of two communities in Cyprus, together with their identities and interests, while also fulfilling the security conditions of the Turkish Cypriot community. . . . Cyprus must remain an independent State with a system of Government in which the Greek and Turkish communities would be able to feel that they belonged to, and identified themselves with, such a State and were able to co-exist in peace, freedom and security without either community running the risk of being subjugated by the other or threatened with the alienation of its national character.[14]

He justified the Turkish Cypriot partition proposals as being necessary responses to the demands of the enosists.

> Partition has been put forward by Turks as a counter claim against the Greek demand of Enosis. If Greeks will continue to demand or insist on Enosis, then a part of Cyprus, at least equal in area to land owned by Turkish Cypriots, will have to be ceded to Turkey as Turkish Cypriots will never accept to bear allegiance to Greece. If, however, Cyprus will continue to be an independent State, then Turkish Cypriots will not demand partition but will claim the establishment of a federal system of government in which Turkish and Greek Cypriots will be able to administer their own affairs without being molested by each other. They will of course cooperate with each other in matters of common interest in a central government.[15]

This Turkish Cypriot Administration has functioned ably in directing Turkish Cypriot affairs and could continue to do so indefinitely. If the Greek Cypriots continue in their refusal to reach a settlement with the Turkish Cypriots, the result they most fear, a divided Cyprus, will have materialized.

6 THE INTERCOMMUNAL TALKS

When it became apparent to Greek and Turkish Cypriot leaders that the political controversy between them could not be solved by armed conflict, they agreed, with the encouragement of the interested parties in the Cyprus dispute, that outstanding differences might be resolved by establishing a dialogue. The members of both communities were becoming dissatisfied with the continued armed impasse and desired a final solution to the problem. The intercommunal talks began in Beirut, Lebanon, on June 2, 1968, between Glafkos Clerides, president of the House of Representatives, representing the Greek Cypriots, and Rauf R. Denktaş, president of the Turkish Cypriot Communal Chamber, representing the Turkish Cypriots. Shortly thereafter, the talks moved to Nicosia.

In interviews of Denktaş this writer learned that the major topics under discussion by the two men began on a package-deal basis. The Greek Cypriots' proposals presented during the talks were:

1. Amend the electoral roll.
2. Reduce the Turkish Cypriot participation in the government and Civil Service from 30 percent to 20 percent.
3. Reduce the Turkish Cypriot participation in the House of Representatives to 20 percent.
4. Unify the Supreme Constitutional Court with the High Court of Justice and remove all protective measures for the Turkish Cypriots in the legal machinery.
5. Unify the gendarmerie and the police force under one command and reduce the Turkish Cypriot participation to 20 percent.
6. Abrogate the separate majority rule in certain legislative enactments.
7. Abrogate all veto rights of the president and vice-president of the republic.
8. Reduce the Turkish Cypriot participation in the Civil Service Commission from 30 percent to 20 percent and abrogate all protective provisions for the Turkish Cypriots in this sphere.
9. Divest the vice-president of the republic of all his powers except those of protocol.
10. Unify the Municipalities.
11. Abolish the Greek Cypriot Communal Chamber and give the government all functions appertaining to the Greek Cypriot communal affairs.
12. Form a Cyprus government within which the Turkish Cypriots would have a minority status.

The Turkish Cypriot leaders expressed willingness to agree to most of the Greek Cypriots' proposals, as presented above, but on the condition that:

1. The Turkish Cypriot Communal autonomy, enjoyed under the Cyprus Constitution, be extended to cover local affairs.
2. The partnership status of the Turkish Cypriot community in the Cyprus government be preserved.
3. The independence of Cyprus continue to be guaranteed by Greece and Turkey.
4. A separate Turkish Cypriot police force be established.
5. Turkish Cypriots be given control of irrigation and water resources in their enclaves.

Other items may also be under consideration, but the public has yet to be informed of agreements reached by the two negotiators. The public is to be kept uninformed until the proposals and counterproposals have been thoroughly exhausted or agreed upon.

On March 4, 1969, Clerides and Denktaş agreed to establish two subcommittees, one to deal with matters pertaining to the legislature and the other with the independent authorities, such as the Telecommunications Authority, the Electricity Authority, the Grain Commission, and Water Boards. Any agreement reached by these subcommittees was to be part of an overall settlement. On May 6, the two subcommittees, composed of three representatives from each community, began their talks. Since January, 1970, no subcommittee meetings have been assembled. When no progress could be achieved at the upper-level conferences between Clerides and Denktaş, it is possible that the two communal representatives came to the conclusion that there was no need for the subcommittees to continue their meetings.

Thus far, the talks have achieved no results because the two communities are not flexible enough in their diplomacy to bring about a solution acceptable to both. President Makarios' concessions to the Turkish Cypriots, through Clerides, are considered by Denktaş as merely natural rights enjoyed by people in any free society. The rights extended to the Turkish Cypriots are: (1) the lifting of all economic restrictions; (2) autonomy in matters of religion, education, culture, and personal status. On July 17, Makarios proposed to recognize the Turkish Cypriots as having rights of self-government similar to those enjoyed by the Turks in Western Thrace and Rhodes. The Turkish Cypriots rejected this proposal[1] and refused to accept minority status because it would mean political impotence. Makarios' statement on March 9, 1971, that he "will not sign any agreement which bars enosis," rendered the intercommunal talks meaningless and caused the Turkish Cypriot leaders to reconsider their position.[2]

Glafkos Clerides' statements to the press were also having a negative impact on the intercommunal talks. He informed the media that the Greek

Cypriots could not agree to return to the Zurich-London Agreements under which the Turkish Cypriots were given representation disproportionate to their numbers.[3] Since the beginning of the intercommunal talks, the Greek Cypriot leadership has insisted that the following be assured:

1. A unitary, sovereign, and independent state with a constitution adopted by the people of Cyprus and based on democratic principles and the principles of the United Nations Charter.
2. Enjoyment by all citizens of the republic of equal rights irrespective of race, community, or religion and the incorporation of human rights for all citizens in the constitution.
3. Autonomy to the Turkish Cypriots with regard to matters pertaining to education, culture, religion, and personal status.[4]

Denktaş's counterargument to the above points was that the objective of the Greek Cypriot leadership is to force his community to accept a minority status and to "abandon all idea of being a co-founder of the State, a partner in the independence of Cyprus!" He refutes the Greek Cypriot proposals as follows:

> In Cyprus, even under the partnership venture, the Greek Cypriots' understanding of democratic rule coincided with the nineteenth century concept that the "first business of political democracy is to give full expression to the will of the majority irrespective of the wishes, fears and doubts of the minority." In the modern concept of democratic rule the primary business of political democracy is to defend the rights of all. Where the will of the minority is not given expression within these rights "mob rule" replaces "democratic rule." The concept of the partnership status in Cyprus was evolved in order to establish a modern system of democracy with sufficient safeguards to prevent its ultimate emergence as tyranny or mob rule.[5]

The Turkish Cypriots have proposed to preserve the independence of the Republic of Cyprus under a form of government that has direct representation of the two communities in the operation of the government. The Turkish Cypriots also refute the claim of President Makarios that they desire to establish a state within a state and that they advocate the partition of the island. They proclaim that *Taksim* is merely a counterproposal to enosis.[6] Under the unitary state proposal, the Greek Cypriots, who are in a 78 percent majority, would rule, and the minority, the Turkish Cypriots, would be granted certain rights and privileges as previously indicated.

In respect to the veto power of the vice-president under the 1960 Constitution, the Turkish Cypriots are willing to make provisions in the future constitution to abolish the veto, while in return they demand local autonomy. President Makarios views the proposals of the Turkish Cypriots on local government as an attempt to create a state within a state, which is unacceptable.[7] The Greek Cypriots are against any separatist, federal, or cantonal solution and insist on a unitary form of government in which the majority will rule. The Turkish Cypriots argue that they have to go through a process of political evolution before any additional political concessions can be made. In respect to the electoral roll, it has been agreed by the two communities that the communal balloting should continue at elections and that the election of the leaders of the House by its members should be by the entire House regardless of communal attachments.

Clerides and Denktaş have also reached an agreement about the village level of local government (groups of villages with a total population of 35,000) but have failed to reach a consensus about higher levels. The Turkish Cypriots favor administering the groups of villages on a basis of ethnic homogeneity, whereas the Greek Cypriots desire geographically designated areas, which would bring about decentrailization of authority. The effect of the Turkish Cypriot proposal would be to continue the separation of the two communities. On the subject of the courts, the two communities are substantially in agreement on merging the highest court and the constitutional court into one supreme court, but they have not agreed on the number of justices or on whether Cypriots shall be judged by supreme justices of their own communities. There is a wide area of agreement on the legislative branch, however; the Turkish Cypriots are in favor of having one parliamentary vice-president instead of two. The primary controversy in the executive branch is over the existence of the Turkish Cypriot vice-president. Since the president of the parliament replaces the president of the republic during his absence, the Greek Cypriots are adamant that there is no need for a Turkish Cypriot vice-president. The Turkish Cypriots have agreed to reduce their numbers in the civil service and the police to coincide with the population. One fundamental point of disagreement concerns the extension of the jurisdiction of the police superintendents to minor criminal offenses; the Greek Cypriots are opposed because they feel that such a change might lead toward separate authority and thus partition. It is reported that President Makarios and the Greek government have agreed to grant no concessions beyond their definite limits in any area that might lead to partition. The Turkish Cypriots are steadfast in their demands for local government, and the Turkish government is not likely to push them on this issue because of the sympathetic attitude of the Turkish military leadership.

The intercommunal talks have not functioned as smoothly as was anticipated. Since 1968, the talks have resumed annually and come to an end upon reaching a stalemate. Secretary General Dr. Kurt Waldheim sent Roberto E. Guyer, undersecretary general for special political affairs, to visit Nicosia, Athens, and Ankara between January 30 and February 5, 1972, and encouraged all the interested parties in the Cyprus issue toward the reactivation of

Rauf Raif Denktaş, President of the Turkish Cypriot Communal Chamber (left), and Glafkos Clerides, President of the House of Representatives (right), exchanging notes before the intercommunal talks on June 8, 1972.

The intercommunal talks on June 8, 1972, in Nicosia. The participants were (from left) Professor Orhan Aldıkaçtı, Mr. Rauf Denktaş, U.N. Secretary-General Kurt Waldheim, Mr. Glafkos Clerides, Mr. Michael Dekleris, and Mr. Bibiano F. Osorio-Tafall (back to the camera).

the intercommunal talks. The intercommunal talks began on June 8, in Nicosia, with the participation of the United Nations secretary general, Dr. Waldheim, along with the special representative of the secretary general in Cyprus, Bibiano F. Osorio-Tafall, Clerides, and Denktaş. The Greek government designated Michael Dekleris and Turkey appointed Professor Orhan Aldıkaçtı as constitutional experts who were to attend the talks in an advisory capacity.[8] In respect to the resumption of the intercommunal talks, Dr. Waldheim said: "I hope and believe that by agreeing to the talks, all concerned have marked their determination that the problems must be solved by peaceful negotiations."[9] After his visit to Cyprus, he stopped in Ankara on June 9, where he declared: "The countries which support the continuation of the UN peacekeeping force in Cyprus are ready to continue giving their financial support. But they wish and hope that the problem will be solved in a manner acceptable to all parties. . . . Our ultimate hope for these talks is that they may reach a final result acceptable to both parties."[10] His hopes for an early political settlement are shared by all the Cypriots, though their expectations for an immediate agreement are not being fulfilled. The talks that had reached a stalemate on February 1, 1974 were resumed after four months.

Some United Nations members have suggested the assignment of a United Nations intermediary to the bicommunal talks, but President Makarios has refused to consider it. Previously the failure to reach an agreement was felt to be serving the interests of all parties, therefore the situation was not expected to suddenly deteriorate. However, it is the feeling of some observers that recent developments indicate that the Cyprus crisis could once again become a major issue in the eastern Mediterranean region. The AKEL general secretary Ezekias Papaiannou came to the defense of the communal talks, advocating a solution based on an independent, sovereign, integral, and unitary democratic "demilitarized and unfettered Cyprus" that could become "the center of friendship and cooperation among the peoples of the area and not an imperialist base of plots and aggression."[11]

The Turkish Cypriot position is that *de facto* partition already exists, but Turkish Cypriots are willing to actively participate in the talks in the hope of achieving a better solution that is fair to both sides. Neither enosis nor *Taksim* is an effective solution; therefore, both ideas must be rejected in order to bring about an agreement acceptable to both communities.

The intercommunal talks must continue until the outstanding differences are settled. Time is not the critical element in the Solution of the Cypriot affair. It is already clear that there is no quick or simple solution. If permanent political agreement can be achieved over a long period of time, then a slow pace is justified. There is little basis for immediate optimism. Some individuals in both communities do not have much faith in the talks, and they concur that the possibility of a settlement is very slim. The Turkish Cypriots are of the opinion that the Greek Cypriots are stalling the talks and wish to reach no immediate agreement. They reason that the Greek Cypriots are satisfied with their political, economic, and living conditions and see no need to expedite a settlement.

The Greek Cypriots may be of the opinion that the longer they avoid an agreement the stronger their bargaining position will be, due to possible deterioration of the economic position and the morale of the Turkish Cypriots. This is a political gamble because at the same time, the Greek Cypriots' position may be fragmenting from internal conflicts.[12] It must be remembered also that all Turkish Cypriots between the ages of eighteen and fifty are being trained in the use of arms in the event of another intercommunal armed confrontation. If the talks continue to end in stalemate, the Turks both in Cyprus and Turkey may become desperate and attempt to change the situation through the use of force.

Greece and Turkey's security and national interest in Cyprus must be recognized by both Cypriot communities. Both nations are very much concerned about the well-being and safety of the communities identified with them until such time as Cyprus becomes a distinct national entity. The Cyprus issue has been an emotional one to the Greek and Turkish governments. The Cyprus problem is regarded by Greece and Turkey as a point of national prestige and honor. If either government gives in to political coercion or loses face, the party in power will hardly be expected to survive the public outcry. For the preservation of the independent status of Cyprus, the two communities must work together to achieve a lasting unity.

7 THE IMPACT OF A COUP

The recent war in Cyprus that pitted Greeks against Turks is not an out-growth of a new problem, for historically Greeks and Turks have distrusted one another for hundreds of years. In fact the roots of the current Greco-Turkish controversy go back to 1453, when the Turks conquered Greece's Byzantine Empire. And more specifically, Cyprus has been a point of contention between the two Mediterranean powers since 1821, when the newly independent Greek nation began to covet the island that had been part of the Byzantine Empire prior to the Crusades. Led on by the myth of the Megali Idea ("The Great Idea") after independence, the Greeks began to dream of recreating the Byzantine Empire. Understandably, Turkish distrust of the Greeks grew in the face of the Greeks' grand design. And as their resistance to the Greek ambitions stiffened over the years, the Turks began to vigilantly guard their defenses and became especially opposed to any Greek control of the islands that surround Turkey's Mediterranean Sea coasts, for these islands are Turkey's main defense against its two foes—Greece and the Soviet Union. A kind of temporary balance was achieved with the Treaty of Lausanne in 1923, when the two nations agreed to preserve the existing balance of power between the two states and to block all attempts for territorial expansion by one at the expense of the other. After 1945 peaceful coexistence between Greece and Turkey became even more necessary, for there was a communist threat against both states. However, when Soviet threats against Greece and Turkey diminished in the 1970s as a result of the general détente between the Eastern and Western blocks, the old nationalistic tensions between Greece and Turkey surfaced again, threatening the peace of both nations.

Given this history, the attempt of Athens to bind Cyprus to Greece in 1974 seemed to the Turks a deliberately provocative and unjustified attempt to change the status quo. Turkey could not acquiesce in this encroachment on its defenses, the attempt to dominate the Turkish community on Cyprus, and the attempt to promote the Megali Idea. Greece's political action on Cyprus forced Turkey to react with force. As a result, the Greeks suffered deep humiliation and mortal injury to their aspirations to unite Cyprus with Greece and had to accept the end of any hope for the realization of the Megali Idea.

The chain of events leading up to the coup began when President Makarios gave up the dream of uniting Cyprus with Greece and began to pursue an independent Cyprus under Greek Cypriot control: a few extremists who still insisted on enosis actively began to plot against Makarios. From 1970 to 1974 there were numerous unsuccessful plots against Makarios, which most people assumed were being planned by the EOKA-B under the direction of Grivas, who had returned secretly to Cyprus in 1971. Aware of the extremists' feeling against him, and aware that the junta leader in Athens, Brigadier General Dimitri Ioannides, thought him "red" because the communist party of Cyprus (AKEL or Progressive Party of the Working People, whose membership is about 40,000) supported his policies. President Makarios charged in June, 1974, that Athens had organized a plot to overthrow him under the code name "Operation Apollo." Makarios made no secret of his suspicions. In mid-June he said in a public sermon that the invisible hand was threatening the liberty of Cyprus and menacing his life. On July 3 Makarios wrote a letter to President Phaedon Gizikis of Greece demanding the removal of the 650 mainland Greek officers who were on Cyprus as a result of an agreement with his Cypriot National Guard. Though Makarios argued that the officers' presence was harmful to relations between Athens and Nicosia, his attempt to get the soldiers recalled must be seen in light of his fear of the enosists' plots against him. Athens refused to recall the officers and denied all charges of plotting.

On July 15, the coup Makarios had feared was openly launched by the Greek Cypriot National Guard under the leadership of the mainland Greek officers. However, the coup against President Makarios, called "Operation President," actually began on the evening of July 14, when Athens clandestinely sent to Cyprus about one hundred more army officers on an Olympic Airlines Boeing 727. Besides the Greek Cypriot National Guard, the 950 Greek soldiers based on Cyprus under the Treaty of Alliance also took part in the coup. Makarios was warned of the forthcoming coup by the intelligence branch of Cyprus government, which helped him escape to Paphos, his birthplace where people supported him, before the presidential palace was destroyed by the T-34 Russian tanks and the mortars of the Greek Cypriot National Guard. In a radio message from Paphos, Makarios called upon his supporters to fight the rebels and appealed to the United Nations and the world "to assist the struggle against the rebellion and preserve the independence and democracy of Cyprus." Shortly after the message, the clandestine Radio Free Cyprus was silenced by Greek Cypriot gunboat bombardment off the coast of Paphos. With the assistance of Major Dewan Prem Chand of India, the UNFICYP commander, Makarios was air-lifted by an RAF helicopter from Paphos to the British military base at Akrotiri and finally to London, after a short stop on the island of Malta.

The junta in Athens, with the endorsement of its own soldiers on Cyprus and the backing of the 10,000 men of the Greek Cypriot National Guard, chose Nikos Giorgiades Sampson, an ardent enosist, as the new president of Cyprus.[1] After taking office, Sampson justified the ousting of President Makarios by accusing him of establishing a personal regime based on torture.

However, these allegations against Makarios were not proved. In reality, Athens had decided to act forcefully because Cypriot independence was becoming permanent, and the junta was convinced that enosis could be achieved only if Makarios were overthrown.

Though Sampson was chosen president, he had few real qualifications for the job. Sampson had been associated with newspapers since his youth, and before taking over the presidency of Cyprus, he was editor of *Makhi* ("Struggle"), a right-wing Greek newspaper. He was also one of the right-wing leaders who had maintained a small private army for attacks on the Turkish Cypriot enclaves since 1964. He was proud that he had taken part in the terror campaigns against the British colonial administration prior to the independence of Cyprus, and against the Turkish Cypriots during the civil war between the two island communities after 1964. Politically he was immature. His political ideology can be traced to his imprisonment in England, where he came in contact with members of the Irish Republican Army (IRA). Sampson, a member of EOKA, had killed twenty-six British soldiers after the resumption of guerrilla warfare against the British in 1955. The British had sentenced him to die twice—once for murder and once for possession of arms—but on the day of his execution he was taken to England instead. As a result of a general amnesty, he was released when Cyprus was given its independence in 1960.

Because of his extremist background and his general lack of political qualifications, Sampson was not acceptable as president to most Greek Cypriots. Most Greeks on the island considered Sampson a political stooge of the junta, who sought to maintain control of Cyprus until enosis could be achieved by prearranged, staged coups. In a gesture of appeasement, Sampson promised free elections within a year and expressed interest in restoring unity among Greek Cypriots, now themselves divided over the issue of enosis versus independence. But neither stance brought Sampson any further support from Greeks on the island. In fact, Greek Cypriots were so divided over Sampson and the question of forced enosis that fighting broke out between them.[2]

Nor were Turks pleased with Sampson and the turn of events in Cyprus; Sampson's seizure of the presidency of Cyprus was anathema to all Turks because Sampson had always hated Turks and they knew it. As long as the enosist plots against Makarios had failed, Turkey had no reason to intervene in Cyprus, but when the enosists' plot succeeded in 1974 and Sampson was placed in the presidency, the scene was set for Turkey's direct intervention in Cyprus. Turkey could not countenance the triumph of the enosists, whom it saw as a threat to Turkish Cypriots and to its own national interest.

Vehemently opposed to Sampson and enosis, the Turkish armed forces in particular pressured Prime Minister Bülent Ecevit to act to prevent Greece's seizure of Cyprus through *de facto* enosis. The coup on Cyprus offered the Turkish military a golden opportunity to act, to establish a permanent foothold on Cyprus and to strengthen its own security as well as the security of the Turkish Cypriots. However, Ecevit was opposed to unilateral action. Instead, he hoped to persuade Great Britain to fulfill its obligations under the 1960 accords and join Turkey in a military operation to insure the independence of Cyprus. However, the talks in London between Ecevit and British Prime Minister Harold Wilson and Foreign Secretary James Callaghan were fruitless for the Turkish military because London's national interest on Cyprus was in no jeopardy. After his visit to London, Ecevit demanded that the 650 Greek officers on Cyprus be withdrawn by Athens and that President Sampson be replaced. Otherwise, he warned, the Turkish army would intervene on Cyprus. Greece, Great Britain, and the United States were all under the impression that Turkey was once again bluffing, as it had done in previous years. The West, especially the United States, underestimated the Turkish passion and resolution to safeguard their rights on Cyprus and their determination to avoid the creation of a Cuba forty miles off their coast. But Ankara was steadfast in its determination not to permit the beginning of a *de facto* enosis and the "enslavement" of its compatriots on Cyprus. The Turkish parliament endorsed the proposition of going to war with Greece if the need arose.

That the United States so badly underestimated the Turks' determination is not surprising, for American policy toward Cyprus since 1963 has been murky and at times labyrinthine. After the coup on Cyprus, the State Department considered the Cypriot political situation an internal matter and favored the continuation of the status quo. To the American foreign policy makers, the factual situation dictated that the status quo should be accepted as an accomplished fact regardless of its moral or legal premises. The United States, however, did state its opposition to enosis and vowed that it supported Cypriot "independence and territorial integrity and its constitutional arrangements." However, when the deposed president, Archbishop Makarios, came to Washington, D.C., on July 22, 1974, to appeal for United States support, he was received coolly. Though it supported the Cypriot independence Makarios had advocated, the United States was not enthusiastic about Makarios himself, for during his tenure as president he had flirted with communist nations and closely identified his regime with the nonaligned nations. Washington's chief objective was to preserve the peace between the Greeks and the Turks in the area. It felt no urgency to recreate a future political base for Archbishop Makarios. Consequently, he left Washington without a United States commitment to support his reinstatement. However, the Soviet Union, which was also watching the crisis with interest, denounced the overthrow of Makarios, accused the Athens junta of armed aggression, and demanded Makarios' reinstatement and the future independence of Cyprus.

Though cool to Makarios' mission, the United States was working during this period to defuse the crisis. During this period Undersecretary of State for Political Affairs Joseph J. Sisco was dispatched to Athens and Ankara to apply political leverage and to aid in finding a solution to the crisis. America was opposed to war between two of its allies and wished to protect its military bases in both countries by extending to them its good offices. Athens was pressured by Sisco to replace Sampson with a more moderate Greek Cypriot and to withdraw its 650 officers from Cyprus. The junta in Greece refused to comply with Sisco's suggestions because they represented a capitulation to the demands of the Turks. Nor was Sisco any more successful with the Turks; Ankara was not impressed with his arguments against an invasion of Cyprus. Prime Minister Ecevit cited the 1964 and 1967 Cyprus crises and chided the United States for preventing positive action then by Turkey that could have prevented the latest crises. Ankara theorized that Athens would attempt to achieve enosis by a series of coups.

When the junta in Athens refused to reach a compromise with Turkey over the restoration of a constitutional leadership on Cyprus, Ankara decided to act. On July 20, 1974, at 6 A.M., the Turkish force of about six thousand men in three brigades, equipped with armored personnel carriers and tanks from Mersin, under naval and air cover landed six miles to the west of Kyrenia. The Turkish naval landing force was composed of thirty landing crafts, two large transports, and an escort of four destroyers.[3] The Turkish invasion met little resistance because the major Greek National Guard armor units were deployed three miles away in the eastern part of Kyrenia, where the invasion was expected. Air transport troop carriers and helicopters were also used to drop Turkish commando detachments in the 10-mile Turkish corridor between Kyrenia and Nicosia. The Turkish paratroopers faced no resistance because the landing areas were under the control of the Turkish Cypriot paramilitary forces. Turkey considered its action legal under the Treaty of Guarantee, Article IV, which states that "each of the three guaranteeing powers reserves the right to take action with the sole aim of reestablishing the state of affairs created by the present Treaty." Ankara viewed its operations on Cyprus as a "police action" with the sole aim of preserving the integrity and independence of the island and blocking any conspiracy for enosis. Turkey also considered its action to be in compliance with the United Nations Charter, Article 2 (4), which states: "All members shall refrain in their international relations from the threat or use of force against the territorial integrity or political independence of any state, or in any other manner inconsistent with the purpose of the United Nations." Also contributing to Turkey's decision to invade Cyprus was the fact that Turkey's $20 million annual financial assistance to the Turkish Cypriots since 1964 was proving to be a burden on its budget. And also, Ankara was determined to open a wedge to a seaport through which the Turkish Cypriots could import and export, thus ending the Greek Cypriot monopolization of the island's economy.

When it became apparent that the Turks were not bluffing and that a Turkish invasion of Cyprus was really underway, the United States and

Great Britain feverishly tried to prevent war between Greece and Turkey, for they believed that Greece was too weak militarily to withstand Turkey's forces,[4] and they believed that prolonged fighting would harm the NATO alliance. The United States tried to get Turkey to call off its invasion of Cyprus by threatening to cut off all economic and military aid to Turkey, which amounted to about $180 million annually. The Turkish government met this threat with indifference, however, because they knew that the United States House of Representatives was already considering cutting aid as a reprisal for Turkey's cultivation of the opium poppy. To counter the United States' economic pressures on Turkey, nations such as the Soviet Union,[5] Iraq, Libya,[6] and Pakistan,[7] among others, extended diplomatic and economic aid to Turkey during its military undertaking on Cyprus.

Actually Turkey saw the United States' threat to cut off military aid as one more effort by the United States to keep Turkey from pursuing its legitimate national interest.[8] As far as Turkey was concerned, these efforts had begun in 1964 when President Johnson's veiled threats had caused Turkey to abandon its first invasion plans. If Turkey had resented Johnson's interference then, it doubly resented the United States' threats now, especially since the United States was also moving to try to ban Turkish poppy-growing, which Turkey considered a vital crop for its peasants.

There is no doubt that the Turkish decision in 1974 to resume growing poppies against the wishes of the United States contributed to the already deteriorating relations between the two allies. In 1971 the Turks had agreed to ban poppy-growing in return for $38,800,000 in compensation from the United States. But Ankara was never happy with the agreement, because opium poppy cultivation was really the only crop Turkish peasants could grow on their poor land. Consequently, when Turkish-American relations became strained over Cyprus, a Turkish government already resentful of American interference in their domestic affairs saw no reason to deny their farmers this means of livelihood. Two additional facts also persuaded the Turks to start growing poppies again. First, it became apparent that Turkey's ban on poppies had caused a shortage of opium in the world's pharmaceutical industry. But most infuriating to Turks was the news that the United States was thinking of asking Indian and American farmers to grow poppies in order to remedy the shortage. However, when Turkey resumed poppy-growing, the government tried to placate the United States by pledging strict policing of the poppy-growing areas and by instituting harsh penalties for smuggling and for illegal use of opium,[9] for despite its differences with the United States over poppies and over Cyprus, Turkey has never ceased to realize that its alliances with the West are indispensible. Turkey has not intended to alienate the West, but rather has only tried to pursue a policy of self-reliance, firmly insisting on its right to define its own national interests.

Relations between the Turks and Americans were also undermined by the fact that during the Turkish invasion the Incirlik Air Base at Adana, which is jointly operated by Turkish and American forces, was used as a crucial springboard for Turkish air attacks against Greek forces on Cyprus. Because Turks resented American pressure against their Cyprus invasion, they closed this NATO base to all American air force flights during the Cyprus crisis. Though the United States presently has two squadrons of nuclear-armed Phantoms at Incirlik Air Base, if the relations between Ankara and Washington do not improve, the Turkish government may request the removal of the American Phantoms.[10] Needless to say, though the Turkish invasion of Cyprus is long past, relations between Ankara and Washington are still tense and may remain so for some time.

Besides undermining already strained Turkish-American relations, Turkey's invasion of Cyprus raised other specters on the world scene. There were fears that in the event of a Greco-Turkish war, Bulgarian troops might attack the Greek port of Kavalla in order to gain direct access to the Aegean Sea. And too, it was feared that the Soviet Union might be concerned about the Turkish-controlled Dardanelles and might even stage a counterthrust against Greece in order to gain for itself a free hand from the Black Sea to the Mediterranean. These fears were increased on July 19 when the Soviet Union reinforced and placed on alert its several airborne divisions in Bulgaria and also strengthened its Mediterranean fleet.[11]

While fears and tensions throughout the world were building as a result of the Turkish invasion of Cyprus, Greece itself began to react. Greece began mobilization of some 200,000 reservists, considered a declaration of war against the Turks, and massed troops along the ninety miles of mutual border on the Evros River in Thrace. Greece announced that it considered the Turkish action a "flagrant violation of treaties concerning Cyprus, threatening the international peace and aiming at the arbitrary creation by Turkey of a situation endangering vital Greek interests."[12] Both Greece and Turkey began to mobilize for war.[13] On July 20, United States Undersecretary of State Joseph J. Sisco was informed by General Ioannides that Greece would declare war on Turkey unless Ankara accepted a ceasefire and withdrew from Cyprus.

However, though Greece talked tough and moved to the brink of war, the Greek junta in Athens proved unprepared and unequal to the struggle. The real possibility of war with a militarily superior Turkey exposed the weaknesses of the Athens military dictatorship and toppled it from power. For when the junta decided to go to war against Turkey, the mobilized Greek reserves discovered that the military depots did not contain adequate supplies of rifles, ammunition, machine guns, rockets, clothes, or even boots.[14] After the junta was ousted, an investigation revealed that to cover up the economic crisis in Greece, the junta had sold to Libya and other Arab and African countries vast quantities of Greek military supplies. When the military shortfall was discovered, and when it became obvious that the junta was powerless to block the Turkish military advances against the beleagured Greek forces on Cyprus, the junta resolved to turn over the government to a civilian authority.

Members of the junta in Athens were military extremists blindly committed to enosis. They lost power not only because they were unprepared militarily, but because they could not see that their intransigent and uncompromising stand on the Cyprus issue was bound to lead to a war with Turkey that they could not hope to win. Finally, the junta had no choice but to reinstitute civilian rule in Greece so that Greece's honor could be salvaged from the wreckage of the enosis adventure. In July, 1974, General Phaeden Gizikis, figurehead president for the Greek military junta, asked the former premier Constantine Karamanlis to return from his self-imposed exile and form a new civilian government.

Always opposed to an enosist coup on Cyprus, in 1960 Karamanlis played a major role in setting up Cypriot independence. He had been the premier of Greece from 1955 until his resignation in 1963, when he quarreled with King Paul over a dispute concerning the royal family and was charged with financial mismanagement and rigging elections. In 1963 Karamanlis was defeated in a general election by the late George Papandreou and had lived in Paris until his return to Athens on July 24, 1974. On his return to Athens, Karamanlis assured the Greek people that he was not a tool of the military dictatorship, and went on to say: "I agreed to take over on two conditions: one, that the armed forces would return to their duties and would not interfere in my government's policies; two, that the country's political forces would support my endeavour. . . . I wish to declare that both conditions are being observed in their totality." Not wishing to have Greece destroyed by Turkey and the major part of it absorbed by the communist nations adjacent to it, on August 16, in a speech to his nation, Caramanlis stated that Greece would not go to war with Turkey over Cyprus due to "weakness inherited from the sinful past" and that Athens was without "the power to correct the injustices to which she is subjected." Hereafter, Athens chose to conduct its battle against Ankara on the diplomatic front, admitting that a war with Turkey would be a disastrous defeat for Greece. Brought by the Turkish invasion to the brink of war, Greece had to retreat, purge itself of the enosist junta, form a new government, and begin to try to arrange a negotiated settlement of the Cyprus problem.

The prime minister of Turkey, Bülent Ecevit, welcomed the return of Karamanlis to Athens, saying "I am convinced that this heralds the beginning of a new era for democracy and freedom in our region. We can easily bury the memories of the past." Ankara welcomed the opportunity to try again to settle the Cyprus crisis by negotiations, to be held this time in Geneva.

Meanwhile on Cyprus, Nikos Sampson, who had been the puppet of the junta, resigned as *de facto* president of Cyprus on July 23, 1974. He was replaced by Glafkos Clerides, the speaker of the House of Representatives, who acted as interim president of Cyprus until Archbishop Makarios could return from the West, where he had fled when his administration was overthrown. However, since the radical enosists on Cyprus opposed Makarios' return, the extremist EOKA-B warned that Makarios' return would bring only division and strife in Cyprus. To try to sabotage his return, they launched assassination campaigns against his supporters. For example, in Nicosia on August 30 the EOKA-B tried to murder Dr. Vassos Lyssarides, who was Makarios' personal physician as well as chairman of the United Democratic Union of the Center (a socialist party) and director of the party's newspaper *Ta Nea*. Though Lyssarides escaped unharmed, his companion in the car was killed. He was Doros Loizou, a poet and leader of the socialist party youth section. Though Dr. Lyssarides accused the United States Central Intelligence Agency of masterminding the assassination plot, the charge was never substantiated. But while the EOKA-B[15] resisted the reinstatement of Makarios, the new government in Athens sanctioned the archbishop's return to power. On July 24, Greek Foreign Minister George Mavros, released from a junta prison only the day before, said that Athens recognized Archbishop Makarios as the *de jure* president of Cyprus. Because he had the blessing of Athens and the support of his own people, Makarios' return was inevitable. On December 7 he returned to Cyprus to resume leadership of the government.

Given the new government in Athens, the reinstatement of constitutional leadership on Cyprus, and the placating mood of the Turks, the conference on Cyprus that began on July 25, 1974, in Geneva seemed promising. The main intention of the tripartite conference, which lasted from July 25 to July 31, was to make urgently needed ceasefire arrangements on Cyprus and to preserve the NATO alliance. By providing a forum for the representatives of Great Britain, Greece, and Turkey to state the policies of their government, the conference prevented further escalation of the fighting on Cyprus.

At the Geneva conference, Great Britain was represented by Foreign Secretary James Callaghan, Greece by Foreign Minister George Mavros, who served in the cabinet of the late George Papandreou, and Turkey by Foreign Minister Turan Güneş. As a prerequisite for the conference, Greece had requested that Turkey withdraw its troops from Cyprus or from the territories captured after the United Nations unanimous ceasefire resolution of July 20, which was reaffirmed on July 22. At this time, the Turkish invasion force had under its control a narrow corridor from the landing beach in Kyrenia to the Turkish section of Nicosia. However, since Prime Minister Ecevit was under pressure from the armed forces not to abandon in negotiations what the troops had won on the battlefield, Turkey refused to comply with the Greek request. Turkey won the point and was not required to pull back to the ceasefire lines of July 22 as precondition for the conference. On the other hand, Turkey wanted two assurances: a guarantee to protect minority rights that the Greek Cypriot majority could not overturn, and assurance that the majority community would not misuse its power once again to the detriment of the Turks, as it had done since 1960.

The preliminary accord agreed on in Geneva permitted the Turks to retain troops on Cyprus at a reduced level and also recognized the existence on Cyprus of two autonomous administrations. The Turks were determined to keep the beach-head in the seaport of Kyrenia and the road to Nicosia, so that their forces would never be land-locked as they had been from 1960 to 1974, when the Turkish supply routes had been hampered by the continuous surveillance by Makarios' government. The Greek Cypriots wished to check all the supplies sent to the Turkish military force on Cyprus in order to prevent arms smuggling to the Turkish Cypriot paramilitary forces. The weapon supplies to the military forces of Makarios were under no supervision; thus, the Greek National Guard was armed with all kinds of sophisticated armaments from Athens, the Arab states, and the communist states.

When the Geneva talks resumed on August 8, in accordance with the interim agreement and ceasefire accord of July 30, 1974, both the Greek and Turkish Cypriot leaders were to join the tripartite talks on August 10, represented by Glafkos Clerides and Rauf Denktaş, respectively. The purpose of the talks was to reach a settlement on the details of the ceasefire accord and to revamp the Cyprus constitution to give Turkish Cypriots a larger degree of autonomy under vice-president Denktaş.

However, on August 14, the talks collapsed when Greece rejected Turkish proposals for establishing two separate autonomous units within a federal or cantonal system in an independent Cyprus. The Turkish proposal would have created a federal Cyprus, with the Turkish Cypriot administration being concentrated on the northern part of the island and the Greek Cypriots on the southern section. Furthermore, the Turkish Cypriot autonomous administration was to have its own police and security forces, as they had had since 1964. Turkey saw its plan as a way to prevent enosis once and for all and to end Greek Cypriot infringement on the natural rights of Turkish Cypriots. But the Greeks rejected the proposals because they thought the Turks were asking for too many concessions, considering their people were the minority group on the island. And too, the Greeks may have been unwilling to lose face by accepting an enemy's terms. At any rate, their refusal ended the promise many had seen in the Geneva conference.

Collapse of the tripartite talks in Geneva precipitated the resumption of the fighting and the acceleration of the Turkish troops' advances on the eastern and western parts of Cyprus. Turkey decided to use military force to gain the political concessions it had failed to achieve through negotiations since 1964. Ankara reinforced its troops, amassing about 35,000–40,000 men and approximately 250–300 tanks. By August 16, 1974, the Turkish forces had succeeded in slicing the northern part of Cyprus from Morphou or Kokkina Bay through the Green Line in Nicosia to Famagusta. However, Turkey made clear that the Turkish military objectives did not exceed the political ones it had attempted to reach at the Geneva conference.

On August 16, Turkey declared a unilateral ceasefire on Cyprus, which was accepted by the interim President Clerides, and which stated its readiness to resume the tripartite peace talks in Geneva. Both Great Britain and Greece chastised Turkey for the military operations on Cyprus and refused to accept the Turkish peace offering after a *fait accompli*. The British [16] and Greek negative responses to the Turkish invitation for peace talks did not deter the Turks from entrenching themselves on one-third of the island.

Meanwhile, the Soviet Union began to express a greater interest in the area. Formerly the Soviets had merely denounced the overthrow of President Makarios as "totally undisguised armed aggression by the Greek military regime" and had demanded the reinstatement of Makarios as president and the restoration of Cyprus as a sovereign republic. But on August 22 the Soviet Union tried to make itself an active party to the Cyprus talks by suggesting that the Geneva talks include an 18-nation international peace conference under United Nations auspices, a conference to be attended by the fifteen members of the United Nations Security Council as well as Greece, Cyprus, and Turkey. The underlying objective of the Soviet Union was to demilitarize Cyprus, to force the British to evacuate their two bases, and to prevent the island from being turned into a possible NATO base. Athens was not very eager to have the Soviets interfere in the Cyprus issue, feeling that their presence would only complicate the crisis; nevertheless, Karamanlis and Clerides accepted the Soviet proposal. Turkey, however, rejected the Soviet suggestion.

Whereas the Soviet Union sought to intrude itself into the Cyprus talks for its own political reasons, the United States has been pulled into the complex crisis from the start because Greece and Turkey are both its NATO allies. Since each of these NATO nations has looked to the United States for support, or at least tacit approval of its actions, the United States has been in a difficult position, bound to displease at least one, and probably both governments, by whatever action it took. For example, because President Johnson's letter dissuaded the Turks from invading Cyprus in 1964 and because the United States Congress made an emotional issue of Turkey's opium poppy industry, Ankara has complained that Washington is pro-Greek. More recently, however, the reluctance of the United States to try to avert either the plot against Makarios or the 1974 Turkish invasion has caused Greece to accuse the United States of being pro-Turkish. The United States denied these latest Greek charges and has tried to steer a middle course between the Mediterranean belligerents. Speaking for the United States government, Dr. Henry Kissinger has admitted that the United States is opposed to enosis and has encouraged Greece and Turkey to compromise. He declared that "the sovereignty, political independence, and territorial integrity of Cyprus must be maintained. It will be up to the parties to decide on the form of government they believe best suited to the particular conditions of Cyprus. They must reach accommodation on the areas to be administered by the Greek and Turkish Cypriot communities."[17] Dr. Kissinger even offered to play the role of mediator between the parties to find a solution to the problem of Cyprus. But Greece rejected the offer, convinced the United States had betrayed Greece by not stopping the Turkish invasion of Cyprus.

One result of the successful Turkish invasion, then, was that a wave of anti-American feeling swept Greece. Accusing the United States of being pro-Turkish, an angry Greece pulled its military forces out of NATO on August 14.[18] A few days later, on August 19, there were anti-American demonstrations in Athens and Nicosia, which led to the murders of American Ambassador Rodger P. Davies and an embassy secretary.[19] Other consequences of the Greeks' anti-Americanism may become apparent in the future, for the American hands-off foreign policy during the invasion has given anti-American elements in Greece an excuse to demand a renegotiation of the agreements providing for United States military bases in Greece.[20]

At present, United States military installations are located in Athens, where the air force has a base for reconnaissance planes and transport; in Piraeus, home port for the Sixth Fleet; and in Crete, which has a NATO missile-firing range at Namfi, north of Suda Bay, an air-weapons range, and an air field at Tymbakion. Moreover, Crete's Suda Bay serves as the United States antisubmarine warfare base and the Sixth Fleet's resupply facilities. Also, the United States has nuclear warheads stockpiles on Crete and near the Bulgarian border. In all, 4,000 military personnel and 6,000 dependents are stationed on American military bases in Greece.[21] Greece is also a member of NATO's computer-operated, early-warning radar system, which runs from the Arctic Circle in Norway to Asia Minor. In addition, independently of NATO, the United States has seven military and five communications sites under a bilateral treaty with Greece.

Karamanlis, who is well aware of American strategic interests in the Mediterranean, is reviewing the status of the United States military bases in Greece, apparently with two ends in view. For one thing, he wants to preserve strict Greek neutrality in case of another Arab-Israeli war. In keeping with this stance, he has announced that although the junta permitted American supply flights bound for Israel to cross Greece in 1973, such flights will no longer be allowed. But probably his main intention is to use the bases as political leverage, a possible way to pressure the United States into coaxing Turkey into a compromise with Athens on the Cyprus issue. Despite this political stance, however, Karamanlis is surely also aware that while American bases in Greece are convenient, they are not a necessity and, furthermore, that the bases do provide Greece with protection against communist encroachment. Though Premier Karamanlis has always been a staunch ally of the West, the anti-American feeling in his country has forced him to adopt an anti-American stance in order to publicize the Greek displeasure with the American stand on Cyprus and in order to gain his people's support in his country's elections on November 17. The elections were significant because, for the first time since 1964, six million Greeks participated in elections that were free. In preparation for the free elections, Greece had even lifted in September the thirty-eight-year ban on communist activities. The communists, who were allowed to campaign legally, gained 9 percent of the votes and eight seats. Former Economics Minister Andreas Papandreou's Panhellenic Socialist Movement (Pasok), whose leftist platform was against the king, the junta, the establishment, the United States, and NATO, got twelve seats with 14 percent of the votes. The moderate Center Union-New Forces party of George Mavros, whose platform was against the reinstatement of the monarchy and in favor of the punishment of the former military junta, obtained 20 percent of the votes and 60 seats. Karamanlis and his New Democracy party, whose backers are the former National Radical Union (ERE), which was in power from 1955 to 1963, won 54 percent of the popular votes and 220 of the 300 seats in the single-chamber parliament.

With this mandate from the Greek electorate, Karamanlis is expected to initiate domestic and national policies in the best interests of the Greek people. His strong stand against the military junta, his leadership during the Cyprus crisis, and his quick return to democracy have won him respect and have been a credit to his statesmanship. On December 8 the abolition of the monarchy and the declaration of Greece as a republic further strengthened the political position of Prime Minister Karamanlis.

Meanwhile, in Turkey there was also a change in government, a change that marked the beginning of a period of political instability that still continues in Turkey. On September 18, 1974, Prime Minister Ecevit resigned after an unsuccessful attempt to form a new coalition government. He agreed, however, to serve as a caretaker premier until a new government was formed. On November 13, Turkish President Fahri Korutürk named Sadı Irmak, an independent senator, to succeed Ecevit, but he was forced to resign on March 13, 1975, when he failed to form a new coalition government. Irmak was succeeded by former Premier Süleyman Demirel, who was forced by Turkey's military commanders to resign from office on March 12, 1971 —some call it a "coup by communique." Demirel, who heads a very unstable coalition government, is to serve as an interim premier until elections can be held. However, partly because of the effects of United States policy on politics in Turkey, these elections have never been held; consequently, Turkey's domestic political situation remains uncertain and clouded.

How have United States politics contributed to political instability in Turkey? Because the United States' congressional elections occurred on November 20, 1974, the Congress became more responsive to the Greek-American lobby than it might have been in a nonelection year. Knowing that the Greek-American ethnic vote could be significant for the outcome of the November elections, despite Defense Department objections,[22] Congress began to threaten to cut military aid to Turkey as a way of pressuring Ankara to move quickly toward a Cyprus settlement favorable to the Greeks.

The military aid that Congress sought to use as political leverage had risen to $40.5 million between July and November, an increase of $13 million over the previous quarter due to the delivery of four F-4 Phantom fighter-bombers to Turkey. In all, during 1974 Turkey received $180 million in American military loans and grants.

Congressional response to the Greek-American lobby became apparent on September 17 and 18 when first the House of Representatives and then the Senate attached to the foreign aid bill of 1975 an amendment that suspended military aid to Turkey unless and until President Ford certified that Ankara was actively negotiating in good faith with Greece and Cyprus. Senator Thomas F. Eagleton of Missouri was author of the Senate amendment to the foreign aid bill that would have stopped military aid to Turkey. On October 15, 1974, President Ford vetoed the amended foreign aid bill; this veto Congress failed to override in a 135–223 vote. In his veto message to both houses of Congress, Ford stated that stopping aid to Turkey was "entirely destructive" to United States efforts to bring about Cyprus peace negotiations. Furthermore, he said, cutting off this aid might imperil United States relations with Turkey and, consequently, "weaken us in the crucial eastern Mediterranean." Moreover, on October 17, Ford vetoed other legislation that called for an immediate cutoff of weapons supply to Turkey. On October 18, however, President Ford reluctantly signed a compromise version of the bill, which stipulated that military aid to Turkey would be cutoff if there were no substantial progress toward a Cyprus settlement by December 10. In addition, Turkey was warned to stop sending United States supplies to its forces on Cyprus and was also warned not to increase its forces or break the ceasefire. But on December 4, since progress had been made in the Clerides-Denktąs negotiations on Cyprus, the Senate voted to postpone until February 10, 1975, the deadline to cut off the United States military aid to Turkey.[23] However, this date was revised when the House and Senate passed on December 10, 1974, a foreign aid bill of $2.69 billion. According to the December 17 bill, President Ford could suspend the ban on aid to Turkey until February 5, 1975. On that date, then, United States military aid to Turkey was finally cut.[24] The political disagreements between the executive and the legislative branches of the United States government over aid to Turkey are due to the following factors, some of which can be attributed to the aftermath of Watergate: (1) legislative determination to have a greater voice in foreign affairs; (2) legislative effort to curb Secretary of State Henry Kissinger's freedom in the Cyprus negotiations, because of the allegations that he is pro-Turkish; (3) legislative desire to cut off military aid to Turkey because Turkey had used American weapons to invade Cyprus; (4) political pressure by the Greek-American lobby on the members of Congress; and (5) congressional displeasure with the Turkish decision to grow opium poppies. Responding to the legislative pressure, Secretary of the State Kissinger said on December 7, 1974, about aid to Turkey that "the U.S. military assistance to Turkey is not, and has never been, granted as a favor. It has been the view of the U.S. government since 1947 that the security of Turkey is vital to the security of the eastern Mediterranean, to N.A.T.O. Europe, and therefore to the security of the Atlantic community."[25]

In making the move to cut military aid to Turkey, the United States Congress was not acting strictly to enforce the Foreign Assistance Act of 1961[26] and the Foreign Military Sales Act of 1968.[27] Congress cut assistance to Turkey not because Turkey had used American weapons to invade Cyprus, but because the legislators were under strong political pressure brought by the Greek-American lobby in an election year.[28] This is further supported by the fact that the American arms flow to Turkey may begin again if there is "substantial progress" in the Cyprus peace talks.

But whatever the causes of the cessation of United States military aid to Turkey, the effect of the move has been to harden the Turkish determination not to make any concessions to the Greeks lest Turkey look like a puppet state of the United States.[29] Moreover, the United States pressure on behalf of the Greeks has contributed to the political instability that makes Turkish elections impossible at this time. For, inside Turkey, political parties are afraid to assume a firm stance on the Cyprus issue because, on the one hand, they might bring on further United States displeasure and even retribution, and on the other hand, they might alienate their own people if they seem to be bending to United States pressure. As a result, then, of the United States decision to withdraw its military aid, dialogue inside Turkey about the Cyprus issue has largely ceased. This situation seems potentially perilous, for until the new elections are held in Turkey, the caretaker government of Prime Minister Süleyman Demirel will be hampered in pursuing a conciliatory policy with Greece. And there is also the threat that the Turkish military establishment, which considers itself the guardian and the preserver of the fatherland, would try to force out of power any civilian government that allowed United States political pressure to force it into a Cyprus settlement that made major concessions to the Greeks.[30] Clearly, then, the result of unchecked political pressure by the United States could force both Turkey and Greece to harden their stand on Cyprus, making a negotiated settlement nearly impossible.

For other reasons too, the United States' recent attempts to pressure Turkey into a Cypriot settlement seem pointless, for even if an agreement on Cyprus were reached, there would still be major issues preventing Greco-Turkish solidarity. Before there can be permanent accord between these two powers, there must be agreement about several serious problems, including Cypriot refugees, the demilitarization of Greece's Aegean Islands,[31] the future of the Turkish minority in Thrace, and, perhaps most important for the future, the question of oil-drilling rights in the Aegean.

One of the problems that keeps emotions between Greeks and Turks running high centers on the present plight and future relocation of the Greek refugees on Cyprus. After the beginning of the second Turkish offensive on

August 14, thousands of Greek Cypriot refugees fled to the southern part of the island to escape the war and are now awaiting a favorable settlement. Greek extremists, active members in EOKA-B and Greek officers from the mainland—about three hundred men captured by the Turks—were separated from the other war prisoners and sent to Turkey for further interrogation and detention. They were returned and released at the Green Line in Nicosia in October, 1974.[32] On the other hand, about 160,000 Greek Cypriots who fled from the northern area found shelter with relatives, while 20,000 more are living in tents on Cyprus. The United States Congress voted to extend $25 million in aid to improve the living conditions of these Greek Cypriot refugees.[33] The Turks firmly refuse to allow the Greek refugees to return to their homes, for the Turks hope to keep the land they now occupy under Turkish control. This has become a major political issue. The Greek leaders insist on making any agreement contingent upon the right of the Greeks to return to their homes. And to strengthen their bargaining position, they had not allowed Turkish refugees under their control to go to the Turkish sector. In the southern, Greek-controlled areas of the island, about 10,000 Turkish Cypriot refugees who had taken refuge at the British military base in Akrotiri were transferred to Turkey between January 18 and 26, 1975. The British government did not consult Makarios before it decided to grant a Turkish request to transfer Turkish Cypriot refugees to Asia Minor. Later, Turkey moved the refugees back to the Turkish-held sector in Cyprus for resettlement. Though refugees are still an issue, the two sides, beginning in September, 1975, continued to exchange wounded or sick persons as well as some prisoners of war of military age. At the conclusion of the Vienna talks on August 3 between Clerides and Denktaş, the Greek Cypriots agreed on the transfer of 9,500 Turkish Cypriot refugees from the south of the island to the north. The transfer started on August 10; at its conclusion all the 140,000 Turks were living in the north and about 500,000 Greeks were living in the south. As part of the Vienna package, 8,500 Greek Cypriots will be allowed to stay in the north and 800 more Greek Cypriots were to be permitted to join them so that they can be reunited with their families. UNFICYP was to have unrestricted access to Greek villages in the north to note observance of the guarantees relating to educational and religious rights. The Vienna accords have not been fully implemented yet.[34]

Another extremely serious issue separating Greeks and Turks exists independently of the Cyprus issue—the dispute over oil-drilling rights in the Aegean. In 1974, Greece discovered offshore oil in the northern Aegean off the Greek island of Thassos, near the Turkish border. To capitalize on its discovery, Greece claimed that Turkey had no right to explore oil in the Aegean, arguing that the Aegean seabeds were part of the continental shelf of the Greek islands. Turkey, ignoring the Greek claims, gave drilling concessions to a state-owned petroleum company, arguing that the Aegean seabeds were an extension of the continental shelf of Turkey. In partnership with

Geophysical Surveys, Inc., an American firm from Dallas, Texas, the Turks were to start their preliminary survey by seismic studies in June, 1974. But due to the Greco-Turkish crisis, the firm withdrew from the agreement under pressure from the State Department. Consequently, Turkey joined with a Norwegian firm, and the preliminary experiments were conducted in February, 1975. Greece warned Turkey that its action would be considered in violation of Greek sovereign rights and that Greece would go to war to defend these rights. In response, Ankara informed Athens that the Aegean Sea is of vital importance to both states and should not be considered a Greek lake.[35] Turkey maintains that the seabed should be divided between the two countries on a line running through the sea halfway between Greece and Turkey's mainland. Athens's proposal to submit the oil dispute to the International Court of Justice at The Hague has not been accepted thus far by Turkey because the Turks have made a counterproposal for bilateral negotiations. The two states held ministerial talks in Rome on May 17–19 and drafted a memorandum on the points of difference to be dealt with by the court. At the Rome conference the foreign ministers of Greece and Turkey, Dimitrios Bitsios and İhsan Sabri Çağlayangil, also reached an agreement that the head of their governments were to confer in Brussels on May 31, during the NATO meeting. The premiers, after meeting President Ford on May 30, met for three hours at the Belgian government's international conference center in the Palais Degmont and discussed the major outstanding issues between the two countries. The communiqué issued by the two governments pledged that "efforts should be made to create and maintain a good climate of relations between Greece and Turkey so that existing problems might be resolved and so that the two countries might re-establish cooperation to their mutual advantage."[36] One of the topics discussed concerned the exploration of oil in the Aegean Sea. Since oil has become critically important throughout the world, the oil dispute dividing Greece and Turkey looms in the background of the Cyprus quarrel, never openly discussed but surely on everyone's mind. And the oil dispute will undoubtedly surface openly when Cyprus ceases to be an issue, probably aggravating once again the old tension and anger between Greece and Turkey.[37]

Since there are so many issues besides Cyprus exacerbating relations between Greece and Turkey, it is probably futile for Greek supporters to seek peace by pressuring the United States to favor Greece at the expense of Turkey in the Cyprus issue. Meanwhile, American attempts to influence a solution favorable to one party or the other may be contributing to political instability in both Greece and Turkey, instability that prevents both nations from making the major concessions that are necessary to reach a compromise on all these critical issues. For both nations feel keenly the need to save face. Neither government can seem to bend to United States desires without losing self-respect, the confidence of its own people, and both the respect and confidence of other nations. And during a period of domestic political instability, neither government can afford to suffer the blow to its pride that submitting to the other side would represent.

Because political tensions inside both Greece and Turkey are apparently making it difficult for either country to move independently toward a conciliatory stance, hope for a Cyprus settlement seems to reside in the resumption of tripartite talks between Greece, Turkey, and the representatives of the two Cypriot communities. Diplomatic talks have resumed between the Greek and Turkish representatives with the backing of the allies of the two countries. On March 10, 1975, United States Secretary of State Kissinger met for two days with the Turkish leaders in Ankara. Dr. Kissinger and the foreign minister of Turkey, Melih Esenbel, advocated renewing the talks as soon as possible. The United Nations Security Council recommended on March 12 that the parties to the Cyprus conflict resume negotiations under the "personal auspices" of Secretary General Kurt Waldheim. The Cyprus talks on the political future of the island between Clerides and Denktaş convened in Vienna, Austria, on April 28. At the end of one week of talks, it was agreed to reopen Nicosia international airport. The airport will be repaired by the United Nations, and a committee will arrange its operations for full civilian use.[38] The representatives of the two communities met on May 12, in Nicosia, and on August 2, in Vienna. The talks dealt with the legal aspects of the powers and functions of a central government and the transference of refugees.

The talks will continue, however, and each of the parties will come to the conference with certain desires and objectives. Some of these issues have been voiced before and have already been rejected by the opposite side, so that it does not seem practical to expect an early compromise between the disputants about the structure of the Cypriot government, the distribution of population, or the guarantees of civil rights for Cypriot citizens. For example, Turkish Cypriots, who now hold 40 percent of the island but would consider settling for 28 percent, favor local autonomy within a bizonal federation, with an exchange of population and resettlement of the Greek and Turkish Cypriots within their own administrative zones. Both Greeks and Turks agree that, under such a bizonal federal system, each ethnic community would administer the internal affairs of its citizens, while having a common, unified external policy. As far as relocation of population is concerned, the Turkish plan is similar to the Greco-Turkish accord of the 1920s, which from 1922 to 1924 permitted a million and a half Greeks to leave Turkey to live in Greece and an equal number of Turks to migrate to Turkey from Greece. However, the preliminary agreement reached in principle between Makarios, Clerides, and Karamanlis is contrary to the Turkish proposals. Objectives and principles announced in Athens stressed: (1) the right of the 180,000 Greek Cypriot refugees to return to their homes; (2) Turkish withdrawal to a territory approximating the proportion of the Turkish Cypriot population; (3) no forcible population exchange; (4) creation of a strong central government; and (5) complete demilitarization of Cyprus. Turkey has already rejected these Greek proposals.[39]

Clearly, the main issue dividing the disputants seems to be the question of what kind of governmental structure should be adopted in Cyprus. Whereas the Turkish Cypriots favor a bizonal federation, the Greek Cypriots reject it, arguing that according to time-honored democratic principles, it is their desire for a strong central government. President Makarios is opposed to a bizonal federal system because he believes it is the forerunner of *Taksim*. He favors, rather, a unitary system, in which the Greek Cypriot majority would be in control of the state, and the Turkish Cypriots would be extended constitutional safeguards and autonomy in their cultural affairs. Turkish Cypriots, however, fear that they will once again be relegated to political impotence under a unified system. Consequently, the Turks rejected the unitary system, and their counterproposal was rejected by Makarios.[40]

As a possible compromise, on November 6, 1974, Clerides publicly urged acceptance of separate geographical areas linked by a federal government as the only realistic solution for Cyprus. He said, "I see no prospect of the Turks accepting any settlement that does not include federation and some geographical basis for it." He went on to say that Greek Cypriot thinking before Turkish invasion had been based on "false assumptions, terrible mistakes and illusions. . . . We could treat the Turkish Cypriot community as a simple minority, without taking into account it was backed by Turkey with a population of 33 million."[41] However, whatever settlement is finally reached about the structure of government, both ethnic communities' domestic affairs will be under their own administrative system.

Tired of the continued political deadlock over the formation of a two-ethnic domestic administrative system and alarmed by a Greek proposal to establish a unitary government, the Turkish Cypriots proclaimed on February 13, 1975, the formation of a separate state and offered to join in a federation with the Greek Cypriots. This *de facto* partition of the island was especially triggered by a Greek proposal, submitted to Rauf Denktaş on February 10, that provided for the establishment of several cantons with predominantly Greek and Turkish population under a strong central Cypriot government. The Turks were opposed to what looked like the reinstatement of the 1960 constitutional system, which they thought might once again allow them to be dominated by the Greek Cypriots. Although President Makarios condemned the Turkish partitioning action, Ankara dismissed the *de facto* partition of the island, an outgrowth of recent developments. Turkey considered the move not to be directed against the independence of Cyprus, but saw it as a recognition of the need for a federal system that would include autonomous Greek and Turkish Cypriot states. However, Turkey has indicated that outright partition of Cyprus between Greece and Turkey would be unacceptable because it would establish a new border with Greece in the Mediterranean.[42] Despite the Greek opposition, on February 19, a fifty-member

Constituent Assembly was established in Nicosia and charged with drafting the constitution for the Turkish Cypriot federal state. The Constituent Assembly consisted of twenty-five members from the Legislative Assembly and twenty-five members from the various trade unions and organizations. The assembly was under the chairmanship of a constitutional law expert from Turkey, Suat Bilge. In a referendum, on June 8, the Turkish Cypriots gave 99.4 percent approval—70 percent of the electorate cast ballots—to the constitution of the Turkish Cypriot state. The constitution provides: (1) a Legislative Assembly composed of thirty members which is elected for a five-year period by general election; (2) a president elected for a period of seven years by universal suffrage; (3) a prime minister and ten cabinet members are appointed by the president of the federal state, and they are responsible to him; and (4) a supreme court to act as an appellate court or high administrative court composed of a president and four members. The Turkish Cypriot federal state is to have its own army and police force.[43] Diplomats hope that the Greeks will adopt a pragmatic approach and, in spite of the unilateral Turkish political action in the northern part of the island, continue the talks to achieve an early settlement. Both communities on Cyprus support the continuation of the communal talks,[44] but so far neither side has shown any political flexibility.

To overcome the outstanding issues dividing them, both Cypriot communities must be willing to accept a compromise, so that the interests of all Cypriots can be served. Certain concessions and preconditions seem to be necessary preludes to settling the Cyprus dispute. First, Greece and Turkey should be guarantors of a sovereign and independent Cyprus. Second, Greece and Turkey should reach a binding agreement that they will not be party in any way—financially, militarily, or morally—to the instigation of guerrilla warfare against an ethnic group on the island.[45] The resurrection of any guerrilla warfare on Cyprus will surely have ramifications beyond the borders of Cyprus, and will ultimately invite war between Greece and Turkey. Third, both Greece and Turkey should be allowed a specific number of troops on Cyprus, and the two ethnic communities should be permitted to possess the armaments needed for the preservation of domestic peace and security. Further, the buildup of armaments by either community should not be permitted. Fourth, Greco-Turkish military cooperation and collaboration must be solidified within the structure of NATO. But the alignment of the two nations with the Western security system should not just serve the defense structure of NATO, but also the respective Greek and Turkish national interests.

Since Western European states have seemed reluctant to concern themselves with issues that Greece and Turkey have considered vital, both Greece and Turkey are justified in reevaluating the value of their NATO alignments. For instance, if Turkey decides that its membership in NATO serves the interest of Western Europe but that Western Europe feels no urgency to support what Turkey considers its own national interest, then the Turks might consider withdrawing from NATO and adopting a neutral foreign policy. Such a neutral policy might strengthen considerably Turkey's diplomatic influence with the nonaligned states. However, Greece's military withdrawal from NATO would probably weaken its own security and hamper the defense strategy of NATO against the Warsaw Pact members.

Concerning the settlement of the Cyprus issue, one thing is clear. If a negotiated agreement is to be reached, all parties must remain flexible and open to reasonable compromise. Turkey must not allow the past political blunders of the extremist military junta[46] to prejudice them toward the Karamanlis government in Athens. A stable and friendly civilian government in Athens will benefit the entire area.[47] The tragic events on Cyprus in the past are eloquent testimony that a handful of extremists must not be permitted to chart the course of events with little concern for consequences to an entire region. Moreover, Turkey must be flexible in its negotiating posture with Greece, so that Athens can regain its tarnished pride, honor, and dignity. Only confident, self-respecting nations can afford to compromise when compromise is necessary. And, of course, Greek and Turkish Cypriots must be relentless in their efforts to bring harmony, prosperity, cooperation, and peace to their troubled island as well as to Greece and Turkey.

8 SUMMARY AND CONCLUSION

Cyprus, the island of Aphrodite, the goddess of love, has attracted world attention since the 1963 inception of the intercommunal hostilities. The contemporary crisis in Cyprus is the consequence of the unsatisfied desires—predating the independence of Cyprus—of Greek Cypriots for enosis and Turkish Cypriots for *Taksim*. In 1974, there are still sharp political divisions between the two ethnic communities. An uneasy truce does exist, kept by the United Nations peace-keeping force on the island, but with intermittent outbreaks of violence. The hostilities were the result of the two communities' inability to function under the formula for self-government as provided for by the Zurich-London Agreements of 1959. Cooperation between the two communities never materialized because of their distrust and unwillingness to unite for the success of the Cyprus Republic, the persistent demand for enosis, the long-standing antagonisms, and the intrusion of foreign interests.

The two communities have retained their exclusiveness and separation even in mixed villages and towns. The Greek and Turkish Cypriots follow the customs and political aspirations of their motherlands. Each ethnic group uses its own language, separate religions, schools, social and cultural programs, and public information centers; each group possesses different loyalties; they share no common purpose; and intermarriage is rare. The Greek Cypriots are heavily influenced by the Orthodox Church of Cyprus, whose head has been Archbishop Makarios III since 1953. He has been president of the Republic since 1960. The archbishop of Cyprus serves as a secular leader as well as a spiritual leader of his community. The role of religion in the Turkish Cypriot politics diminished after the Kemalist revolution in Turkey in 1923.

After the island came under the British administration in 1878, little encouragement was given for communal cooperation. Until the Cyprus independence from Great Britain in 1960, the two ethnic groups retained their ethnic and cultural separation but lived in mixed villages and towns in relative harmony. As there were no solid foundations for communal cooperation, each community concentrated on issues that were to the best interest of its own ethnic group. The outbreak of the hostilities in 1963 forced thousands of Turkish Cypriots to leave their villages of mixed populations and take refuge in areas that were under the control of their own ethnic groups. The attempts to encourage their return to the mixed villages were not successful.

The British colonial administration was instrumental in modernizing some facets of Cypriot society, but the British failed to encourage communal understanding and cooperation in preparation for a statehood. The enosis movement gained momentum after the 1920s under the supervision and guidance of the church. Since there was no uniform schooling for all of the Cypriots, each community strengthened its own national traditions by bonding itself to the mother country—Greece or Turkey.

Under the zealous leadership of the church, the Greek Cypriots committed themselves to the cause of enosis. Greece also took an active role in vigorously supporting enosis, which became the basis for the deterioration of the diplomatic relations between Athens and Ankara. The Greek Cypriot commitment to enosis antagonized the British colonial administration and the Turkish Cypriots. British efforts to liberalize the island rule achieved little support from the Greek Cypriots, who instead accentuated self-determination and enosis. Turkey, in order to prevent enosis, took a more active interest in its ethnic constituency.

The Greek Cypriot desire for enosis was never concealed from the British colonial administration. Great Britain was sympathetic to the cause of the enosists but persistently opposed it. The British government had agreed with Turkey that if Cyprus were evacuated or if Russia restored to Turkey its three eastern provinces seized in 1877, Cyprus would be returned to the Porte. London also wished to preserve her alliance with the Turks, which was important for its defenses in the Middle East. Great Britain, in order to nourish the support of the Greek Cypriots, who are in the majority, instituted the first Cypriot Constitution in 1882. It established a Legislative Council with elected representation, but its operations were hindered because the Greek Cypriots elected to the council refused to cooperate with the colonial government. They demanded constitutional reforms under which each community would have proportional representation based on population. The Greek Cypriot legislatures were not genuinely interested in constitutional reforms, but in enosis. The British colonial administration's determination to block the enosis movement forced the Greek Cypriot support of the Legislative Council to diminish.

When offered enosis by Great Britain, Greece reluctantly allowed the opportunity to pass by. In 1914, when Turkey joined forces with the Central Powers, Great Britain formally annexed Cyprus and a year later offered it to Greece as an inducement to enter the war on the Allied side. King Constantine refused the offer because his forces were not prepared for a war. The offer was retracted when Greece chose to remain neutral. The British annexation of Cyprus was never recognized by Turkey, since the Treaty of Sevres of 1920 was never recognized by the Kemalists. The Turkish Republic under the leadership of Mustafa Kemal Atatürk recognized the British annexation of Cyprus when it was a signatory to the Treaty of Lausanne of 1923. On May 1, 1925, Cyprus officially became a British crown colony.

The enosis campaign continued under the guise of the doctrine of self-determination. Great Britain was opposed to complete independence for Cyprus because neither of the two communities were politically ready for state-hood. The Greek Cypriot antagonism toward British rule became militant in 1931 and resulted in mob violence. The British reacted by strengthening their forces on the island and revoking the Constitution and the Legislative Council. The leaders of the Greek Cypriot protesters were deported, and civil liberties were curtailed. The repressive measures by the British against the enosists forced them to go underground. In the 1930s, the British colonial administration was under the illusion that the great majority of the people of Cyprus were not in favor of enosis.

After World War II, the Labour party came to power in London following the elections of 1945. The Labour government expressed the desire to grant a liberal constitution for Cyprus and at the same time permitted the deported leaders of the 1931 uprising to return to the island. The British plans to se-cure the cooperation of the church leaders in the formation of a Consultative Assembly for the writing of a new constitution were rejected, because no ref-erence was made to self-determination and enosis. The slogan of the church leaders was "union and only union" with Greece. The 1948 constitutional proposals, which extended a potential majority representation to the Greek Cypriots in the Legislative Council, were rejected because they excluded self-determination and enosis. Thus, the church relentlessly continued to de-mand enosis.

In 1950, a plebiscite was conducted under the leadership of the bishop of Citium, Michael Christodoulos Mouskos, and Archbishop Makarios II, who instructed the Greek Cypriots to vote for enosis. All the Greek Cypriots over the age of eighteen participated in the voting. At the polls, 97 percent of the Greek Cypriots supported the enosis cause of the church. The same year, the bishop of Citium was elected Archbishop Makarios III. He made a pledge to the Greek Cypriot community that he would reject all plans short of enosis. Following his ascendence to head the Orthodox Church of Cyprus, Makarios III concentrated more on secular affairs than spiritual. Under the able leadership of the archbishop, the Greek Cypriots rejected the British at-tempt to introduce a limited self-government combined with colonial status.

The church was unconcerned about the Turkish Cypriot community or Turkey's interest in the future of the island. The archbishop had failed to realize that the Turkish Cypriots and Turkey's national interest had to be taken under consideration before any political settlement could be made in regard to Cyprus. The Turkish Cypriots distrusted the church leadership because it advocated enosis without indicating any willingness to recognize their rights as a minority and the protection of their cultural identity. The Turkish Cypriots became active and were instrumental in Turkey's involve-ment in the talks concerning the future of Cyprus. Turkey's increased inter-est in Cyprus revitalized the Greco-Turkish feud.

When the enosists could not attain political results on Cyprus and abroad in support of enosis, the church took an active part in the organization of the guerrilla fighters—EOKA—in 1952, which was to come under the leadership of Colonel George Grivas. Great Britain considered its presence on Cyprus vital for the protection of its strategic interest in the Middle East and reacted strongly to the organized guerrilla warfare. Turkey vehemently opposed enosis and supported the British policy on Cyprus, reiterating its interest in the future of the island. The Turks also warned Greece that its participation in the Cyprus crisis might have adverse consequences on the Greco-Turkish friendship and alliances. Because of the proximity of Cyprus to Turkey, that country did not hesitate to exert increasing pressure on the others that were involved in finding a settlement to the Cypriot problem. The Turkish Cypriots were of the opinion that in the event of the British withdrawal from Cyprus, the island should be returned to its former ruler.

EOKA's terror campaign was launched in 1955 and continued until 1959. To ease the tensions between the two ethnic communities on the island, Great Britain resorted to diplomatic talks between Greece and Turkey. The Tripartite Conference in 1955, in London, took place between the representatives of the three countries, who hoped to reach an agreement pertaining to the future of Cyprus. When the conference failed to reach any agreement, Great Britain strengthened its military forces on the island and appointed Field Marshal Sir John Harding as the new governor. Governor Harding launched sweeping military operations to suppress the operations of EOKA and capture Grivas. On both counts he failed. In 1956, on the political front Governor Harding initiated negotiations with the archbishop, but they broke down, and the church leader was exiled to the Seychelles Islands.

As the EOKA guerrilla warfare intensified against the British colonial administration in all parts of the island, the tension between the Greek and Turkish Cypriots escalated, and civil war seemed imminent. The Turkish Cypriots organized their own underground movement called Volkan (Volcano); later it was named the Türk Müdafaa Teşkilate (Turkish Resistance Movement) or TMT. The objective of TMT was to protect Turkish Cypriots and deter those who challenged the guidance of their leaders. The EOKA members were also antagonized by the willingness of certain Turkish Cypriots to assist the British forces in the interrogation of the captured guerrilla members and to join the sweeping operations in tracking down the terrorists. A number of Turkish Cypriots lost their lives in serving the British colonial government.

In 1958, Great Britain's proposal for a seven-year period of partnership between the three governments was set aside because of Greece's demand for enosis and Turkey's counterclaim for *Taksim*. The same year, the intercommunal strife picked up momentum, increasing tensions between Greece and Turkey. Sir Hugh Foot, who had succeeded Governor Harding in 1957, proposed a five-year cooling-off period to be followed by self-determination.

Foot's proposal was rejected by Greece and Turkey. The Macmillan Plan failed to receive acceptance by Greece because it was held to be tantamount to *Taksim*.

Greece and Turkey sued for diplomatic negotiations so that a consensus on a Cyprus settlement could be reached. The Zurich and London Agreements of 1959 between Great Britain, Greece, Turkey, and Greek and Turkish Cypriots established the foundation of the Republic of Cyprus. The agreements represented a compromise that safeguarded the national interests of all the parties. The British were able to retain two sovereign base areas, and Greece and Turkey secured the right to station troops on the island under the Treaty of Alliance. Furthermore, the Treaty of Guarantee required the Republic of Cyprus to remain independent and respect its Constitution, which barred enosis and *Taksim*. Great Britain, Greece, and Turkey had the right to intervene to safeguard the independence, territorial integrity, and the Constitution of Cyprus. The power of the ethnic communities in the Republic of Cyprus was divided in proportion to the ethnic composition of the population.

Archbishop Makarios reluctantly accepted the agreements while the Turkish Cypriots expressed their satisfaction. After the Cyprus independence in 1960, the diverse interests and distrust between the two ethnic communities complicated the functioning of a constitutional government. When the two communities were unable to be flexible in their policies, the Constitution proved to be too rigid for the smooth operation of the government.

In 1963 President Makarios proposed thirteen sweeping amendments to the Constitution that he argued would be necessary to the smooth functioning of the government. The Turks rejected these proposals on the grounds that they would unify the state under a majority rule. The Greek Cypriots advanced the argument that the Turkish Cypriots had secured a representation in the Cyprus parliament disporportionate to their distribution of population. Makarios' proposals for the unification of the government under the domination of the Greek Cypriots were rejected by the Turks. Furthermore, the method advanced by Makarios for the constitutional changes was illegal and contrary to the agreements reached at Zurich and London. The Turks asserted that Makarios' whole scheme was to attain enosis.

The independence of Cyprus was consummated amid the cynicism and skepticism of the two communities toward each other, hampering cooperation and the smooth functioning of the republic. Each community, expecting hostilities, trained irregular forces as early as 1961 or 1962. The Turkish Cypriots were obstinate in upholding their constitutional rights and blocking enosis. The Greek Cypriots refused to live by the constitutional provisions because they opposed the veto power of the vice-president, the separate majority vote in the legislative branch, the 70–30 ratio in the public service, the opposition of the Turkish Cypriot members of the House to vote for the tax bill, the deadlock over the collection of custom duties, and the control of separate municipalities by each community independently as crippling to the governmental operations. They believed that these powers to the Turks were disporportionate to their numerical strength. The intransigent positions of the two communities on these political issues produced the constitutional crises.

On Christmas Eve, 1963, violence broke out between the two communities in Nicosia, and the hostilities quickly spread all over the island. The forces of Greece and Turkey stationed on Cyprus joined their own respective ethnic compatriots, which strained relations between the two NATO members and brought them to the brink of war. The Turkish Cypriot members withdrew from the government, leaving the control of the state in the hands of the Greek Cypriots. The United Kingdom forces were able to prevent the escalation of the hostilities between the two communities until the arrival of the United Nations peace-keeping force in March, 1964.

Since the development of the crisis on Cyprus, the affairs of the two communities have been conducted by their own authorities. In 1967 the Turkish Cypriots instituted the Turkish Cypriot Provisional Administration to conduct the community's affairs until a constitutional settlement was reached. Each of the two communities has its own defense force: the Greek Cypriot National Guard, which is the military arm of the Greek Cypriot-controlled government, contains about 15,000 men, and the Turkish Defense Organization, which consists of approximately 5,000 men. The armed forces of the two communities have experienced extensive training under mainland Greek and Turkish military officers, and both sides are heavily armed. In November, 1967, the fighting around the villages of Ayios Theodoros and Kophinou nearly precipitated war between Greece and Turkey. Hostilities were averted, thanks to the efforts of the United States special presidential emissary, Cyrus Vance. The negotiations and agreements between Greece and Turkey established a *modus vivendi* until the coup d'état by the enosists against President Makarios in 1974. The coup precipitated the invasion of Cyprus by Turkey to block the materialization of the Megali Idea, and, furthermore, to fulfil its treaty commitments in preserving the sovereign independence of the island. Cyprus, since the Turkish invasion in 1974, has been a *de facto* bizonal federation within which each ethnic community has an autonomous jurisdiction. The 1960 Constitution was, in effect, abrogated by the Greek Cypriots in 1963, but the island and its government are no longer monopolized by the Greek Cypriots as they were from 1964 until 1974.

The intercommunal talks that were activated in 1968 have been continuing irregularly between Glafkos Clerides and Rauf R. Denktaş. Regardless of the intermittent stalemate in the talks, the face-to-face dialogue between the two politicians must continue if a settlement to the Cyprus crisis is to be reached. When the Clerides-Denktaş talks resumed, they were looked upon with optimism, but as time passed and no agreement was reached, pessimism set in. The stalemate in the talks, accompanied by the dispute over the oil-drilling rights and demarcation of offshore oil-bearing areas in the Aegean Sea, has marred Greco-Turkish relations. The political relations of Turkey and Cyprus have also deteriorated with the regime of General Dimitri Ioannidis of Greece because of the plot instigated by Athens to overthrow Makarios and back the enosists on the island.

The United Nations peace-keeping operations since 1964 have been able to keep armed confrontations on Cyprus to a minimum and helped to restore and maintain peace and order. The UNFICYP presence on Cyprus is indispensable until Cypriot political life returns to normal. The United Nations peace-keeping strength fluctuates between 4,000 and 7,000 men from Great Britain, Canada, Denmark, Finland, and Sweden. The UNFICYP maintains permanent posts at the potential trouble spots between the defenses of the Greek Cypriot National Guard and the Turkish Cypriot fighters or Mücahit (freedom fighters). The manning of these posts by the UNFICYP prevents the expansion of the defense posture of either of the factions. The UNFICYP continues to preserve the unsteady peace with every six-month extension of its operations by the United Nations Security Council. UNFICYP has preserved the peace, but underlying causes of the dispute have not been settled.

In 1965 the United Nations mediator, Galo Plaza Lasso, submitted his report on Cyprus to Secretary General U Thant, but none of the recommendations could be implemented. The report, which was opposed to enosis and *Taksim*, was rejected by Turkey. Galo Plaza resigned in December, 1965, and a replacement was not appointed. A special representative of the secretary general, a Mexican diplomat, Bibiano F. Osorio-Tafall, has succeeded Galo Plaza. The Mexican diplomat is making an important contribution in encouraging the continuation of the intercommunal talks until a final settlement is reached. The United Nations mediation efforts have been unsuccessful, but they nonetheless help perpetuate peace and provide an atmosphere of calm in which a dialogue between the representatives of the two communities can take place.

If a constitutional settlement between the two ethnic groups is to be brought about, both must be flexible and willing to compromise. The armed confrontation between the two communities must be ended so that normal relations can be established. This continued confrontation minimizes the chances for peace while maximizing the possibility of a conflict; moreover, it does nothing to add to security nor to strengthen each community's yearning to compromise. Both sides are convinced that vigilance must be maintained despite assurances of good faith. Until normalcy can be established, each community will justify its actions as being necessary, providing a source of perpetual irritation to the other community.

Greece and Turkey both have security and cultural interests in Cyprus. Turkey's strategy is the result of its geographical proximity to Cyprus. The ties of the two Cypriot communities to their motherlands are very strong, and it is difficult for Cypriots to regard Greece and Turkey as external parties. In order to acquire the acquiescence of the two countries to an agreement, a settlement must exclude both enosis and *Taksim*.

The Greek Orthodox Church is openly endorsing enosis, disregarding the Turkish Cypriot opposition to it. Some church leaders in unison with the enosists are accusing President Makarios of obstructing the cause of enosis. Grivas, who directed the EOKA campaign against the British colonial administration from 1955 to 1959, was always the champion of enosis. After he returned to Cyprus in 1964, he succeeded in organizing and controlling the chaos among the Greek Cypriot fighter groups. He assumed command of the National Guard, whose officers are mainland Greeks, without checking his actions with the ministry of interior or with President Makarios. Grivas was under the direct orders of the military government of Prime Minister George Papadopoulos in Athens. Grivas was recalled to Athens after his military actions against the Turkish Cypriots at Ayios Theodoros and Kophinou. However, in 1971, he returned to Cyprus clandestinely and has organized an underground armed operation against the regime of President Makarios. Grivas refused to contribute to the normalization and coexistence of the two Cypriot communities. He had proclaimed that his organization was dedicated to the realization of enosis.

The majority of the Greek Cypriots in the 1970s wish to end the armed confrontation and to return to the normal way of life. They realize that enosis is an impractical and unattainable goal. The persistent demand for enosis by the church and Grivas sympathizers will escalate the antagonisms between the two ethnic communities on Cyprus.

After 1963, President Makarios continued to give lip service to enosis but sought to maintain his independence in policy matters. He wished to retain the political autonomy of Cyprus while establishing his symbolic link with Greece. Under its archbishop, the church of Cyprus has always been autonomous. Archbishop Makarios' background had prepared him for independence rather than a role as a representative official of Athens, which enosis would provide. Since the Turkish threat of intervention in 1967, President Makarios has reduced the economic and military pressures on the Turkish Cypriots. President Makarios must press hard to find a solution to the Cyprus issue, because the prolongation of the status quo may invite another outbreak of violence.

The Greek Cypriot communists were in favor of enosis during the 1947–49 civil war in Greece between the royalists and the communists. The communists on Cyprus were in favor of enosis because it was expected that Greece would fall under the communist regime. When the communist guerrillas were crushed in Greece, with the financial and military assistance of the Western nations, the Cypriot communists' interest in enosis tapered off. After 1955, AKEL campaigned for unconditional self-determination in lieu of enosis because such a union would entail the moving of NATO forces into the island. AKEL, which is proportionately the strongest communist party in the noncommunist world, conforms with the policy of Moscow, supporting the independence, the sovereignty, and the territorial integrity of Cyprus. AKEL has a better opportunity for growth in an independent Cyprus. In compliance with the orders of the Kremlin, AKEL is backing President Makarios on his stand for Cyprus's independence and nonaligned foreign policy.

The interest of the Soviet Union has been to prevent Cyprus from becoming a viable NATO base or a partner in any Western military block. The Soviet Union wishes to weaken the eastern flank of NATO by intensifying divisions within the alliance. Moscow sought to avert a Turkish invasion of Cyprus and encouraged President Makarios to abrogate the treaties because they limited the sovereignty of the republic. The Soviet Union and its satellites are in favor of the abrogation of the two British sovereign military bases[1] and the withdrawal of the American intelligence radio facilities from the island.[2] They support an independent Cyprus because it will assure the continued role of AKEL in the government and a possible agreement for naval and air bases on Cyprus for the Soviet Union.

The communists are in favor of the Cypriot political instability because they are its sole benefactors. The Soviet Union desires a rapprochement with Turkey and is using Cyprus as a lever to achieve it. The Turks are avowed anticommunists and highly value their military alliances with the Western powers for their security. However, they are disappointed and bitter because of the lack of political support from their allies over the Cyprus issue. Turkey's allies in NATO were opposed to its military intervention on Cyprus. Therefore, Turkey, to gain wider international support for its cause on Cyprus, deemed it necessary to be more closely aligned with the nonaligned and the communist states. The Soviet Union encourages the straining of Turkey's relations with the West and the deterioration of the alliance. It has extended support to the Turkish Cypriot cause by degrees. In 1965, the Kremlin supported Turkey's proposal for Cypriot federation as a solution to the Cypriot crises. Federal solution is unacceptable to the Greek Cypriots and Greece, because it is considered a step toward partition.

After the invasion of Cyprus by Turkey on July 20, 1974, the Turks occupied 40 percent of the island and expelled the Greek Cypriots from their homes. The Turkish objective is to settle Turkish Cypriot refugees on the lands occupied by its military forces. Since the intercommunal hostilities of 1963, approximately 20,000 Turkish Cypriots have been moved from about one hundred villages to the Turkish sectors and have been taken care of by the Turkish government. Following the coup against President Makarios, which failed because of the Turkish invasion, thousands of Turkish Cypriots, seeking security and refuge, moved from their homes to the Turkish sectors in the southern part of the island. The Turkish Cypriot refugees consider their settlement in the northern part of Cyprus to be permanent.

The Turks are willing to consider the return to the Greeks of some of the lands that are now under their occupation, but they refuse to permit the return of a large percentage of Greek Cypriots to the Turkish sector. The return of 180,000 Greek Cypriot refugees would jeopardize Turkish security because the Greeks have threatened to instigate an underground guerrilla war against the Turks. The Turks thus hope that the strain of caring for 180,000 refugees will weaken Greek resolve and that Greece will be forced to accept establishment of a bizonal federation on Cyprus. The Greeks, however, hope that American pressure on Turkey will weaken Turkish intransigence. President Makarios is adamantly opposed to a federal system, but Glafkos Clerides is more reconciled to acceptance of the geographical separation of the two communities under their own separate governing systems.

A unitary system under Greek Cypriot domination with constitutional safeguards for the Turkish Cypriots has been strongly rejected. From 1964 to 1974 the Greek Cypriots did not exhibit a sincere enough interest to gain the trust of the Turkish Cypriots. Therefore, the Turkish Cypriots fear that a unified state under the reign of the majority will relegate them once again to an inferior position and Hellenize the island. The Turkish Cypriots are in favor of a local autonomy within a bizonal federation. Under the bizonal federation, each ethnic group would administer its own internal affairs, while having a common external policy. The Greek leadership's attempt to return to the situation that existed prior to 1974 or prior to 1964 is futile. The Turkish Cypriots, with the strong military backing of Turkey, refuse to be relegated to political impotence under a unified system. Any Cypriot settlement must take into consideration both Greek and Turkish national interests. Both nations are proceeding cautiously in order to avoid another accord that might be stillborn. The intercommunal talks between Glafkos Clerides and Rauf Denktaş must be pragmatic, and the new political developments that occurred with the invasion of Cyprus by Turkey must be accepted.

Greco-Turkish economic cooperation and military alliance are of paramount importance for their sovereign independence against the Soviet Union's imperialism. The Greeks and the Turks will be forced to reevaluate their placing complete dependence for security on the United States because of the American refusal to prevent the communist onslaught against the South Vietnamese in 1975. As stated in Kissinger's book *American Foreign Policy*, (1969): "Regional groupings supported by the United States will have to take over major responsibility for their immediate areas, with the United States being more concerned with the overall framework of order than with the management of every regional enterprise." The American foreign policy objective since 1968 has not been focused on containing communism but on perpetuating its own national interest, sometimes at the expense of its commitment to an ally, as happened in the case of South Vietnam. The United States is abandoning the moralistic considerations that have dominated its foreign policy since the period of President Woodrow Wilson. The United

States wants freedom of action in its foreign policy and is reassessing its policy to be less ideological and more oriented to survival. The makers of American foreign policy are more pragmatically oriented and will concentrate more on the United States' national interest, which is the basic principle of realpolitik.

The long-term national interest of both Greece and Turkey is much more important than the political future of the personalities involved. President Makarios' return to Cyprus might have prevented a civil war among the Greek Cypriots' left and right groups, but it was anathema to the Turks. The Turkish Cypriots have no faith in the promises of Makarios because of his political maneuvering from 1964 to 1974. As a gesture for harmony and peace between the two Cypriot communities, President Makarios should resign from state and political offices and devote himself to his ecclesiastical duties. The Turks will not accept him as the head of a federated state; President Makarios' willingness to exit from office would assist the evolution of a political compromise.

The difficult task ahead of the Greek and Turkish Cypriots is to create a federated state in which the forces of nationalism will have a chance to develop. The development of Cypriot nationalism will mean security for both Greece and Turkey. Cypriotism, a form of patriotism, should emphasize self-government in which the two communities will be able to govern themselves and be coequal under the federal laws. The accumulation of military power by each community must be avoided as it will ultimately cause only death and destruction, increasing the suspicion and fear that only hardens ethnic intransigence. The paramount desire of all Cypriots should be what is best for Cyprus and its citizens. Justice and equality must be the uppermost objectives. A united Cypriot citizenry can become a reality with the development of the proper state of mind. If the two communities fail in this endeavor, Cypriot identity will disintegrate and the two ethnic authorities will grow until each unites with its own motherland. Ethnic pride and arrogance must be forsaken for Cypriotism.

APPENDIXES

A: THE CYPRUS CONVENTION

I. CONVENTION OF DEFENSIVE ALLIANCE BETWEEN
GREAT BRITAIN AND TURKEY, WITH RESPECT TO
THE ASIATIC PROVINCES OF TURKEY. SIGNED
AT CONSTANTINOPLE, 4TH JUNE, 1878

Source: Sir George F. Hill, *A History of Cyprus,* vol. IV (Cambridge: Cambridge University Press, 1952), pp. 300–304.

Her Majesty the Queen of the United Kingdom of Great Britain and Ireland, Empress of India, and His Imperial Majesty the Sultan, being mutually animated with the sincere desire of extending and strengthening the relations of friendship happily existing between their two empires, have resolved upon the conclusion of a Convention of Defensive Alliance with the object of securing for the future the territories in Asia of His Imperial Majesty the Sultan.

Their Majesties have accordingly chosen and named as their Plenipotentiaries, that is to say:

Her Majesty, the Queen of the United Kingdom of Great Britain and Ireland, Empress of India, the Right Honourable Austen Henry Layard, Her Majesty's Ambassador Extraordinary and Minister Plenipotentiary at the Sublime Porte;

And His Imperial Majesty the Sultan, His Excellency Safvet Pasha, Minister for Foreign Affairs of His Imperial Majesty;

Who, after having exchanged their full powers, found in due and good form, have agreed upon the following Articles:

Art. I. If Batoum, Ardahan, Kars, or any of them shall be retained by Russia, and if any attempt shall be made at any future time by Russia to take possession of any further territories of His Imperial Majesty the Sultan in Asia, as fixed by the Definitive Treaty of Peace, England engages to join His Imperial Majesty the Sultan in defending them by force of arms.

In return, His Imperial Majesty the Sultan promises to England to introduce necessary Reforms, to be agreed upon later between the two Powers, into the government, and for the protection of the Christian and other subjects of the Porte in these territories.

And in order to enable England to make necessary provision for executing her engagement, His Imperial Majesty the Sultan further consents to assign the Island of Cyprus to be occupied and administered by England.

Art. II. The present Convention shall be ratified, and the ratifications thereof shall be exchanged, within the space of one month, or sooner if possible.

In witness whereof the respective Plenipotentiaries have signed the same, and have affixed thereto the seal of their arms.

Done at Constantinople, the fourth day of June, in the year one thousand eight hundred and seventy-eight.

(L.S.) A. H. Layard
(L.S.) Safvet

II. ANNEX TO THE PRECEDING CONVENTION. SIGNED AT CONSTANTINOPLE, 1ST JULY, 1878

The Right Honourable Sir A. H. Layard, G.C.B, and His Highness Safvet Pasha, now the Grand Vizier of His Majesty the Sultan, have agreed to the following Annex to the Convention signed by them as Plenipotentiaries of their respective Governments on the 4th June 1878:

It is understood between the two High Contracting Parties that England agrees to the following conditions relating to her occupation and administration of the Island of Cyprus:

I. That a Mussulman religious Tribunal (Mehkeme-i Sheri) shall continue to exist in the island, which will take exclusive cognizance of religious matters, and of no others, concerning the Mussulman population of the island.

II. That a Mussulman resident in the island shall be named by the Board of Pious Foundations in Turkey (Evkaf) to superintend, in conjunction with a Delegate to be appointed by the British Authorities, the administration of the property, funds, and lands belonging to the mosques, cemeteries, Mussulman schools, and other religious establishments existing in Cyprus.

III. That England will pay to the Porte whatever is the present excess of revenue over expenditure in the island; this excess to be calculated upon and determined by the average of the last five years, stated to be 22,936 purses, to be duly verified hereafter, and to the exclusion of the produce of State and Crown lands let or sold during that period.

IV. That the Sublime Porte may freely sell and lease lands and other property in Cyprus belonging to the Ottoman Crown and State (Arazi Mirie ve Emlak-i Humayun) the produce of which does not form part of the revenue of the island referred to in Article III.

V. That the English Government, through their competent authorities, may purchase compulsorily, at a fair price, land required for public improvements, or for other public purposes, and land which is not cultivated.

VI. That if Russia restores to Turkey Kars and the other conquests made by her in Armenia during the last war, the Island of Cyprus will be evacuated by England, and the Convention of the 4th of June, 1878, will be at an end.

Done at Constantinople, the 1st day of July, 1878.

A. H. Layard
Safvet

III. ADDITIONAL ARTICLE. SIGNED AT THERAPIA, 14TH AUGUST, 1878

The Right Honourable Sir A. Henry Layard, G.C.B., and His Highness Safvet Pasha, Grand Vizier and Minister for Foreign Affairs of His Imperial Majesty the Sultan, having met together this day, have, in virtue of their full powers, signed the following additional Article to the Convention of the 4th June, 1878, signed by them as Plenipotentiaries of their respective Governments.

It is understood between the High Contracting Parties, without prejudice to the express provisions of the Articles I, II, and IV of the Annex of the 1st July, 1878, that His Imperial Majesty the Sultan, in assigning the Island of Cyprus to be occupied and administered by England, has thereby transferred to and vested in Her Majesty the Queen, for the term of the occupation and no longer, full powers for making Laws and Conventions for the Government of the island in Her Majesty's name, and for the regulations of its Commercial and Consular relations and affairs free from the Porte's control.

Done at Constantinople, the 14th day of August, 1878.

A. H. Layard
Safvet

IV. Agreement Between Great Britain and Turkey
for Commuting the Ottoman Crown Property,
Revenues, etc., of Cyprus for a Fixed Annual Payment of £5,000. Constantinople, 3rd February, 1879

It having been agreed between Her Britannic Majesty's Government and that of His Imperial Majesty the Sultan that all the rights reserved to the Ottoman Crown and Government, under Article IV of the Annex to the Convention signed at Constantinople on the 4th of June, 1878, shall be commuted by a fixed annual money payment, the Undersigned the Right Honourable Austen Henry Layard, Her Britannic Majesty's Ambassador Extraordinary and Minister Plenipotentiary to the Sublime Porte, and His Excellency Alexandre Carathéodory Pasha, His Majesty's Minister for Foreign Affairs, being duly authorized so to do, hereby declare that:

All property, revenues, and rights reserved to the Ottoman Crown and Government in the said Article IV of the Annex to the Convention of the 4th June, including all revenue derived from tapous, mahloul, and intikal are commuted hereby for a fixed annual payment of £5,000 to be made by Her Britannic Majesty's Government to that of His Imperial Majesty the Sultan, every year during the British occupation of Cyprus, to be calculated from the beginning of next financial year.

Done at Constantinople, the 22nd January, 3rd February, 1879.

A. H. Layard
Al. Carathéodory

V. Copy of the Imperial Firman of 1st July 1878,
as Recorded in the Sher'i Court of Nicosia.

To my aiding Vazir Sadiq Pasha, Vali of the Vilayet of the Archipelago, . . .

To Ahmed Pasha, one of my honoured Mir-i-Miran, Mütasarrif of the Island of Cyprus. . . .
To the Naib and Mufti of Cyprus. . . .
To the Members of the Council and Notables of the people. . . .
Be it known, on the arrival of my high Imperial Cypher, that the delivery, in a temporary manner, to Her of the Island of Cyprus having been desired and requested by the illustrious British Government in consequence of reasons known, and on a

discussion of the matter in my Privy Council of Illustrious Ministers; considering that the said Government has up to now, according to the requirement of the friendship and sincerity which have of old existed between my exalted Government and Her, given by actual deeds very many proofs of Her benevolent designs and intentions towards my Government, and that, consequently, it would be congruous with the exigencies of the circumstances and of the case that the said Government should possess the said Island temporarily, it has been deemed expedient that the temporary administration of the said Island be handed over to the said Government with the condition (in accordance with the Convention that has been framed, sealed and signed in that behalf), that there shall be a Sher'i Court in the Island as heretofore, which will continue to conduct the Sher'i affairs of the Moslem community of the Island; that an official shall be appointed by the Imperial Evqaf Ministry, also from amongst the Moslem community, in order to administer, in conjunction with an official to be appointed by the said Government, the sacred mosques and the properties, real estate and lands belonging to the Moslem cemeteries, schools and other religious institutions found in the Island. That the surplus remaining after deduction of local expenses from the total of my Imperial dues now paid to my exalted Government by the said Island shall be annually paid to my Government. That the miri and vaqf lands found in the said Island shall be freely sold or farmed out, and the monies accruing from them shall be included in the said Imperial dues. And that the said Government shall be empowered to purchase at suitable prices, and through the officer in charge, the necessary unsown lands for public works, and for other purposes of general utility. And this decision having been referred to and submitted for my noble Majesty's sanction, and my high Imperial Iradeé having been appended and issued for the carrying out of the same accordingly, you, the above-mentioned Vali, Mütasarrif, Naib, Mufti and others, are hereby ordered to proceed to the handing over to the officers of the said Government of the temporary administration of the said Island, and to be careful to see that no act or deed is done contrary to my Imperial approbation.

Written on this thirtieth day of the month Jemadhi-ul-akhir, in the year one thousand two hundred and ninety-five.

B: BRITISH HIGH COMMISSIONERS
AND GOVERNORS, 1878–1960

HIGH COMMISSIONERS

July 22, 1878	Lt. General Sir Garnet Wolseley, G.C.M.G., K.C.B.
June 23, 1879	Colonel Robert Biddulph, G.C.B., G.C.M.G.
March 9, 1886	Sir H. E. Bulwer, G.C.M.G.
April 5, 1892	Sir Walter Sendall, K.C.M.G.
April 23, 1898	Sir W. F. Haynes Smith, K.C.M.G.
October 17, 1904	Sir C. A. King Harman, K.C.M.G.
October 12, 1911	Major Sir Hamilton Goold-Adams, G.C.M.G., C.B.

| January 8, 1915 | Major Sir J. E. Clauson, K.C.M.G., C.V.O. |
| July 31, 1920 | Malcolm Stevenson, C.M.G. |

GOVERNORS

May 1, 1925	Sir Malcolm Stevenson, K.C.M.G.
November 30, 1926	Sir Ronald Storrs, K.C.M.G., C.B.E.
October 29, 1932	Sir Reginald Edward Stubbs, G.C.M.G.
November 8, 1933	Sir Herbert Richmond Palmer, K.C.M.G.
July 4, 1939	Sir William Denis Battershill, K.C.M.G.
October 3, 1941	Sir Charles Campbell Woolley, K.C.M.G.
October 24, 1946	Reginald Fletcher, Lord Winster, P.C., K.C.M.G.
August 4, 1949	Sir Andrew Barkworth Wright, K.C.M.G., C.B.E., M.C.
September 28, 1955	Field-Marshall Sir John Harding, Chief of the Imperial Staff, G.C.B., C.B.E., D.S.O., M.C.
December 3, 1957	Sir Hugh Mackintosh Foot, G.C.M.G., K.C.V.O., O.B.E.

C: THE ZURICH AGREEMENT

(FEBRUARY 11, 1959)

Source: Great Britain. Colonial Office. *Conference on Cyprus: Documents Signed and Initialled at Lancaster House on February 19, 1959* (Cmnd. 679. London: Her Majesty's Stationery Office, 1959), pp. 5–9.

BASIC STRUCTURE OF THE REPUBLIC OF CYPRUS

1. The State of Cyprus shall be a Republic with a presidential regime, the President being Greek and the Vice-President Turkish elected by universal suffrage by the Greek and Turkish communities of the Island respectively.

2. The official languages of the Republic of Cyprus shall be Greek and Turkish. Legislative and administrative instruments and documents shall be drawn up and promulgated in the two official languages.

3. The Republic of Cyprus shall have its own flag of neutral design and colour chosen jointly by the President and the Vice-President of the Republic.

Authorities and communities shall have the right to fly the Greek and Turkish flags on holidays at the same time as the flag of Cyprus.

The Greek and Turkish communities shall have the right to celebrate Greek and Turkish national holidays.

4. The President and the Vice-President shall be elected for a period of five years.

In the event of absence, impediment or vacancy of their posts, the President and the Vice-President shall be replaced by the President and the Vice-President of the House of Representatives respectively.

In the event of a vacancy in either post, the election of new incumbents shall take place within a period of not more than 45 days.

The President and the Vice-President shall be invested by the House of Representatives, before which they shall take an oath of loyalty and respect for the Constitution. For this purpose, the House of Representatives shall meet within 24 hours after its constitution.

5. Executive authority shall be vested in the President and the Vice-President. For this purpose they shall have a Council of Ministers composed of seven Greek Ministers and three Turkish Ministers. The Ministers shall be designated respectively by the President and the Vice-President who shall appoint them by an instrument signed by them both.

The Ministers may be chosen from outside the House of Representatives.

Decisions of the Council of Ministers shall be taken by an absolute majority.

Decisions so taken shall be promulgated immediately by the President and the Vice-President by publication in the official gazette.

However, the President and the Vice-President shall have the right of final veto and the right to return the decisions of the Council of Ministers under the same conditions as those laid down for laws and decisions of the House of Representatives.

6. Legislative authority shall be vested in a House of Representatives elected for a period of five years by universal suffrage of each community separately in the proportion of 70 per cent for the Greek community and 30 per cent for the Turkish community, this proportion being fixed independently of statistical data. (N.B.— The number of Representatives shall be fixed by mutual agreement between the communities.)

The House of Representatives shall exercise authority in all matters other than those expressly reserved to the Communal Chambers. In the event of a conflict of authority, such conflict shall be decided by the Supreme Constitutional Court which shall be composed of one Greek, one Turk and one neutral, appointed jointly by the President and the Vice-President. The neutral judge shall be president of the Court.

7. Laws and decisions of the House of Representatives shall be adopted by a simple majority of the members present. They shall be promulgated within 15 days if neither the President nor the Vice-President returns them for reconsideration as provided in Point 9 below.

The Constitutional Law, with the exception of its basic articles, may be modified by a majority comprising two-thirds of the Greek members and two-thirds of the Turkish members of the House of Representatives.

Any modification of the electoral law and the adoption of any law relating to the municipalities and of any law imposing duties or taxes shall require a simple majority of the Greek and Turkish members of the House of Representatives taking part in the vote and considered separately.

On the adoption of the budget, the President and the Vice-President may exercise their right to return it to the House of Representatives, if in their judgment any question of discrimination arises. If the House maintains its decisions, the President and the Vice-President shall have the right of appeal to the Supreme Constitutional Court.

8. The President and the Vice-President, separately and conjointly, shall have the right of final veto on any law or decision concerning foreign affairs, except the par-

ticipation of the Republic of Cyprus in international organizations and pacts of alliance in which Greece and Turkey both participate, or concerning defence and security as defined in Annex I.

9. The President and the Vice-President of the Republic shall have, separately and conjointly, the right to return all laws and decisions, which may be returned to the House of Representatives within a period of not more than 15 days for reconsideration.

The House of Representatives shall pronounce within 15 days on any matter so returned. If the House of Representatives maintains its decisions, the President and the Vice-President shall promulgate the law or decision in question within the time-limits fixed for the promulgation of laws and decisions.

Laws and decisions, which are considered by the President or the Vice-President to discriminate against either of the two communities, shall be submitted to the Supreme Constitutional Court which may annul or confirm the law or decision, or return it to the House of Representatives for reconsideration, in whole or in part. The law or decision shall not become effective until the Supreme Constitutional Court or, where it has been returned, the House of Representatives has taken a decision on it.

10. Each community shall have its Communal Chamber composed of a number of representatives which it shall itself determine.

The Communal Chambers shall have the right to impose taxes and levies on members of their community to provide for their needs and for the needs of bodies and institutions under their supervision.

The Communal Chambers shall exercise authority in all religious, educational, cultural and teaching questions and questions of personal status. They shall exercise authority in questions where the interests and institutions are of a purely communal nature, such as sporting and charitable foundations, bodies and associations, producers' and consumers' co-operatives and credit establishments, created for the purpose of promoting the welfare of one of the communities. (N.B.—It is understood that the provisions of the present paragraph cannot be interpreted in such a way as to prevent the creation of mixed and communal institutions where the inhabitants desire them.)

These producers' and consumers' co-operatives and credit establishments, which shall be administered under the laws of the Republic, shall be subject to the supervision of the Communal Chambers. The Communal Chambers shall also exercise authority in matters initiated by municipalities which are composed of one community only. These municipalities, to which the laws of the Republic shall apply, shall be supervised in their functions by the Communal Chambers.

Where the central administration is obliged to take over the supervision of the institutions, establishments, or municipalities mentioned in the two preceding paragraphs by virtue of legislation in force, this supervision shall be exercised by officials belonging to the same community as the institution, establishment or municipality in question.

11. The Civil Service shall be composed as to 70 per cent of Greeks and as to 30 per cent of Turks.

It is understood that this quantitative division will be applied as far as practicable in all grades of the Civil Service.

In regions or localities where one of the two communities is in a majority approaching 100 per cent, the organs of the local administration responsible to the central administration shall be composed solely of officials belonging to that community.

12. The deputies of the Attorney-General of the Republic, the Inspector-General, the Treasurer and the Governor of the Issuing Bank may not belong to the same community as their principals. The holders of these posts shall be appointed by the President and the Vice-President of the Republic acting in agreement.

13. The heads and deputy heads of the Armed Forces, the Gendarmerie and the Police shall be appointed by the President and the Vice-President of the Republic acting in agreement. One of these heads shall be Turkish and where the head belongs to one of the communities, the deputy head shall belong to the other.

14. Compulsory military service may only be instituted with the agreement of the President and the Vice-President of the Republic of Cyprus.

Cyprus shall have an army of 2,000 men, of whom 60 per cent shall be Greek and 40 per cent Turkish.

The security forces (gendarmerie and police) shall have a complement of 2,000 men, which may be reduced or increased with the agreement of both the President and the Vice-President. The security forces shall be composed as to 70 per cent of Greeks and as to 30 per cent of Turks. However, for an initial period this percentage may be raised to a maximum of 40 per cent of Turks (and consequently reduced to 60 per cent of Greeks) in order not to discharge those Turks now serving in the police, apart from the auxiliary police.

15. Forces, which are stationed in parts of the territory of the Republic inhabitated, in a proportion approaching 100 per cent, by members of a single community, shall belong to that community.

16. A High Court of Justice shall be established, which shall consist of two Greeks, one Turk and one neutral, nominated jointly by the President and the Vice-President of the Republic.

The President of the Court shall be the neutral judge, who shall have two votes.

This Court shall constitute the highest organ of the judicature (appointments, promotions of judges, etc.).

17. Civil disputes, where the plaintiff and the defendant belong to the same community, shall be tried by a tribunal composed of judges belonging to that community. If the plaintiff and defendant belong to different communities, the composition of the tribunal shall be mixed and shall be determined by the High Court of Justice.

Tribunals dealing with civil disputes relating to questions of personal status and to religious matters, which are reserved to the competence of the Communal Chambers under Point 10, shall be composed solely of judges belonging to the community concerned. The composition and status of these tribunals shall be determined according to the law drawn up by the Communal Chamber and they shall apply the law drawn up by the Communal Chamber.

In criminal cases, the tribunal shall consist of judges belonging to the same community as the accused. If the injured party belongs to another community, the composition of the tribunal shall be mixed and shall be determined by the High Court of Justice.

18. The President and the Vice-President of the Republic shall each have the right to exercise the prerogative of mercy to persons from their respective communities

who are condemned to death. In cases where the plaintiffs and the convicted persons are members of different communities the prerogative of mercy shall be exercised by agreement between the President and the Vice-President. In the event of disagreement the vote for clemency shall prevail. When mercy is accorded the death penalty shall be commuted to life imprisonment.

19. In the event of agricultural reform, lands shall be redistributed only to persons who are members of the same community as the expropriated owners.

Expropriations by the State or the Municipalities, shall only be carried out on payment of a just and equitable indemnity fixed, in disputed cases, by the tribunals. An appeal to the tribunal shall have the effect of suspending action.

Expropriated property shall only be used for the purpose for which the expropriation was made. Otherwise the property shall be restored to the owners.

20. Separate municipalities shall be created in the five largest towns of Cyprus by the Turkish inhabitants of these towns. However:—

a—In each of the towns a coordinating body shall be set up which shall supervise work which needs to be carried out jointly and shall concern itself with matters which require a degree of cooperation. These bodies shall each be composed of two members chosen by the Greek municipalities, two members chosen by the Turkish municipalities and a President chosen by agreement between the two municipalities.

b—The President and the Vice-President shall examine within four years the question whether or not this separation of municipalities in the five largest towns shall continue.

With regard to other localities, special arrangements shall be made for the constitution of municipal bodies, following, as far as possible, the rule of proportional representation for the two communities.

21. A Treaty guaranteeing the independence, territorial integrity and constitution of the new State of Cyprus shall be concluded between the Republic of Cyprus, Greece, the United Kingdom and Turkey. A Treaty of military alliance shall also be concluded between the Republic of Cyprus, Greece and Turkey.

These two instruments shall have constitutional force. (This last paragraph shall be inserted in the Constitution as a basic article.)

22. It shall be recognised that the total or partial union of Cyprus with any other State, or a separatist independence for Cyprus (i.e., the partition of Cyprus into two independent States), shall be excluded.

23. The Republic of Cyprus shall accord most-favoured-nation treatment to Great Britain, Greece and Turkey for all agreements whatever their nature.

This provision shall not apply to the Treaties between the Republic of Cyprus and the United Kingdom concerning the bases and military facilities accorded to the United Kingdom.

24. The Greek and Turkish Governments shall have the right to subsidize institutions for education, culture, athletics and charity belonging to their respective communities.

Equally, where either community considers that it has not the necessary number of schoolmasters, professor or priests for the working of its institutions, the Greek and Turkish governments may provide them to the extent strictly necessary to meet their needs.

25. One of the following Ministries—the Ministry of Foreign Affairs, the Ministry of Defence or the Ministry of Finance—shall be entrusted to a Turk. If the President and the Vice-President agree they may replace this system by a system of rotation.

26. The new State which is to come into being with the signature of the Treaties shall be established as quickly as possible and within a period of not more than three months from the signature of the Treaties.

27. All the above Points shall be considered to be basic articles of the Constitution of Cyprus.

D: TREATY OF GUARANTEE

(FEBRUARY 19, 1959)

Source: Great Britain. Colonial Office. *Cyprus* (Cmnd. 1093. London: Her
Majesty's Stationery Office, 1960), pp. 86–87.

The Republic of Cyprus of the one part, and Greece, Turkey and the United Kingdom of Great Britain and Northern Ireland of the other part,

I. Considering that the recognition and maintenance of independence, territorial integrity and security of the Republic of Cyprus, as established and regulated by the Basic Articles of its Constitution, are in their common interest,

II. Desiring to co-operate to ensure respect for the state of affairs created by that Constitution,

Have agreed as follows:

ARTICLE I

The Republic of Cyprus undertakes to ensure the maintenance of its independence, territorial integrity and security, as well as respect for its Constitution.

It undertakes not to participate, in whole or in part, in any political or economic union with any State whatsoever. It accordingly declares prohibited any activity likely to promote, directly or indirectly, either union with any other State or partition of the Island.

ARTICLE II

Greece, Turkey and the United Kingdom, taken note of the undertakings of the Republic of Cyprus set out in Article I of the present Treaty, recognize and guarantee the independence, territorial integrity and security of the Republic of Cyprus, and also the state of affairs established by the Basic Articles of its Constitution.

Greece, Turkey and the United Kingdom likewise undertake to prohibit, so far as concerns them, any activity aimed at promoting, directly or indirectly, either union of Cyprus with any other State or partition of the Island.

ARTICLE III

The Republic of Cyprus, Greece and Turkey undertake to respect the integrity of the areas retained under United Kingdom sovereignty at the time of the establishment of the Republic of Cyprus, and guarantee the use and enjoyment by the United Kingdom of the rights to be secured to it by the Republic of Cyprus in accordance with the Treaty concerning the Establishment of the Republic of Cyprus signed at Nicosia on today's date.

ARTICLE IV

In the event of a breach of the provisions of the present Treaty, Greece, Turkey and the United Kingdom undertake to consult together with respect to the representations or measures necessary to ensure observance of those provisions.

In so far as common or concerted action may not prove possible, each of the three guaranteeing powers reserves the right to take action with the sole aim of reestablishing the state of affairs created by the present Treaty.

ARTICLE V

The present Treaty shall enter into force on the date of signature. The original texts of the present Treaty shall be deposited in Nicosia.

The High Contract Parties shall proceed as soon as possible to the registration of the present Treaty with the Secretariat of the United Nations, in accordance with Article 102 of the Charter of the United Nations.

E: TREATY OF ALLIANCE

(FEBRUARY 19, 1959)

Source: Great Britain. Colonial Office. *Cyprus* (Cmnd. 1093. London: Her Majesty's Stationery Office, 1960), pp. 88–90.

The Republic of Cyprus, Greece and Turkey,
I. In their common desire to uphold peace and to preserve the security of each of them,
II. Considering that their efforts for the preservation of peace and security are in conformity with the purposes and principles of the United Nations Charter,
Have agreed as follows:

Article I

The High Contracting Parties undertake to co-operate for their common defence and to consult together on the problems raised by that defence.

Article II

The High Contracting Parties undertake to resist any attack or aggression, direct or indirect, directed against the independence or the territorial integrity of the Republic of Cyprus.

Article III

For the purpose of this alliance, and in order to achieve the object mentioned above, a Tripartite Headquarters shall be established on the territory of the Republic of Cyprus.

Article IV

Greece and Turkey shall participate in the Tripartite Headquarters so established with the military contingents laid down in Additional Protocol No. 1 annexed to the present Treaty.

The said contingents shall provide for training of the army of the Republic of Cyprus.

Article V

The Command of the Tripartitite Headquarters shall be assumed in rotation for a period of one year each, by a Cypriot, Greek and Turkish General Officer, who shall be appointed respectively by the Governments of Greece and Turkey and by the President and Vice-President of the Republic of Cyprus.

Article VI

The present Treaty shall enter into force on the date of signature.

The High Contracting Parties shall conclude additional agreements if the application of the present Treaty renders them necessary.

The High Contracting Parties shall proceed as soon as possible with the registration of the present Treaty with the Secretariat of the United Nations, in conformity with Article 102 of the United Nations Charter.

ADDITIONAL PROTOCOL No. 1

I. The Greek and Turkish contingents which are to participate in the Tripartite Headquarters shall comprise respectively 950 Greek officers, non-commissioned officers and men, and 650 Turkish officers, non-commissioned officers and men.

II. The President and the Vice-President of the Republic of Cyprus, acting in agreement, may request the Greek and Turkish Governments to increase or reduce the Greek and Turkish contingents.

III. It is agreed that the sites of the cantonments for the Greek and Turkish contingents participating in the Tripartite Headquarters, their juridical status, facilities and exemptions in respect of customs and taxes, as well as other immunities and privileges and any other military and technical questions concerning the organization and operation of the Headquarters mentioned above shall be determined by a Special Convention which shall come into force not later than Treaty of Alliance.

IV. It is likewise agreed that the Tripartite Headquarters shall be set up not later than three months after the completion of the tasks of the Mixed Commission for the Cyprus Constitution and shall consist, in the initial period, of a limited number of officers, charged with the training of the armed forces of the Republic of Cyprus. The Greek and Turkish contingents mentioned above will arrive in Cyprus on the date of signature of the Treaty of Alliance.

ADDITIONAL PROTOCOL No. 2

Article I

A Committee shall be set up consisting of the Foreign Ministers of Cyprus, Greece, and Turkey. It shall constitute the supreme political body of the Tripartite Alliance and may take cognizance of any question concerning the Alliance which the Governments of the three Allied Countries shall agree to submit to it.

Article II

The Committee of Ministers shall meet in ordinary session once a year. In a matter of urgency the Committee of Ministers can be convened in special session by its Chairman at the request of one of the members of the Alliance.

Decisions of the Committee of Ministers shall be unanimous.

Article III

The Committee of Ministers shall be presided over in rotation and for a period of one year, by each of the three Foreign Ministers. It will hold its ordinary sessions, unless it is decided otherwise, in the capital of the Chairman's country. The Chairman shall, during the year in which he holds office, preside over sessions of the Committee of Ministers, both ordinary and special.

The Committee may set up subsidiary bodies whenever it shall judge it to be necessary for the fulfillment of its task.

Article IV

The Tripartite Headquarters established by the Treaty of Alliance shall be responsible to the Committee of Ministers in the performance of its functions. It shall submit to it, during the Committee's ordinary session, an annual report comprising a detailed account of the Headquarter's activities.

F: PRESIDENT MAKARIOS' PROPOSALS

TO AMEND THE CYPRUS CONSTITUTION

(NOVEMBER 30, 1963)

Source: Facts About Cyprus (Nicosia, Cyprus: Cyprus Chamber of Commerce And Industry, January 10, 1964).

SUGGESTED MEASURES TO FACILITATE THE SMOOTH FUNCTIONING OF THE STATE AND REMOVE CERTAIN CAUSES OF INTER-COMMUNAL FRICTION

The Constitution of the Republic of Cyprus, in its present form, creates many difficulties in the smooth government of the State and impedes the development and progress of the country. It contains many sui generis provisions conflicting with internationally accepted democratic principles and creates sources of friction between Greek and Turkish Cypriots.

At the Conference at Lancaster House in February, 1959, which I was invited to attend as leader of the Greek Cypriots, I raised a number of objections and expressed strong misgivings regarding certain provisions of the Agreement arrived at in Zurich between the Greek and the Turkish Governments and adopted by the British Government. I tried very hard to bring about the change of at least some provisions of that Agreement. I failed, however, in that effort and I was faced with the dilemma either of signing the Agreement as it stood or of rejecting it with all the grave consequences which would have ensued. In the circumstances I had no alternative but to sign the Agreement. This was the course dictated to me by necessity.

The three years' experience since the coming into operation of the Constitution, which was based on the Zurich and London Agreements, has made clear the necessity for revision of at least some of those provisions which impede the smooth functioning and development of the State.

I believe that the intention of those who drew up the Agreement at Zurich was to create an independent State, in which the interests of the Turkish Community were safeguarded, but it could not have been their intention that the smooth functioning and development of the country should be prejudiced or thwarted, as has in fact been the case.

One of the consequences of the difficulties created by certain constitutional provisions is to prevent the Greeks and Turks of Cyprus from co-operating in a spirit of understanding and friendship, to undermine the relations between them and cause them to draw further apart instead of closer together, to the detriment of the wellbeing of the people of Cyprus as a whole.

This situation causes me, as President of the State, great concern. It is necessary to resolve certain of the difficulties by the removal of some at least of the obstacles to the smooth functioning and development of the State.

With this end in view I have outlined below the immediate measures which I propose to be taken.

1. The right of veto of the President and the Vice-President of the Republic to be abandoned.

The right of veto given under the Constitution of the Republic to the President and the Vice-President can be exercised separately by each one of them against:—

(*a*) laws or decisions of the House of Representatives concerning foreign affairs, defence and security; and

(*b*) decisions of the Council of Ministers concerning foreign affairs, defence and security.

It is a right of final veto and, therefore, different from any measure provided in certain Constitutions whereby the President of the country has a right of limited veto in the sense that he is entitled not to promulgate a law immediately, but to return it for reconsideration. Provisions for the return of laws and decisions for reconsideration exist in the Cyprus Constitution independently from the provision of final veto.

The Constitution of Cyprus has been based on the doctrine of separation of powers between the Executive and the Legislature. The balance between them must be carefully maintained and friction avoided, if it is to work. The right of veto cuts right across the principles involved and could bring the President and Vice-President into direct conflict with the Legislature.

The exercise of the right of veto is a negative power in the sense that it does not enable the President or the Vice-President to take decisions, but it gives them the power to prevent a decision of the Council of Ministers or of the House of Representatives, on matters of foreign policy, defence, or security from taking effect. It is obvious that it cannot be considered as a power which affords the President or the Vice-President the opportunity to deal with an existing situation in a constructive manner.

More difficulties are encountered because of the fact that the right of veto is not vested only in one person but in two persons, the President and the Vice-President of the Republic, thus increasing the occasions when a deadlock may occur. An example in point is the use of the veto by the Vice-President on the subject of the composition of the units of the Army of the Republic.

Under the Constitution the Army of the Republic must consist of 60% Greeks and 40% Turks. The Council of Ministers, by majority, decided that the organisational structure of the Army should be based throughout on mixed units comprising both Greeks and Turks. The Vice-President, who wanted the structure to be based on separate units of Greeks and Turks, exercised his right of veto against the above decision of the Council, with the result that there is no decision on this matter and the Army has remained ineffective.

In the case of the Army, no great harm has resulted, since it is doubtful whether the Republic can really afford its expansion to 2,000 men at present and cope simultaneously with the heavy financial burdens of economic development and expansion of educational and social services. But it is easy to envisage situations where exercise of the veto could result in more far-reaching and damaging repercussions.

Therefore, the right of veto should be abandoned and reliance placed instead on the provisions for the return of laws and decisions for reconsideration, and the various other relevant safeguards.

2. The Vice-President of the Republic to deputise for the President of the Republic in case of his temporary absence or incapacity to perform his duties.

Under the provisions of the Constitution, the Vice-President of the Republic does not deputise for the President in the event of his absence or incapacity to act, but the President of the House of Representatives does so instead.

This provision creates the impression that a person belonging to the Turkish community and elected by it cannot deputise in a post the nature of which bears responsibility to Cyprus as a whole. It produces a situation whereby, in the absence of the President of the Republic, the Vice-President is overlooked and the President of the House of Representatives steps above him.

The practical effect of this is that it hinders the continuity of the smooth functioning of the executive power. The Vice-President of the Republic is a member of the Executive, he participates in the deliberations of the Council of Ministers, he knows the reasons and background of decisions taken and is, therefore, in a much better position to continue with the implementation of such decisions than the President of the House of Representatives, who is not a member of the Executive, and on whom the burden of acting as Head of the Executive is suddenly thrust.

It is for the above reasons that the Vice-President should deputise for the President of the Republic during his temporary absence or incapacity to perform his duties.

As a result of the new status of the Vice-President certain consequential or relative amendments have to be made.

3. The Greek President of the House of Representatives and the Turkish Vice-President to be elected by the House as a whole and not as at present the President by the Greek Members of the House and the Vice-President by the Turkish Members of the House.

Under the provisions of the Constitution the President of the House of Representatives, who must be a Greek, is elected by the Greek Members of the House and the Vice-President, who must be a Turk, is elected by the Turkish Members. Further, the Turkish Vice-President cannot deputise for the President in case of his temporary absence or incapacity.

The function of the President of the House, who presides over the entire Assembly, is one which bears responsibility to the House as a whole and not to a particular section of it. It is, therefore, improper that the election of the President of the House should be carried out by the Greek Members only. As far as can be ascertained there is no other Constitution where the President of the Legislative Assembly is elected by one section of the Assembly.

The participation of Representatives of both communities in electing the President of the House will also create conditions which will gradually train the two communities to cooperate in electing persons to political offices. It will lead both Greek and Turkish Representatives to closer contact with the office of the President of the House and will facilitate the solution of problems which arise in considering legislative measures.

For the same reasons the Vice-President of the House should be elected by the House as a whole and not by the Turkish Members only.

4. The Vice-President of the House of Representatives to deputise for the President of the House in case of his temporary absence or incapacity to perform his duties.

Under the provisions of the Constitution the Vice-President of the House cannot deputise for the President of the House of Representatives. In case of temporary absence or incapacity of the President of the House his duties are entrusted to the oldest Greek Representative or to such Greek Member of the House as the Greek Members may decide. In the case of the Vice-President his duties are performed by the oldest Turkish Representative or by such other Turkish Member as the Turkish Members may decide.

The fact that the Vice-President never presides over the House and never deputises for the President creates a situation whereby neither does he feel that he owes responsibility to the whole House nor do the Greek Members feel that they owe any duty or responsibility towards the Vice-President.

Apart from the fact that this provision of the Constitution tends to show that the Vice-President is a figure Vice-Head it also affects the smooth functioning of the House. It may occur that the oldest Greek or Turkish Member is not the right person to perform the duties of President or Vice-President of the House. If, on the other hand, the Greek or the Turkish Members of the House nominate other Greek and Turkish Representatives to act as President and Vice-President, respectively, by decision taken on each occasion, there will be no experienced Acting President or Vice-President to take over at a given time.

Finally, in view of the non-existence of a permanent Vice-President of the House entitled to deputise for the President, there is no one familiar with the work involved either in regard to the political aspect of the functions of the President or to the duties connected with the administration of the House.

5. The constitutional provisions regarding separate majorities for enactment of certain laws by the House of Representatives to be abolished.

The Constitution provides that any law imposing taxation and any law relating to Municipalities and any modification of the Electoral Law requires separate majorities of the Greek and Turkish Members of the House of Representatives taking part in the vote.

This provision is obviously contrary to all democratic principles. Its effect is that, though a Bill may be unanimously approved by the Council of Ministers and though it may receive the overwhelming majority of votes in the House of Representatives, nevertheless it is defeated if it does not receive the separate majority of the Greek or Turkish Representatives taking part in the vote.

The House of Representatives consists of 35 Greek Members and 15 Turkish Members. If, for example, 35 Greek Members and 7 Turkish Members vote in favour of a Bill, i.e. the Bill receives a total of 42 votes in favour, it can be defeated by 8 Turkish votes. Even 2 Turkish Representatives can defeat a Bill if only 3 Turkish Representatives take part in the vote.

This provision obstructs the enactment of vital legislation, generally, and impedes the development of the country. In particular, it has already caused serious adverse effects on the State by preventing or delaying the enactment of taxation legislation. Thus, on one occasion, by the exercise of the right of separate majorities, the State remained completely without taxation legislation for several months.

When, subsequently, an Income Tax Bill was introduced to the House the Turkish Representatives again used their right of separate majority to defeat the Bill, with the result that the State remained without an Income Tax Law.

In an attempt to minimize the grave consequences of the situation thus created, an unorthodox system has been devised whereby one Income Tax Law was enacted by the House imposing taxation on non-citizens of the Republic and two separate Income Tax Laws were enacted by the Greek and Turkish Communal Chambers imposing a form of income tax on Greeks and Turks, respectively. Thus, the Republic has three income tax systems, which cause administrative dislocation and give rise to a multitude of legal contentions. Further, in view of the fact that the Government has no control over the Communal Chambers, any amendment may at any time be made by the respective Communal Chamber in its income tax legislation, thereby creating incalculable difficulties for assessment purposes. The existence of three separately controlled tax systems requires separate accounting; the consequent slow rate of assessment and collection of the income taxes encourages tax evasion to a level unknown before in Cyprus.

Past experience has shown that the right of separate majorities was not exercised by the Turkish Representative because of disagreement with provisions of the taxation legislation before the House. The Turkish Members used this right against taxation Bills neither because they disagreed with their provisions nor because such Bills were discriminatory against their community, but for matters unconnected with taxation legislation.

A further difficulty in the enactment of taxation legislation, arising out of the separate majorities provisions, is demonstrated by the fact that such legislation submitted to the House requires months of frustrating negotiations.

Even if one assumes that in the future a more prudent use will be made of the right of separate majorities, the application of this procedure will always cause serious difficulties. It may well make it impossible for the Government to effect proper development of the direct taxes as revenue procedure and also as unified instruments of social and economic policy. No government is able to carry out a programme of development unless it can also plan and control its resources.

There is no justification at all for the provision of separate majorities. If such provision were intended as a safeguard against discriminatory legislation, then it is completely unnecessary because there are other provisions in the Constitution affording adequate safeguards and remedies. Any legislation which is discriminatory can be challenged before the Constitutional Court by the Vice-President of the Republic. Furthermore, Article 6 of the Constitution provides that no law or decision of the House of Representatives shall discriminate against any of the two communities or any person as a person or as a member of a community. Any citizen has a right given to him by the Constitution to challenge any law or decision which discriminates in such a manner as to affect his interests directly.

6. Unified Municipalities to be established.

The Constitution provides that separate Municipalities shall be created in the five main towns of the Republic.

Not only does this provision not serve any useful purpose but it has also proved to be unworkable.

The impossibility of finding a way to define geographical areas and create separate Municipalities, based on communal criteria, is due to the fact that never before did the Greek and Turkish Cypriots contemplate living in separate areas.

A factual examination will show that there are many areas in which Greeks and Turks live side by side and that the ownership of property by the two communities does not follow the pattern of communal areas. This fact is clearly apparent from the proposed principles formulated by the Vice-President of the Republic for determining which streets will fall within the Greek Municipality and which will fall within the Turkish Municipality. The Vice-President proposed that:—

> "The frontage of all property abutting on any street will be measured and if the total length of the frontage of the property belonging to the members of the Greek community in that street is greater, then that street will be included in the sector of the Greek Municipality. The same prin-

ciple will apply in the case of a street where the total length of the frontage of the property belonging to the members of the Turkish community is greater"

It should be observed that by this proposal, the Vice-President has tried to find a solution by distinguishing ownership of property on the basis of communal criteria without taking into consideration the occupants of such property. It is an undisputed fact that there are many properties belonging to Turks which have Greek tenants and vice versa. Many streets abutting on or leading into each other will fall in the area of one or the other Municipality and thus the resulting two municipal areas will not have any territorial cohesion. This fact alone demonstrates the impracticability of the division of the town into separate areas on the basis of communal critera.

Apart, however, from the fact that geographical separation is not feasible, the separation of Municipalities will be financially detrimental to the townsmen. There would be duplication of municipal services and the cost of their running might become so prohibitive as to render their proper functioning almost impossible.

The impossibility of agreeing on the separate areas became apparent during the year-long deliberations of the Constitutional Commission. In view of the inability of the Constitutional Commission to reach agreement on this point, the responsibility was transferred to the President and the Vice-President of the Republic by the insertion of Article 177 of the Constitution, whereby the President and the Vice-President were empowered to define boundaries of the areas of each Municipality. Owing to the above difficulties, however, they failed to reach an agreement on the determination of the boundaries.

Under the proviso to Article 173 (1) of the Constitution the President and the Vice-President of the Republic have a duty, within a period of four years from the date of the coming into operation of the Constitution, to examine the question whether or not the separation of the Municipalities in the five main towns shall continue.

It is obvious that the reason why this provision was inserted was that, even at the time when the Zurich Agreement was drafted, doubts were entertained as to the desirability or practicability of such an arrangement and it was, therefore, thought necessary to give the President and the Vice-President power to reconsider the position within a specified period from the date of Independence.

If it were put forward that the separation of the Municipalities in the five main towns was provided for in order to protect the Turkish inhabitants of such towns against any discrimination, other safeguards may be provided in this respect, such as:—

(*a*) the municipal council in each of the five main towns should consist of Greek and Turkish councillors in proportion to the number of the Greek and Turkish inhabitants of such town by whom they shall be elected respectively;

(*b*) there should be earmarked in the annual budget of each such town, after deducting any expenditures for common services, a sum proportionate to the ratio of the Turkish population of such town. This sum should be disposed of for municipal purposes recommended by the Turkish councillors.

7. The administration of Justice to be unified.

The Constitution separates the administration of Justice on the basis of communal criteria by providing that in all cases, civil and criminal, a Greek must be tried by a Greek Judge, a Turk by a Turkish Judge and that cases, however trivial, involving both Greeks and Turks, must be tried by a Mixed Court composed of Greek and Turkish Judges.

This division is not only entirely unnecessary but, what is more important, is detrimental to the cause of Justice. The very concept of Justice defies separation.

The mere fact that a Greek must be tried by a Greek and a Turk by a Turk is in itself a slur on the impartiality and integrity of the Judges. It is inevitable that when a Judge assumes jurisdiction on the basis of communal criteria he begins to think that the interests of his community stand in danger of being jeopardized and that he is there to protect such interests. The Judge will, therefore, gradually lose the sense of being a judge above communal criteria. This is particularly so in mixed cases, where each Judge will eventually come to feel that his presence is necessary in order to protect the party belonging to his community from possible injustice by his brother Judge. As a consequence of this, Judges will lose their respect for each other, will begin to regard each other with suspicion and may develop the mentality, not of a judge, but of an arbitrator appointed by one of the parties to a dispute. This mentality will inevitably seep into the minds of the people as a whole, who will consider Judges as advocates in the cause of their community and expect them to act as such.

It is another consequence of the dichotomy of Justice that the public is bound to compare sentences imposed by Greek Judges on Greeks and by Turkish Judges on Turks and to draw conclusions from such comparisons. In view of the fact that the jurisdiction of Judges is based on communal criteria, the result of such comparisons will be to foster the belief that there exists separate Justice for Greeks and Turks. This will diminish the respect of the people for the administration of Justice.

Thus Justice will not only cease to be done but will also cease to be seen to be done. Nothing is more certain to undermine Justice and to bring it into disrepute than the situation described above.

Apart from the aforesaid most important considerations, the system which has had to be devised in order to implement these provisions of the Constitution is also unnecessarily costly.

In view of the fact that Greek cases are more numerous than Turkish cases, the Greek Judges are burdened with a much larger volume of work than the Turkish Judges. Due to the separation imposed by the Constitution, Turkish Judges, even if not fully occupied and although willing, cannot relieve their Greek colleagues by taking cases in which the parties involved are Greek. There must, therefore, be maintained a greater number of Judges than would be warranted by the number of cases if they could be evenly distributed. The fact that even a trivial case, as well as a preliminary enquiry, must be heard by two Judges if the parties belong to different communities results in unnecessary waste of time and money, delay and hardship to the litigant, and is yet another reason for having a greater number of Judges than would otherwise be necessary.

A further result of the separation of the administration of Justice is the duplication of registry work and therefore of court personnel, thus creating an additional financial burden.

The measure of civilization of a country and its stability greatly depend on the fair administration of Justice and on the confidence enjoyed by its Judiciary. If the principle of Justice is undermined the consequences to the State cannot but be serious and, in Cyprus, if the present system continues, Justice is certain to suffer.

Before the Constitution came into force, the court system prevailing in Cyprus had been operating extremely well for many years, Justice being administered by Greek and Turkish Judges, honourably and impartially, irrespective of community. There can be no greater proof of this than the fact that even at the height of inter-communal strife, when Justice was still unified, never was a shadow of doubt cast on the integrity of the Judges or any complaint made about their impartiality.

There is, therefore, no reason for the imposition of restrictions on the jurisdiction of the Judges of the Republic, on communal criteria, thus establishing a system which is bound to undermine justice and is most impracticable in its application.

8. The division of the Security Forces into Police and Gendarmerie to be abolished.

Since the establishment of Independence the Security Forces of the Republic have been divided into Police and Gendarmerie and operate as two separate and distinct Forces in defined areas and under separate command.

This division of the Security Forces is entirely unnecessary and should be abolished for the following reason:—

(*a*) with the existence of two Forces under separate command, separate Headquarters for each Force had to be established. This has led to unnecessary financial expenditure;

(*b*) the creation of separate commands necessitates concentration of many officers at Headquarters and causes a waste of manpower, especially in the higher ranks. At least 200 officers are engaged in additional administrative posts due to the division and duplication of the administration. There now also exists a greater ratio of officers vis-a-vis men without a corresponding increase in the total numerical strength. This increase in personnel costs the State an additional expenditure of at least £150,000 per annum;

(*c*) due to the division of the Security Forces and their command into two, both at Headquarters level and at Divisional level, the cohesion and strength of the Security Forces is adversely affected and results, inter alia, in lack of uniformity of discipline and in friction between the two separate Forces;

(*d*) in case of an emergency or other grave situation neither Force will have readily available for immediate use the full strength of the Security Forces and their reserves.

Finally, the experience gained in having only one Force, the Police Force, which worked efficiently and effectively for so many years proves that there is no valid reason for the division of the Security Forces into Police and Gendarmerie, a course not even warranted by the size of the Island.

9. The numerical strength of the Security Forces and of the Defence Forces to be determined by a Law.

The Constitution provides that the Security Forces of the Republic shall consist of the Police and the Gendarmerie and shall have a contingent of 2,000 men which may be reduced or increased by agreement of the President and the Vice-President of the Republic.

This is an unworkable provision because, even if the President and the Vice-President agree to increase the numerical strength of the Security Forces, such agreement will be completely ineffectual unless the House of Representatives approves the resulting increase in budgetary expenditure. Under the Constitution the President and the Vice-President cannot, by agreeing to increase the Security Forces, create a charge on the Consolidated Fund.

The question of increasing or decreasing the numerical strength of the Security

Forces should, in the first instance, be decided by the Council of Ministers in the normal way and legislation be introduced to the House for enactment.

The Constitution also provides that the Republic shall have an Army of 2,000 men. This provision is impracticable as no implementation of the numerical strength of the Army can take place unless the House of Representatives approves the financial expenditure required. Furthermore, no provision exists for the increase or decrease, depending on ordinary requirements, of the numerical strength of the Army. Constitutional provision should, therefore, be made that the Republic shall have such Defence Forces as may be regulated by Law.

10. The proportion of the participation of Greek and Turkish Cypriots in the composition of the Public Service and the Forces of the Republic to be modified in proportion to the ratio of the population of Greek and Turkish Cypriots.

The Constitution provides that 70% of the Public Service shall be composed of Greek Cypriots and that 30% shall be composed of Turkish Cypriots. It further provides that this ratio shall be applied, as far as practicable, in all grades of the Public Service.

The Constitution also provides that the Security Forces shall be composed of 70% Greek Cypriots and 30% Turkish Cypriots and that the Army shall be composed of 60% Greek Cypriots and 40% Turkish Cypriots.

It is an accepted fact that the proper administration of a country depends on the efficiency of its Public Service. This is of particular importance in Cyprus owing to the fact that, as a result of Independence, new institutions have been created adding further complexities to the normal problems of administering the country. Furthermore, the Government, by undertaking a five-year development plan which provides for a Government expenditure of approximately £10 million per year, is casting an additional burden on the Public Service.

The percentages of participation of the two communities in the Public Service as fixed by the Constitution bear no relation to the true ratio of the Greek and Turkish inhabitants of the Island which is 81.14% Greeks and 18.86% Turks.

Generally speaking any provision the effect of which is that certain posts in the Public Service or a certain percentage of such posts are reserved for persons belonging to a community, religious group or ethnic minority is contrary to the internationally accepted principles of Human Rights. Thus under Article 21 (2) of the Universal Declaration of Human Rights of the United Nations it is provided that "Everyone has the right of equal access to the Public Service of his country."

It can of course, be argued that the fixing of a percentage of participation of a community in the Public Service of a country is for the purpose of securing to the citizens constituting such community a right of equal access to the Public Service of the country.

The best way of securing the right of equal participation in the Public Service is not by fixing a percentage, but by provisions in the Constitution giving the right to citizens, who applied and were not appointed to the Public Service, to challenge the decision of the appointing authority before the competent court on the ground that they were discriminated against.

If, however, the method to be followed for securing equality of access is by fixing the ratio of participation of a community in the Public Service, then, in order to minimize discrimination, such ratio must be a fair one so as to afford an equal opportunity to the community constituting the minority to participate in the Public

Service, without at the same time preventing the majority of the population from having an equal opportunity of participation in the Public Service of the country.

The present constitutional provision, by specifying that 70% of the Public Service shall be composed of Greek Cypriots, when in fact the Greek Cypriots constitute more than 81% of the population, and that 30% of the Public Service shall be composed of Turkish Cypriots, when in fact the Turkish Cypriots constitute less than 19% of the population, does not afford an equal opportunity to the majority of the citizens of the Republic to participate in the Public Service. It is, therefore, clearly discriminatory.

The implementation of the above provision of the Constitution creates serious problems for the State.

It makes it necessary, in considering appointments and promotions, to use criteria other than those universally accepted, such as qualifications, efficiency and suitability of the candidate, because the appointing authority has to take into consideration the community to which the candidate belongs. As a result the best candidates cannot always be selected. Further, particular hardship is created in the case of promotions. Public servants who possess all the required qualifications and experience for promotion to higher grades may have to be overlooked in favour of less qualified or efficient public servants, solely in order to give effect to an artificially fixed communal ratio of participation in the Public Service. The result of the situation thus created is that the efficiency of the Public Service is adversely affected.

If the provision is to be implemented without affecting the promotion of public servants, the alternative is to create unnecessary posts and impose a further financial burden on the State. The Government now spends 31% of its Ordinary Budget for salaries and other allowances to public servants, not including pensions. It is clear, therefore, that any increase of unnecessary expenditure in expanding the Public Service would be highly detrimental to the economy of the country.

In addition to what is stated above this provision cannot be implemented for the following reason:—

In many cases in which the Public Service Commission decided to allocate posts to the Turkish community, it was found that no qualified Turks were available for appointment, with the result that a number of posts remained vacant and in some cases the Commission had to appoint Greeks on a temporary basis until qualified Turkish candidates might become available.

In some instances the minimum qualifications specified in the schemes of service were lowered in order to enable Turkish candidates to enter the Public Service, but even with such lower standards no Turkish qualified candidate could be found.

The fact that the Commission had to draw from a population forming less than 19% of the population of the Island in order to fill the 30% of the posts in the Public Service made it very difficult to find qualified Turks for many posts.

Further, the exigencies of public business and the pattern of business and professional activity in the Island require that the Public Service should contain an adequate proportion of Greek officers. The language problem of itself demands this.

It can be seen from what is stated above that not only is the provision that the Public Service shall be composed of 30% Turks unjust and discriminatory against the Greeks, but it is also impracticable, it creates serious difficulties and impedes the efficient functioning of the Public Service.

The reasons given above regarding the ratio of participation of the two commu-

nities in the Public Service apply to a great extent to the ratio fixed for the participation of the two communities in the Security Forces.

It must be stated that the 60:40 ratio of participation of Greeks and Turks in the
Army discriminates to an even greater extent against the Greeks.

Nevertheless, in so far as the present ratio of Greeks and Turks in the Public
Service, the Security Forces and the Army exceeds the population ratio, no abrupt
steps should be taken to reduce it. The proper balance can be achieved over a period
of time through normal appointments, thus avoiding hardship or unfairness to existing members of the Services of the Republic.

11. The number of the Members of the Public Service Commission to be reduced
from ten to five.

The Constitution provides that there shall be a Public Service Commission consisting of a Chairman and nine other Members appointed jointly by the President
and Vice-President of the Republic and that seven Members of the Commission shall
be Greeks and three Members shall be Turks.

Practical experience has shown that, for the purposes for which the Public Service
Commission is intended and bearing in mind the nature of the duties it has to perform, it is too large a body to work efficiently.

A smaller body will have a better chance of securing closer cooperation and understanding amongst its Members, and valuable time, wasted in lengthy arguments
resulting from the divergence of opinion of its many Members, will be saved. Generally, a more constructive approach to the problems facing the Commission will
result.

12. All decisions of the Public Service Commission to be taken by simple majority.

The Constitution provides that any decision of the Public Service Commission
shall be taken by an absolute majority vote of its Members.

This general provision, however, is qualified by other provisions making it necessary that in matters of appointments, promotions, transfers and discipline such
majority must include a certain minimum number of Greek and Turkish votes depending on whether the decision relates to a Greek or a Turk. In short, a power of
veto is given to a section of the Greek or Turkish Members to negative majority
decisions.

It is obvious that this procedure for taking decisions by the Public Service Commission creates a situation whereby the Greek and Turkish Members feel that their
paramount purpose, as Members of the Commission, is to protect Greek and Turkish
interests and not to serve the true interests of the Public Service. Thus, even in the
mode of deciding an issue communal criteria are superimposed on the universally
accepted criteria adopted by similar bodies elsewhere. This is of particular signifi-
cance in view of the fact that the Public Service Commission, in addition to being
the appointing authority, is also the disciplinary body for the Public Service.

Furthermore, the procedure laid down in the Constitution creates situations leading to deadlock resulting in a state of uncertainty amongst the public servants and
often preventing the speedy appointment of officers to vital posts.

If this situation is allowed to continue, it will result in undermining the efficiency
of the Public Service.

It may be argued that, in taking decisions, the Public Service Commission may
act in a discriminatory manner. In such a case there is adequate remedy provided by
Articles 6 and 146 of the Constitution. The former Article prohibits discrimination

against any of the two communities or any person as a person or by virtue of being a member of a community, while the latter article provides that any person may make a recourse to the Constitutional Court against any decision, act or omission contrary to any of the provisions of the Constitution, one of which is Article 6, if any legitimate interest which he has either as a person or by virtue of being a member of a community, is adversely affected.

13. The Greek Communal Chamber to be abolished.

The Constitution provides that there shall be two Communal Chambers, one Greek and one Turkish, each having jurisdiction in matters of religion, education, cultural affairs and personal status over members of its repsective community, as well as control over communal co-operative societies.

This provision appears to have its origin in the concept that the Republic ought not to interfere with religious, educational, cultural and other cognate matters the administration of which should be regarded as a safeguarded right in the case of the minority.

When this concept was extended to the Greek majority the result was to place the entire education of the country outside the sphere of Government economic and social policies and to create financial problems and other difficulties for the Communal Chambers, reflecting adversely on the State. With a view to minimizing these difficulties the Communal Chambers should be abolished and a new system should be devised providing for their substitution by appropriate authorities and institutions.

Should the Turkish community, however, desire to retain its Chamber, in the new system, such a course is open to it.

I have dealt with certain of the difficulties created by our Constitution.

In conclusion I would stress that it is not my intention by any of these proposals to deprive the Turkish community of their just rights and interests or proper safeguards. The purpose is to remove certain causes of friction and obstacles to the smooth working of the State.

The main object of a Constitution should be to secure, within its framework, the proper functioning of the State and not to create sources of anomaly and conflict. Experience has proved that our Constitution falls short of this object, and certain of its provisions have created great difficulties in practice. In the interests of our people we must remedy this. I earnestly believe that the proposed settlement of the various points of difficulty will be to the benefit of the people of Cyprus as a whole. I hope that the Turkish Cypriots will share this view.

ARCHBISHOP MAKARIOS,
President of the Republic of Cyprus.
Nicosia,
30th November, 1963.

G: UNITED STATES AND TURKISH VIEWS

ON NATO OBLIGATIONS AND THE CYPRUS

CRISIS: Correspondence between

President Johnson and Prime Minister

İnönü, June 5 and 13, 1964

Source: "Correspondence between President Johnson and Prime Minister İnönü,
June 1964," *The Middle East Journal*, Vol. XX, No. 3, Summer 1966. pp. 386–393.

WHITE HOUSE STATEMENT

At the request of the Government of Turkey, the White House is today releasing
the texts of letters exchanged on June 5, 1964, between President Johnson and the
then Prime Minister of Turkey İsmet İnönü on the Cyprus crisis. Steps subsequent
to this exchange of letters led to the visit of Prime Minister İnönü to Washington
later in that month and constructive discussions by the President and the Prime
Minister of the issues involved.

A joint communiqué released at the conclusion of those discussions welcomed the
opportunity for a full exchange of views by the two leaders and the occasion to consider ways in which the two countries could strengthen the efforts of the United
Nations with respect to the safety and security of Cyprus. The communiqué noted
that "the cordial and candid conversations of the two leaders strengthened the broad
understanding already existing between Turkey and the United States."

The United States continues to value highly the close and friendly relations we
maintain with Turkey.

PRESIDENT JOHNSON'S LETTER TO PRIME MINISTER İNÖNÜ JUNE 5, 1964

Dear Mr. Prime Minister:

I am gravely concerned by the information which I have had through Ambassador
Hare from you and your Foreign Minister that the Turkish Government is contem-
plating a decision to intervene by military force to occupy a portion of Cyprus. I
wish to emphasize, in the fullest friendship and frankness, that I do not consider that
such a course of action by Turkey, fraught with such far-reaching consequences, is
consistent with the commitment of your Government to consult fully in advance with
us. Ambassador Hare has indicated that you have postponed your decision for a few
hours in order to obtain my views. I put to you personally whether you really believe
that it is appropriate for your Government, in effect, to present a unilateral decision
of such consequence to an ally who has demonstrated such staunch support over the
years as has the United States for Turkey. I must, therefore, first urge you to accept
the responsibility for complete consultation with the United States before any such
action is taken.

It is my impression that you believe that such intervention by Turkey is permissible under the provisions of the Treaty of Guarantee of 1960. I must call your attention, however, to our understanding that the proposed intervention by Turkey would be for the purpose of effecting a form of partition of the Island, a solution which is specifically excluded by the Treaty of Guarantee. Further, that Treaty requires consultation among the Guarantor Powers. It is the view of the United States that the possibilities of such consultation have by no means been exhausted in this situation and that, therefore, the reservation of the right to take unilateral action is not yet applicable.

I must call to your attention, also, Mr. Prime Minister, the obligations of NATO. There can be no question in your mind that a Turkish intervention in Cyprus would lead to a military engagement between Turkish and Greek forces. Secretary of State Rusk declared at the recent meeting of the Ministerial Council of NATO in The Hague that war between Turkey and Greece must be considered as "literally unthinkable." Adhesion to NATO, in its very essence, means that NATO countries will not wage war on each other. Germany and France have buried centuries of animosity and hostility in becoming NATO allies; nothing less can be expected from Greece and Turkey. Furthermore, a military intervention in Cyprus by Turkey could lead to a direct involvement by the Soviet Union. I hope you will understand that your NATO allies have not had a chance to consider whether they have an obligation to protect Turkey against the Soviet Union if Turkey takes a step which results in Soviet intervention without the full consent and understanding of its NATO Allies.

Further, Mr. Prime Minister, I am concerned about the obligations of Turkey as a member of the United Nations. The United Nations has provided forces on the Island to keep the peace. Their task has been difficult but, during the past several weeks, they have been progressively successful in reducing the incidents of violence on that Island. The United Nations Mediator has not yet completed his work. I have no doubt that the general membership of the United Nations would react in the strongest terms to unilateral action by Turkey which would defy the efforts of the United Nations and destroy any prospect that the United Nations could assist in obtaining a reasonable and peaceful settlement of this difficult problem.

I wish also, Mr. Prime Minister, to call your attention to the bilateral agreement between the United States and Turkey in the field of military assistance. Under Article IV of the Agreement with Turkey of July 1947, your Government is required to obtain United States consent for the use of military assistance for purposes other than those for which such assistance was furnished. Your Government has on several occasions acknowledged to the United States that you fully understand this condition. I must tell you in all candor that the United States cannot agree to the use of any United States supplied military equipment for a Turkish intervention in Cyprus under present circumstances.

Moving to the practical results of the contemplated Turkish move, I feel obligated to call to your attention in the most friendly fashion the fact that such a Turkish move could lead to the slaughter of tens of thousands of Turkish Cypriots on the Island of Cyprus. Such an action on your part would unleash the furies and there is no way by which military action on your part could be sufficiently effective to prevent wholesale destruction of many of those whom you are trying to protect. The presence of United Nations forces could not prevent such a catastrophe.

You may consider that what I have said is much too severe and that we are disregardful of Turkish interests in the Cyprus situation. I should like to assure you that this is not the case. We have exerted ourselves both publicly and privately to assure the safety of Turkish Cypriots and to insist that a final solution of the Cyprus problem should rest upon the consent of the parties most directly concerned. It is possible that you feel in Ankara that the United States has not been sufficiently active in your behalf. But surely you know that our policy has caused the liveliest resentments in Athens (where demonstrations have been aimed against us) and has led to a basic alienation between the United States and Archbishop Makarios. As I said to your Foreign Minister in our conversation just a few weeks ago, we value very highly our relations with Turkey. We have considered you as a great ally with fundamental common interests. Your security and prosperity have been a deep concern of the American people and we have expressed that concern in the most practical terms. You and we have fought together to resist the ambitions of the Communist world revolution. This solidarity has meant a great deal to us and I would hope that it means a great deal to your Government and to your people. We have no intention of lending any support to any solution of Cyprus which endangers the Turkish Cypriot community. We have not been able to find a final solution because this is, admittedly, one of the most complex problems on earth. But I wish to assure you that we have been deeply concerned about the interests of Turkey and of the Turkish Cypriots and will remain so.

Finally, Mr. Prime Minister, I must tell you that you have posed the gravest issues of war and peace. These are issues which go far beyond the bilateral relations between Turkey and the United States. They not only will certainly involve war between Turkey and Greece but could involve wider hostilities because of the unpredictable consequences which a unilateral intervention in Cyprus could produce. You have your responsibilities as Chief of the Government of Turkey; I also have mine as President of the United States. I must, therefore, inform you in the deepest friendship that unless I can have your assurance that you will not take such action without further and fullest consultation I cannot accept your injunction to Ambassador Hare of secrecy and must immediately ask for emergency meetings of the NATO Council and of the United Nations Security Council.

I wish it were possible for us to have a personal discussion of this situation. Unfortunately, because of the special circumstances of our present Constitutional position, I am not able to leave the United States.[1] If you could come here for a full discussion I would welcome it. I do feel that you and I carry a very heavy responsibility for the general peace and for the possibilities of a sane and peaceful resolution of the Cyprus problem. I ask you, therefore, to delay any decisions which you and your colleagues might have in mind until you and I have had the fullest and frankest consultation.

Sincerely,
Lyndon B. Johnson

PRIME MINISTER İNÖNÜ'S RESPONSE
TO THE PRESIDENT JUNE 13, 1964

Dear Mr. President,

I have received your message of June 5, 1964 through Ambassador Hare. We have, upon your request, postponed our decision to exercise our right of unilateral action in Cyprus conferred to us by the Treaty of Guarantee. With due regard to the spirit of candour and friendship in which your message is meant to be written, I will, in my reply, try to explain to you in full frankness my views about the situation.

Mr. President,

Your message, both in wording and content, has been disappointing for an ally like Turkey who has always been giving the most serious attention to its relations of alliance with the United States and has brought to the fore substantial divergences of opinion in various fundamental matters pertaining to these relations.

It is my sincere hope that both these divergences and the general tone of your message are due to the haste in which a representation made in good-will was, under pressure of time, based on data hurriedly collected.

In the first place, it is being emphasized in your message that we have failed to consult with the United States when a military intervention in Cyprus was deemed indispensable by virtue of the Treaty of Guarantee. The necessity of a military intervention in Cyprus has been felt four times since the closing days of 1963. From the outset we have taken a special care to consult the United States on this matter. Soon after the outbreak of the crisis, on December 25, 1963, we have immediately informed the United States of our contacts with the other guaranteeing powers only to be answered that the United States was not a party to this issue. We then negotiated with the United Kingdom and Greece for intervention and, as you know, a tri-partite military administration under British command was set up on December 26, 1963. Upon the failure of the London conference and of the joint Anglo-American proposals, due to the attitude of Makarios and in the face of continuing assaults in the island against the Turkish Cypriots, we lived through very critical days in February and taking advantage of the visit of Mr. George Ball to Ankara, we informed again the United States of the gravity of the situation. We tried to explain to you that the necessity of intervention to restore order in the island might arise in view of the vacuum caused by the rejection of the Anglo-American proposals and we informed you that we might have to intervene at any time. We even requested guarantees from you on specific issues and your answers were in the affirmative. However, you asked us not to intervene and assured us that Makarios would get at the United Nations a severe lesson while all the Turkish rights and interests would be preserved.

We complied with your request without any satisfactory result being secured at the United Nations. Moreover the creation of the United Nations force, decided upon by the Security Council, became a problem. The necessity for intervention was felt for the third time to protect the Turkish community against the assaults of the terrorists in Cyprus who were encouraged by the doubts as to whether the United Nations forces would be set up immediately after the adoption of the Security Council resolution of March 4, 1964. But assuring us that the force would be set up very shortly, you insisted again that we refrain from intervening. Thereupon we postponed our intervention once again, awaiting the United Nations forces to assume their duty.

Dear Mr. President,

The era of terror in Cyprus has a particular character which rendered ineffective all measures taken so far. From the very outset, the negotiations held to restore security and the temporary set-ups have all helped only to increase the aggressiveness and the destructiveness of the Makarios administration. The Greek Cypriots have lately started to arm themselves overtly and considered the United Nations as an additional instrument to back up their ruthless and unconstitutional rule. It has become quite obvious that the United Nations have neither the authority nor the intent to intervene for the restoration of constitutional order and to put an end to aggression. You are well aware of the instigative attitude of the Greek Government towards the Greek Cypriots. During the talks held in your office, in the United States, we informed you that under the circumstances we would eventually be compelled to intervene in order to put an end to the atrocities in Cyprus. We also asked your Secretary of State at The Hague whether the United States would support us in such an eventuality and we received no answer. I think, I have thus reminded you how many times and under what circumstances we informed you of the necessity for intervention in Cyprus. I do remember having emphasized to your high level officials our due appreciation of the special responsibilities incumbent upon the United States within the alliance and of the necessity to be particularly careful and helpful to enable her to maintain solidarity within the alliance. As you see, we never had the intention to confront you with a unilateral decision on our part. Our grievance stems from our inability to explain to you a problem which caused us for months utmost distress and from your refusal to take a frank and firm stand on the issue as to which party is on the right side in the dispute between two allies, namely, Turkey and Greece.

Mr. President,

In your message you further emphasized the obligation of Turkey, under the provisions of the Treaty, to consult with the other two guaranteeing powers, before taking any unilateral action. Turkey is fully aware of this obligation. For the past six months we have indeed complied with the requirements of this obligation. But Greece has not only thwarted all the attempts made by Turkey to seek jointly the ways and means to stop Greek Cypriots from repudiating international treaties, but has also supported their unlawful and inhuman acts and has even encouraged them.

The Greek Government itself has not hesitated to declare publicly that the international agreements it signed with us were no longer in force. Various examples to that effect were, in due course, communicated in detail, orally and in writing, to your State Department.

We have likewise fulfilled our obligation of constant consultation with the Government of the United Kingdom, the other guaranteeing power.

In several instances we have, jointly with the Government of the United Kingdom, made representations to the Greek Cypriots with a view to restoring constitutional order. But unfortunately, these representations were of no avail due to the negative attitude of the Greek Cypriot authorities.

As you see, Turkey has earnestly explored every avenue of consulting continuously and acting jointly with the other two guaranteeing powers. This being the fact, it can not be asserted that Turkey has failed to abide by her obligation of consulting with the other two guaranteeing powers before taking unilateral action.

I put it to you, Mr. President, whether the United States Government which has felt the need to draw the attention of Turkey to her obligation of consultation, yet earnestly and faithfully fulfilled by the latter, should not have reminded Greece, who repudiates treaties signed by herself, of the necessity to abide by the precept "pacta sunt servanda" which is the fundamental rule of international law. This precept which, only a fortnight ago, was most eloquently characterized as "the basis of survival" by your Secretary of State himself in his speech at the "American Law Institute," is now being completely and contemptuously ignored by Greece, our NATO ally and by the Greek Cypriots.

Dear Mr. President,

As implied in your message, by virtue of the provisions of Article 4 of the Treaty of Guarantee, the three guaranteeing powers have, in the event of a breach of the provisions of that Treaty, the right to take concerted action and, if that proves impossible, unilateral action with the sole aim of re-establishing the state of affairs created by the said Treaty. The Treaty of Guarantee was signed with this understanding being shared by all parties thereto. The "Gentleman's Agreement" signed on February 19, 1959 by the Foreign Ministers of Turkey and Greece, is an evidence of that common understanding.

On the other hand, at the time of the admission of the Republic of Cyprus to the United Nations, the members of the organization were fully acquainted with all the international commitments and obligations of the said Republic and no objections were raised in this respect.

Furthermore, in the course of the discussions on Cyprus leading to the resolution adopted on March 4, 1964 by the Security Council, the United States Delegate, among others, explicitly declared that the United Nations had no power to annul or amend international treaties.

The understanding expressed in your message that the intervention by Turkey in Cyprus would be for the purposes of effecting the partition of the island has caused me great surprise and profound sorrow. My surprise stems from the fact that the data furnished to you about the intentions of Turkey could be so remote from the realities repeatedly proclaimed by us. The reason of my sorrow is that our ally, the Government of the United States, could think that Turkey might lay aside the principle constituting the foundation of her foreign policy, i.e., absolute loyalty to international law, commitments and obligations, as factually evidenced in many circumstances well known to the United States.

I would like to assure you most categorically and most sincerely that if ever Turkey finds herself forced to intervene militarily in Cyprus this will be done in full conformity with the provisions and aims of international agreements.

In this connection, allow me to stress, Mr. President, that the postponement of our decision does naturally, in no way affect the rights conferred to Turkey by Article 4 of the Treaty of Guarantee.

Mr. President,

Referring to NATO obligations, you state in your message that the very essence of NATO requires that allies should not wage war on each other and that a Turkish intervention in Cyprus would lead to a military engagement between Turkish and Greek forces.

I am in full agreement with the first part of your statement, but the obligation for the NATO allies to respect international agreements concluded among themselves as well as their mutual treaty rights and commitments is an equally vital requisite of the alliance. An alliance among states which ignores their mutual contractual obligations and commitments is unthinkable.

As to the concern you expressed over the outbreak of a Turco-Greek war in case of Turkey's intervention in Cyprus in conformity with her rights and obligations stipulated in international agreements, I would like to stress that Turkey would undertake a "military operation" in Cyprus exclusively under the conditions and for the purpose set forth in the agreements. Therefore, a Turco-Greek war so properly described as "literally unthinkable" by the Honorable Dean Rusk could only occur in case of Greece's aggression against Turkey. Our view, in case of such an intervention, is to invite to an effective collaboration, with the aim of restoring the constitutional order in Cyprus, both Greece and the United Kingdom in their capacity as guaranteeing powers. If despite this invitation and its contractual obligations Greece were to attack Turkey, we could in no way be held responsible of the consequences of such an action; I would like to hope that you have already seriously drawn the Greek Government's attention on these matters.

The part of your message expressing doubts as to the obligation of the NATO allies to protect Turkey in case she becomes directly involved with the USSR as a result of an action initiated in Cyprus, gives me the impression that there are as between us wide divergence of views as to the nature and basic principles of the North Atlantic Alliance. I must confess that this has been to us the source of great sorrow and grave concern. Any aggression against a member of NATO will naturally call from the aggressor an effort of justification. If NATO's structure is so weak as to give credit to the aggressor's allegations, then it means that this defect of NATO needs really to be remedied. Our understanding is that the North Atlantic Treaty imposes upon all member states the obligation to come forthwith to the assistance of any member victim of an aggression. The only point left to the discretion of the member states is the nature and the scale of this assistance. If NATO members should start discussing the right and wrong of the situation of their fellow-member victim of a Soviet aggression, whether this aggression was provoked or not and if the decision on whether they have an obligation to assist the member should be made to depend on the issue of such a discussion, the very foundations of the Alliance would be shaken and it would lose its meaning. An obligation of assistance, if it is to carry any weight, should come into being immediately upon the observance of aggression. That is why Article 5 of the North Atlantic Treaty considers an attack against one of the member states as an attack against them all and makes it imperative for them to assist the party so attacked by taking forthwith such action as they deem necessary. In this connection I would like to further point out that the agreements on Cyprus have met with the approval of the North Atlantic Council, as early as the stage of the United Nations debate on the problem, i.e., even prior to the establishment of the Republic of Cyprus, hence long before the occurrence of the events of December 1963.

As you will recall, at the meeting of the NATO Ministerial Council held three weeks ago at The Hague, it was acknowledged that the treaties continued to be the basis for legality as regards the situation in the island and the status of Cyprus. The fact that these agreements have been violated as a result of the flagrantly unlawful acts of one of the parties on the island should in no way mean that the said agreements are no longer in force and that the rights and obligations of Turkey by virtue of those agreements should be ignored. Such an understanding would mean that as long as no difficulties arise, the agreements are considered as valid and they are no longer in force when difficulties occur. I am sure you will agree with me that such an understanding of law cannot be accepted. I am equally convinced that there could be no shadow of doubt about the obligation to protect Turkey within the NATO Alliance in a situation that can, by no means, be attributed to an arbitrary act of Turkey. An opposite way of thinking would lead to the repudiation and denial of the concept of law and of Article 51 of the United Nations Charter.

In your message, concern has been expressed about the commitments of Turkey as a member of the United Nations. I am sure, Mr. President, you will agree with me if I say that such a concern, which I do not share, is groundless especially for the following reasons: Turkey has distinguished herself as one of the most loyal members of the United Nations ever since its foundation. The Turkish people has spared no effort to safeguard the principles of the United Nations Charter, and has even sacrificed her sons for this cause. Turkey has never failed in supporting this organization and, in order to secure its proper functioning, has borne great moral and material sacrifices even when she had most pressing financial difficulties. Despite the explicit rights conferred to Turkey by the Treaty of Guarantee, my Government's respect for and adherence to the United Nations have recently been demonstrated once more by its acceptance of the Security Council resolution of March 4, 1964 as well as by the priority it has given to the said resolution.

Should the United Nations have been progressively successful in carrying out their task as pointed out in your message, a situation which is of such grave concern for both you and I, would never have arisen. It is a fact that the United Nations operations in the island have proved unable to put an end to the oppression.

The relative calm which has apparently prevailed in the island for the past few weeks marks the beginning of preparations of the Greek Cypriots for further tyranny. Villages are still under siege. The United Nations forces, assuaging Turkish Cypriots, enable the Greeks to gather their crops; but they do not try to stop the Greeks when the crops of Turks are at stake and they act as mere spectators to Greek assaults. These vitally important details may not well reach you, whereas we live in the atmosphere created by the daily reports of such tragic events.

The report of the Secretary-General will be submitted to the United Nations on June 5, 1964. I am seriously concerned that we may face yet another defeat similar to the one we all suffered on March 4, 1964. The session of March 4th had further convinced Makarios that the Treaty of Guarantee did not exist for him and thereupon he took the liberty of actually placing the United Nations forces under his control and direction. From then on the assassination of hostages and the besieging of villages have considerably increased.

Dear Mr. President,

Our allies who are in a position to arbiter in the Cyprus issue and to orient it in the right direction have so far been unable to disentangle the problem from a substantial error. The Cyprus tragedy has been engendered by the deliberate policy of the Republic of Cyprus aimed at annulling the treaties and abrogating the constitution. Security can be established in the island only through the proper functioning of an authority above the Government of Cyprus. Yet only the measures acceptable to the Cypriot Government are being sought to restore security in Cyprus. The British administration set up following the December events, the Anglo-American proposals and finally the United Nations command have all been founded on this unsound basis and consequently every measure acceptable to Makarios has proved futile and has, in general, encouraged oppression and aggression.

Dear Mr. President,

You put forward in your message the resentment caused in Greece by the policy pursued by your Government. Within the content of the Cyprus issues, the nature of the Greek policy and the course of action undertaken by Greece indicate that she is apt to resort to every means within her power to secure the complete annulment of the existing treaties. We are at pains to make our allies understand the sufferings we bear in our rightful cause and the irretrievable plight in which the Turkish Cypriots are living. On the other hand, it is not the character of our nation to exploit demonstrations of resentment. I assure you that our distress is deeply rooted since we can not make you understand our rightful position and convince you of the necessity of spending every effort and making use of all your authority to avert the perils inherent in the Cyprus problem by attaching to it the importance it well deserves.

That France and Germany have buried their animosity is indeed a good example. However, our nation had already given such an example forty years ago by establishing friendly relations with Greece, right after the ruthless devastation of the whole Anatolia by the armies of that country.

Dear Mr. President,

As a member of the Alliance our nation is fully conscious of her duties and rights. We do not pursue any aim other than the settlement of the Cyprus problem in compliance with the provisions of the existing treaties. Such a settlement is likely to be reached if you lend your support and give effect with your supreme authority to the sense of justice inherent in the character of the American nation.

Mr. President,

I thank you for your statement emphasizing the value attached by the United States to the relations of alliance with Turkey and for your kind words about the Turkish nation. I shall be happy to come to the United States to talk the Cyprus problem with you. The United Nations Security Council will meet on June the 17th. In the meantime, Mr. Dirk Stikker, Secretary General of NATO, will have paid a visit to Turkey. Furthermore, the United Nations mediator Mr. Tuomioja will have submitted his report to the Secretary-General. These developments may lead to the emergence of a new situation. It will be possible for me to go abroad to join you, at a date convenient for you, immediately after June 20th.

It will be most helpful for me if you would let me know of any defined views and designs you may have on the Cyprus question so that I may be able to study them thoroughly before my departure for Washington.

Finally, I would like to express my satisfaction for the frank, fruitful and promising talks we had with Mr. G. Ball in Ankara just before forwarding this message to you.

Sincerely,
İsmet İnönü
Prime Minister of Turkey.

H: THE BASIC PROVISIONS OF THE

PROVISIONAL CYPRUS TURKISH

ADMINISTRATION

(DECEMBER 29, 1967)

Source: United Nations. Security Council. *Special Report by the Secretary-General on Recent Developments Regarding Cyprus.* S/8323, 3 January 1968, Annex 1. pp. 1–4. See also Turkish Communal Chamber (Cyprus) *Special News Bulletin*, No. 1258. December 30, 1967. *Halkın Sesi*, December 29, 1967.

Section 1: Until all provisions of the 16 August 1960 Constitution of the Republic of Cyprus are applied, all Turks living in Turkish areas shall be attached to the Provisional Turkish Administration.

LEGISLATIVE MATTERS

Section 2: The necessary legislation for Turkish areas shall be made by the House of the Provisional Turkish Administration which shall be composed of the Turkish members of the House of Representatives and members of the Turkish Communal Chamber. The Vice-President of the House of Representatives shall be the President of the House.

Section 3: The members of the House shall continue to possess all the powers embodied in the Constitution dated 16 August 1960.

Section 4: The House shall function in accordance with those provisions of the Rules and Regulations of the House of Representatives and of the Turkish Communal Chamber which are capable of being applied.

Section 5: The Laws enacted in accordance with the 16 August 1960 Constitution before 21 December 1963 shall be in full force and operation.

Section 6: The House may empower the Executive Council to make any rules and regulations for application within the Turkish areas.

EXECUTIVE MATTERS

Section 7: The executive power in Turkish areas shall be exercised by the Executive Council on the Provisional Turkish Administration.

Section 8: The Executive Council shall be composed of the three Ministers envisaged in Article 46 of the 16 August 1960 Constitution and of six other members. The Vice-President of the Republic shall be the President and the President of the Turkish Communal Chamber shall be the Vice-President of the Executive Council.

Section 9: The Executive Council shall be composed of members responsible for Defence Matters (including internal and external relations); Agricultural and Natural Resources; Health Services; Educational, Cultural and Teaching matters; Social Services, Municipalities, Vakfs and Co-operative matters; Judicial matters; Financial and Budgetary matters; Works and Communications; and Economic matters.

Section 10: Vacancies occurring in the Executive Council through the resignation of members or through other reasons, shall be filled by appointments made by the President on the recommendation of the Vice-President.

Section 11: The President, the Vice-President and the Members of the Executive Council shall not be engaged in any private work incompatible with their official duties.

Section 12: The Executive Council shall have power to effect any changes in the Administrative System and to define the functions of the System.

Section 13: The Defence and Security Services of the Provisional Turkish Administration shall be ensured by an Organization to be established for the purpose by the Executive Council.

Section 14: All kinds of assistance from Turkey shall be utilized in accordance with the conditions upon which the assistance has been given.

Section 15: The functions of the Public Service Commission as envisaged in the 16 August 1960 Constitution shall be exercised in respect of all public officers of the Provisional Turkish Administration by a commission composed of three members. The members of the Turkish Public Service Commission shall be appointed by the President upon the recommendation of the Vice-President of the Executive Council.

COURT MATTERS

Section 16: The Court matters in the Provisional Turkish Administration shall be dealt with by independent Turkish Courts.

Section 17: Turkish Judges shall be appointed by the President upon the recommendation of the Vice-President of the Executive Council of the Provisional Turkish Administration.

Section 18: Matters concerning the establishment of Turkish Courts, their jurisdiction and duties and the status of the Judges shall be regulated by the introduction of temporary rules and regulations.

Section 19: The above provisions which have been accepted for application in Turkish areas shall remain in force until all the provisions of the 16 August 1960 Constitution are applied.

I: THE DRAFT CONSTITUTION OF
THE TURKISH FEDERATED STATE
OF CYPRUS

Source: Typescript provided in July, 1975 by Rauf Denktaş to Salih.

PART I. GENERAL PROVISIONS

The characteristics of the Turkish Federated State of Cyprus:

ARTICLE 1

The Turkish Federated State of Cyprus is a secular Republic based on the principles of supremacy of democracy, social justice and law.

The powers of the Federated State:

ARTICLE 2

The Turkish Federated State of Cyprus shall exercise all powers except for the powers expressly given to the Federal Republic of Cyprus on definite subjects and for this purpose shall set up the necessary organs.

Official Language:

ARTICLE 3

The Official language of the Turkish Federated State of Cyprus is Turkish.

Fundamental Rights and Liberties:

ARTICLE 4

(1) Every person has the right to personal immunity, inalienable and unwithdrawable fundamental rights and liberties prescribed in the European Convention on Human Rights and Fundamental Liberties.

(2) Fundamental rights and liberties can be restricted, without affecting their essence, only by legislation for reasons such as public interest, public order, general conduct, social justice, national security, public health and for providing security to life and property of persons.

The right to elect, to be elected and to participate in a public referendum:

ARTICLE 5

(1) Every male and female Turkish citizen who has completed the age of eighteen has the right to elect and to participate in a public referendum and every person who has completed the age of twenty one has the right to be elected.

(2) Elections shall be held in accordance with the principles of free, equal, secret, direct ballot and by universal suffrage, open counting and enumeration.

(3) The procedure in connection with elections and public referendum and the qualifications for electing and being elected shall be prescribed by law.

Political Parties:

ARTICLE 6

(1) The organs, administration, programs and activities of political parties must be in accordance with the principles of democratic and secular republic based on human rights and liberties and in accordance with the principles set by Ataturk. Parties not being in accordance with the above shall be closed permanently.

(2) Proceedings in connection with the closing of political parties shall be within the jurisdiction of the Supreme Court sitting as a Constitutional Court.

National Service:

ARTICLE 7

(1) National Service is the right and duty of every Turkish citizen.

(2) The way in which the national service will be performed, either in the security forces or in the public service, and the establishment of the security forces and their powers and duties, shall be regulated by law.

PART II. THE LEGISLATURE

The Assembly of the Turkish Federated State of Cyprus:

ARTICLE 8

The legislative powers of the Turkish Federated State of Cyprus shall be exercised by the Assembly of the Federated State of Cyprus which shall be composed of thirty deputies elected for five years by general election.

Taking the oath:

ARTICLE 9

The members of the Assembly of the Turkish Federated State of Cyprus shall take the following oath before assuming their duties:—

"I affirm on my honour to preserve the integrity of the Turkish Federated State of Cyprus, to respect human rights and the principles of democratic and secular state under the rule of law and the ideals of Ataturk and to work for the welfare of my nation."

The duties and powers of the Assembly of the Turkish Federated State of Cyprus:

ARTICLE 10

The Assembly shall have power to enact, amend and repeal laws, to debate and approve bills in connection with the budget and final accounts, to give general or special amnesty and to decide whether death penalties given and finalised by Courts should be carried out. The power to ratify agreements shall rest with the Assembly.

The procedure of the Assembly of the Turkish Federated State of Cyprus:

ARTICLE 11

(1) The Assembly of the Turkish Federated State of Cyprus shall meet without summons on the first working day of the month of October every year.

(2) The quorum for meetings of the Assembly of the Turkish Federated State of Cyprus shall be the absolute majority of the full number of its members and a resolution shall be decided upon by the absolute majority of the members present and voting.

(3) The Assembly of the Turkish Federated State of Cyprus shall carry out its functions in accordance with standing orders made by it.

(4) The Assembly shall determine the time and period of its recess.

(5) The Assembly of the Turkish Federated State of Cyprus may be summoned to an extraordinary session by the President of the Turkish Federated State of Cyprus, the President of the Assembly of the Turkish Federated State of Cyprus and on the request of seven deputies.

Elections for the Assembly of the Turkish Federated State of Cyprus:

ARTICLE 12

(1) The Turkish Federated State of Cyprus shall be divided into electoral constituencies on the basis of population. The electoral system and the number of deputies to be elected for each electoral constituency shall be regulated by law.

(2) An Assembly which has been dissolved, shall continue to exercise the powers of the Assembly until a new Assembly is elected in its place.

(3) By-elections shall be held every year on a fixed date. No by-elections shall be held within one year of the general elections.

(4) In case there are no means for the holding of elections due to emergency reasons the elections may be postponed by the Assembly of the Turkish Federated State of Cyprus up to a period of one year. Any decision for the postponement of the elections shall be taken by a two-thirds majority of the full number of members.

New elections for the Assembly of the Turkish Federated State of Cyprus:

ARTICLE 13

(1) The Assembly of the Turkish Federated State of Cyprus may decide on its dissolution and the holding of general elections by an absolute majority of the full number of members.

(2) In case of the creation of circumstances leading to difficulties between the executive and legislative bodies in the proper functioning of the State and the continuation of these circumstances, the President of the Turkish Federated State of Cyprus may decide to dissolve the Assembly of the Turkish Federated State of Cyprus.

(3) Before deciding to dissolve the Assembly, the President of the Turkish Federated State of Cyprus shall consult the President of the Assembly and the Council of Ministers of the Turkish Federated State of Cyprus.

Immunity of Deputies:

ARTICLE 14

(1) Deputies shall not be held responsible for their votes given or statements made in the Assembly of the Turkish Federated State of Cyprus and for repeating and disclosing these outside the Assembly.

(2) Where it is alleged that a deputy has committed an offence before or after the elections, he cannot be arrested or prosecuted without the leave of the Assembly of the Turkish Federated State of Cyprus. Such leave is not required in the case of an offence punishable with death or imprisonment for five years or more in case the offender is taken in the act. Provided that the competent authority must notify forthwith the Assembly of the Turkish Federated State of Cyprus.

(3) A sentence imposed on a deputy before or after the elections shall not be carried out until after his term of office ends. The period during which a deputy is in office shall not be reckoned for the purposes of prescription.

The termination of a Deputy's term of office:

ARTICLE 15

Where a sentence imposed on a deputy for an offence preventing him from being elected has become final, he resigns, he is under any disqualification, he accepts a duty not compatible with the office of a deputy and he does not attend the meetings of the Assembly of the Turkish Federated State of Cyprus for a period of one month without any reason or leave, his terms of office shall come to an end.

The Assembly of the Turkish Federated State of Cyprus shall decide on questions relating to termination of term of office of a deputy.

Duties not compatible with the office of a Deputy:

ARTICLE 16

(1) The members of the Assembly of the Turkish Federated State of Cyprus shall not accept any office in any State or other public institution and shall not directly or indirectly be charged with any of their engagements.

(2) Other duties and functions not compatible with the membership of the Assembly of the Turkish Federated State of Cyprus shall be prescribed by law.

Remuneration

ARTICLE 17

The remuneration of the deputies shall be defined by law.

The enactment of laws:

ARTICLE 18

(1) Only the Council of Ministers of the Turkish Federated State of Cyprus and the deputies are authorized to introduce bills.

(2) Bills introduced by the Council of Ministers of the Turkish Federated State of Cyprus or bills proposed by members and adopted by the Council of Ministers of the Turkish Federated State of Cyprus shall be debated with priority.

(3) The President of the Turkish Federated State of Cyprus shall either promulgate within ten days any law enacted by the Assembly of the Turkish Federated State of Cyprus or return it to the Assembly for reconsideration or refer it to public referendum on the request of the Council of Ministers. Where the Assembly of the Turkish Federated State of Cyprus approves the law returned by a two-thirds majority of the full number of its members, either after amending it or as it is, the law shall be promulgated by the Head of State.

(4) Laws approved by public referendum shall be promulgated by the Head of State in the Official Gazette within ten days.

The Debate and approval of the Budget:

ARTICLE 19

(1) The Draft Budget shall be submitted by the Council of Ministers of the Turkish Federated State of Cyprus to the Assembly of the Turkish Federated State of Cyprus at least two months before the beginning of the financial year.

(2) The Budget committee shall complete its work on the subject at the latest within one month.

(3) The Deputies cannot make proposals, during the debate of the draft budget at the general meeting of the Assembly of the Turkish Federated State of Cyprus, which aim at increasing the expenses or decreasing certain items of income.

Payment of Taxes:

ARTICLE 20

(1) Every person is bound to pay taxes according to his means for meeting public expenses.

(2) Financial burdens shall only be imposed by law. The minimum and maximum limits of financial burdens may be prescribed by law. The financial burdens may be amended by a resolution of the Council of Ministers of the Turkish Federated State of Cyprus within these limits.

(3) No retrospective financial burdens shall be imposed.

PART III. THE EXECUTIVE

The Duties and Powers of the Executive:

ARTICLE 21

The executive duties and powers of the Turkish Federated State of Cyprus shall be carried out and exercised by the President and the Council of Ministers of the Turkish Federated State of Cyprus.

The President of the Turkish Federated State of Cyprus:

ARTICLE 22

The President of the Turkish Federated State of Cyprus shall be elected by universal suffrage for a period of seven years.

The Taking of the Oath by the President of the Turkish Federated State of Cyprus:

ARTICLE 23

The President of the Turkish Federated State of Cyprus shall take the oath on his investiture in the following way:

"I affirm on my honour to preserve the integrity of the Turkish Federated State of Cyprus, to conform with and defend the Constitution and laws of the Turkish Federated State of Cyprus, to respect human rights and the principles of democratic and secular state under the rule of law and the ideals of Ataturk and to work for the welfare of my nation."

The relations of the President of the Turkish Federated State of Cyprus with his political party:

ARTICLE 24

In the event of the President of the Turkish Federated State of Cyprus being a member of a political party he shall not be bound by the decisions of his party and he shall act independently of it.

The duties and powers of the President of the Turkish Federated State of Cyprus:

ARTICLE 25

(1) The President of the Turkish Federated State of Cyprus shall be the head of Turkish Federated State of Cyprus and the commander of the Security forces.

(2) The President of the Turkish Federated State of Cyprus shall secure respect for the Constitution of the Turkish Federated State of Cyprus, the carrying out of public affairs in any uninterrupted and orderly manner and the continuation of the state.

(3) Where the security of the state is in danger and the organs mentioned in the Constitution cannot function the President of the Turkish Federated State of Cyprus shall take the necessary exceptional and temporary measures in consultation with the Council of Ministers, the President of the Assembly, the President of the Supreme Court and the Attorney General of the Turkish Federated State of Cyprus.

The responsibilities of the President of the Turkish Federated State of Cyprus:

ARTICLE 26

(1) The Assembly of the Turkish Federated State of Cyprus may accuse the Head of State for treason by a decision taken by at least a two-thirds majority of the full number of its members upon a proposal submitted by at least the one-third of the full number of its members.

(2) The Head of State shall be tried by the Supreme Court sitting as a Constitutional Court. In case the Supreme Court finds the accusation justified the term of office of the Head of State shall be terminated.

Deputising for the President of the Turkish Federated State of Cyprus:

ARTICLE 27

In the event of the President of the Turkish Federated State of Cyprus being temporarily absent from his office because of illness or travel abroad or in the event of a vacancy in the office of the President due to any reason, the Prime Minister of the Turkish Federated State of Cyprus shall act in his place until the President resumes his office or until a new President is elected. In such a case the Prime Minister shall appoint one of the members of the Council of Ministers to act in his place.

The Council of Ministers of the Turkish Federated State of Cyprus:

ARTICLE 28

(1) The Council of Ministers of the Turkish Federated State of Cyprus shall be composed of the Head of State, the Prime Minister and the Ministers.

(2) The President of the Turkish Federated State of Cyprus shall appoint the Prime Minister, and on the proposal of the Prime Minister, the Ministers. The President shall terminate their appointment when necessary. It shall not be essential for Ministers to be appointed from amongst the members of the Assembly of the Turkish Federated State of Cyprus.

(3) The Prime Minister shall secure coordination amongst the Ministries, the application of the general policy of the Council of Ministers and of Laws.

(4) The Head of State shall preside over the Council of Ministers. Upon the request of the Head of State the Prime Minister may preside over the Council of Ministers for a definite agenda.

(5) The Prime Minister and deputies who are appointed Ministers shall not lose their membership of the Assembly of the Turkish Federated State of Cyprus. Ministers appointed to the Council of Ministers of the Turkish Federated State of Cyprus from outside the Assembly shall benefit from immunity in the same way as deputies but shall not vote in the assembly of the Turkish Federated State of Cyprus.

The responsibilities of the Council of Ministers of the Federated State of Cyprus:

ARTICLE 29

(1) The Prime Minister shall be responsible to the Assembly of the Turkish Federated State of Cyprus for the program of the Council of Ministers of the Turkish Federated State of Cyprus and for its application or for any important political action.

(2) Any motion of no-confidence to be submitted to the Assembly against the Prime Minister in connection with the subjects mentioned in the first paragraph shall be signed by at least seven deputies.

(3) A decision as to whether the motion of no-confidence shall be included on the agenda or not shall be taken at the second meeting after it is submitted. The motion of no-confidence shall not be put to vote before the passing of one day from the completion of the general debate on the motion.

(4) In case the absolute majority of the full number of the members of the Assembly approves a vote of no-confidence, the Prime Minister shall submit his resignation to the Head of State.

Decrees having the force of Laws:

ARTICLE 30

(1) In the event of urgency in economic matters, the Council of Ministers may issue decrees having the force of law. A decree having the force of law shall come

into force on its publication in the Official Gazette. Decrees having the force of law shall remain in force until they are repealed or amended by the Assembly of the Turkish Federated State of Cyprus or cancelled by the Supreme Court sitting as a Constitutional Court.

(2) New public burdens shall not be imposed and personal and political rights and liberties shall not be restricted by decrees having the force of law.

Foreign Assistance:

ARTICLE 31

The Turkish Federated State of Cyprus shall have power to receive any assistance from foreign states and international organizations in cultural, social, economic, financial, and technical fields.

State of Emergency:

ARTICLE 32

(1) The Council of Ministers of the Turkish Federated State of Cyprus may proclaim a state of emergency up to a period of two months for reasons such as the creation of circumstances which necessitate war, the carrying out of a revolution, the endangering of the life of the Turkish Federated State of Cyprus, internally or externally, and for widespread acts of violence aimed at the elimination of the liberal and democratic law and order recognized by the Constitution of the Turkish Federated State of Cyprus.

(2) The decision to declare a state of emergency shall be laid forthwith before the Assembly of the Turkish Federated State of Cyprus for approval.

(3) The state of emergency shall be regulated by law.

The Executive Structure:

ARTICLE 33

(1) The Ministries shall be established, in accordance with the number and principles provided by law, upon the proposal of the Prime Minister and the approval of the Head of State. The internal organization of the Ministries shall be regulated by regulations to be made by the Council of Ministers.

(2) The Turkish Federated State of Cyprus shall be administered by division into administrative and local organizations.

(3) The executive bodies of local organizations shall come to power by election. The duties and powers of independent organizations shall be defined by law.

The appointment of Public Officers:

ARTICLE 34

(1) The appointment of the members of the public and security services shall be made by the President of the Federated State of Cyprus. The Head of State may delegate this power to other authorities or organizations.

(2) The President and members of the Supreme Court, the Attorney General, the Auditor General and the members of the Board of Auditors shall be appointed by decision of the Council of Ministers. Senior officials shall be appointed by decree

carrying the signatures of the Minister concerned, the Prime Minister and the Head of the State.

Financial Control:

ARTICLF 35

(1) The Board of Auditors which is an organ of financial control shall control and inspect public income and expenses and shall inform the Assembly and the Council of Ministers of the Turkish Federated State of Cyprus of the result. The Board of Auditors shall assist the Assembly and the Council of Ministers on financial matters.

(2) The establishment and functions of the Board of Auditors shall be regulated by law

PART IV. THE JUDICIARY

Judicial Powers:

ARTICLE 36

(1) The judicial powers shall be exercised in the Turkish Federated State of Cyprus by independent courts.

(2) The establishment, duties, and powers of courts shall be regulated by law.

(3) Judges shall be independent in their duties and they shall give judgment in accordance with the Constitution, the laws, legal principles and the opinion dictated by their conscience.

(4) The qualifications, appointment, rights and responsibilities of judges shall be regulated by law in accordance with the principles of the independence of courts and confidence in judges.

The Supreme Court of the Turkish Federated State of Cyprus:

ARTICLE 37

(1) There shall be a Supreme Court of the Turkish Federated State of Cyprus composed of a President and four members.

(2) The Supreme Court shall carry out the duties of the Constitutional Court, the Court of Appeal and the High Administrative Court.

(3) The Supreme Court shall have jurisdiction to act as the Constitutional Court, with the President and four members attending the sittings. The Supreme Court shall have jurisdiction to act as the Court of Appeal or the High Administrative Court with the President and two members or just three members attending the sittings.

(4) The decisions of the Supreme Court shall be final and conclusive. The establishment, functioning, duties and powers of the Supreme Court shall be regulated by law.

PART V. TRANSITIONAL PROVISIONS

Transitional Article 1.

(1) The provisions—
　　　(*a*) of the Constitution of the 16th August 1960 and of laws enacted thereunder until the 21st December 1963;

(*b*) of the Basic Articles of the 28th December 1967 of the Turkish Cypriot Administration and their amendments and of laws enacted thereunder; and

(*c*) of the Resolutions accepted at the joint meetings of the Executive Council and Legislative Assembly of the Autonomous Turkish Cypriot Administration held on the 13th and 18th February 1975 and of laws enacted in accordance with these Resolutions which are not contrary to, or inconsistent with, the provisions of this Constitution shall continue to be in force.

(2) Until the laws and organs provided for by the Constitution are enacted and established all laws in force shall remain in force and all existing organs shall continue functioning.

Transitional Article 2.

When the Constitution of the Federal Republic of Cyprus comes in force the necessary amendments shall accordingly be made to the Constitution of the Turkish Federated State of Cyprus.

Constituent Assembly:
Transitional Article 3.

Upon the first meeting of the Assembly of the Turkish Federated State of Cyprus set up under this Constitution the legal existence of the Constituent Assembly shall come to an end and the Constituent Assembly shall automatically dissolve.

The Head of State:
Transitional Article 4.

The office of the present Head of State shall come to an end on the date on which the Head of State elected in accordance with this Constitution is invested.

Council of Ministers:
Transitional Article 5.

The President of the Turkish Federated State of Cyprus elected in accordance with this Constitution shall form the Council of Ministers of the Turkish Federated State of Cyprus under this Constitution upon the holding of the elections for the Assembly of the Turkish Federated State of Cyprus and the beginning of the Assembly's term. The term of office of the present Council of Ministers shall thus end.

Elections:
Transitional Article 6.

As long as there is no state of emergency the election of the deputies and of the Head of State shall take place within six months from the date of the coming into force of this constitution. The dates for holding the elections shall be fixed by the Constituent Assembly.

J: GREEK-TURKISH MILITARY

BALANCE (1975)

Source: Trevor N. Dupuy, Grace P. Hayes, John A. C. Andrews, *The Almanac of World Military Power* (3rd edition. New York: R. R. Bowker Co., 1974), pp. 122–125 (Turkey), and pp. 94–97 (Greece).

Paxton, John (ed.) *The Statesman's Year-Book: Statistical and Historical Annual of the States of the World for the Year 1974–1975* (New York: St. Martin's Press, 1974). pp. 1379–1380 (Turkey), and p. 986 (Greece).

Turkey

General

Area: 301,380 square miles
Population: 38,200,000
Total Active Armed Forces: 607,500
Gross National Product: $16.9 billion ($444 per capita)
Annual Military Expenditures: $3 billion
Steel Production: 2.00 million metric tons
Fuel Production: Coal: 13.8 million metric tons
                Oil: 3.64 million metric tons
Electric Power Output: 9.7 billion kwh
Merchant Marine: 328 ships; 713,767 gross tons
Civil Air Fleet: 16 jet and 7 propjet transports

Army

Personnel: 514,000
Organization:
four armies: one in European Turkey, protecting the northern approach to the Straits; one in western Anatolia, concentrated near the Asiatic side of the Straits; one in the Aegean region facing Greece; and one in eastern Anatolia, concentrated near the Soviet frontier.
    6 army corps; two for each army
    1 armored division (M-48 tanks)
    1 mechanized infantry division
   12 infantry divisions
    4 armored cavalry brigades
    4 armored brigades (M-48 tanks)
    3 mechanized infantry brigades
    2 parachute battalions
    2 SSM battalions ("Honest John")
Major Equipment Inventory:
    1,500 medium tanks (M-47 and M-48)

   light tanks (M-24 and M-41)
   tank destroyers (M-36)
   armored cars (M-8)
500 + APCs (M-113 and M-59)
   105mm and 155mm self-propelled guns
   105mm, 155mm, and 203mm howitzers
   40mm, 75mm, and 90mm AA artillery pieces
   "Honest John" launchers
40 light aircraft
100 + helicopters (AB-206, Bell 47, CH-47)
Reserves: There are over 800,000 trained reservists

Navy

Personnel: 38,500
Major Units:

 15 destroyers (DD)
  1 frigate
 16 submarines (SS)
  2 submarine support ships
  2 submarine rescue ships
  6 submarine chasers (PC)
 15 escort/minesweepers (PF/MSF)
 16 coastal minesweepers (MSC)
  4 inshore minesweepers (MSI)
  3 fleet minelayers (MMF)
  6 coastal minelayers (MMC)
 11 torpedo boats (PT)
  7 patrol gunboats (PGM)
 38 patrol boats and motor launches (YP and smaller classes)
 52 landing craft
 38 minor landing craft
 43 coastal craft
  2 repair ships
 12 S-ZE "Trackers" (forming 1 ASW squadron)
  1 training ship (ex-yacht)
  7 oilers
  1 transport
  7 boom defence vessels
  4 gate vessels
  2 tugs
  2 tenders
  3 helicopters (AB-205; ASW)
Reserves: 70,000 trained reserves
Naval bases: At Gölcük in the Gulf of Izmit, at Iskenderun and at Izmir.

Air Force

Personnel: 55,000
Organization: 2 tactical air forces
             6 interceptor squadrons (F-5A, F-102A)
           10 fighter-bomber squadrons (F-104G, F-5A, F-100C)
            2 reconnaissance squadrons (RF-84F)
            4 transport squadrons (C-47, C-54, C-130, D-18, "Viscount," "Transall")
            2 SAM battalions ("Nike-Hercules": 6 batteries)
Major Aircraft Types:
   466 combat aircraft:
        40 F-4E phantom II fighter-bombers
      147 F-5A/B interceptor/fighter-bombers
       78 F-104G fighter-bombers/interceptors
   100–125 F-100 C fighter-bombers
       36 F-102A interceptors
       40 RF-84F reconnaissance aircraft
 275 other aircraft:
       10 C-47 transports
        6 C-45 transports
        3 "Viscount" transports
        3 C-54 transports
        4 C-103E transports
       16 "Transall" C-160 transports (from Luftwaffe)
       20 miscellaneous transports
     130 trainer/support aircraft (including T-33A, TF-102A, TF-104G, T-37A, T-34, T-41, T-11, F-100F, and F-5B)
       23 helicopters (UH-1, H-19)
       60 helicopters from the Soviet Union
Major Air Bases: Izmir, Adana, Bandırma, Dıyarbakır, Esenboğa, Sivas, Etimesgut, Eskişehir, Yesilköy, Merzifon, Balıkesir
Reserves: 80,000 trained reserves. The total number of men that the three services could mobilize is estimated at over 2 million.
Paramilitary forces:
   Gendarmerie: 75,000 (3 mobile brigades)
   National Guard: 20,000
Equipment on order:
       40 F-4 Phantom fighter-bombers
        4 submarines being built in West Germany
        5 surface-to-surface guided missile patrol boats
     250 M-48 tanks
       40 F-104 G fighter-bombers/interceptors
     150 medium tanks from West Germany (Leopard)
       40 Alpha-Jet trainer-light strike

U.S. Foreign Aid:

Military aid $3,030,000,000   (1950–1973)
Economic aid $2,138,200,000   (1947–1973)

GREECE

General

Area: 50,943 square miles
Population: 9,234,000
Total Active Armed Forces: 159,000
Gross National Product: $13.6 billion ($1,477 per capita)
Annual Military Expenditures: $1.311 billion
Electric Power Output: 10.6 billion kwh
Merchant Marine: 2,056 ships: 13.1 million gross tons
Civil Air Fleet: 12 jet, 9 propjet, and 13 piston transports

Army

Personnel: 118,000
Organization:
      3 corps (2 on northern frontier assigned to NATO)
      11 infantry divisions (8 under strength)
      1 armored division
      1 commando brigade
      2 SSM battalions ("Honest John")
      1 SAM battalion ("Hawk")
Major Equipment Inventory:
   250 medium tanks (M-47)
   270 medium tanks (M-48)
    50 medium tanks (AMX-30)
      light tanks (M-24 and M-41)
      APCs (M-2, M-59, and M-113)
      105mm, 155mm and 175mm self-propelled guns
      105mm, 155mm, and 203mm self-propelled howitzers
      armored cars (M-8 and M-20)
      scout cars (M-3)
      "Hawk" SAMs
      "Honest John" SSMs
      40mm, 75mm, and 90mm AA guns
   20 light aircraft, helicopters
Reserves: About 350,000 reservists available for mobilization

Navy

Personnel: 18,000
Major Units:
    11 destroyers (DD)
    4 destroyer escorts (DE)
    7 diesel submarines (SS)
    2 minelayers (MMC)
    5 escorts/minesweepers (MSO)
    5 submarine chasers (PC)
    4 missile boats
    5 patrol gunboats (PG)
    7 patrol escorts (PF)
    21 coastal minesweepers (MSC)
    14 torpedo boats (PT)
    1 landing ship dock (LSD)
    8 landing ships tank (LST)
    6 landing ships medium (LSM)
    8 landing craft (LCU/LCT)
    13 landing craft mechanized (LCM)
    34 landing craft vehicle-personnel (LCVP)
    17 auxiliaries
    8 HU-16 maritime patrol aircraft
    1 repair ship
    2 depot ships
    1 salvage vessel
    8 oilers
    5 surveying craft
    3 lighthouse tenders
    5 water carriers
    11 fleet tugs
Reserves: About 50,000 trained reservists

Air Force

Personnel: 23,000
Organization:
    6 fighter-bomber squadrons (F-104G and F-84F)
    4 day interceptor squadrons (F-5A)
    1 all-weather interceptor squadron (F-102A)
    2 reconnaissance squadrons (RF-84F and RF-5)
    2 transport squadrons (Noratlas, C-47, C-119, D-28)
    2 helicopter squadrons (Alouette 11, Bell 47, AB-104, H-19)
    1 ASW/search and rescue squadron (under Navy control)
    1 SAM wing (1 battalion each of Nike-Ajax and Nike-Hercules)

Major Aircraft Types:
  228 combat aircraft
    36 F-104G fighter-bombers
    72 F-84F fighter-bombers
    18 F-102A all-weather interceptors
    72 F-5A interceptors
    15 RF-84F reconnaissance aircraft
    15 RF-5 reconnaissance aircraft
  251 + other aircraft
    40 Nord 2501D "Noratlas" transports
    10 C-119G transports
    31 Do-28B/D transports
    70 + helicopters (Bell 47, AB-205, U11-19D, etc.)
    100 trainer/support aircraft
Reserves: About 30,000 trained reservists
Paramilitary forces:
  Gendarmerie: 25,000
  National Guard: 50,000
Equipment on order:
   4 diesel submarines (SS)
   3 destroyer escorts (DE)
  40 F-1 Mirage fighter-bombers
   5 guided missile patrol boats (PTFG) (to be armed with "Exocet" SSMs)
 100 medium tanks (AMX-30)
  60 A7D long-range attack-bombers (LTV Aerospace Corporation)
  40 T2 jet trainers
  12 C130 transport aircraft

U.S. Foreign Aid:

Military aid $1,585,000,000   (1950–1973)
Economic aid $1,062,800,000   (1948–1973)

NOTES

CHAPTER 1

1. *Cyprus Mail*, May 17, 1972.

2. Cyprus was never part of Hellenic Greece. The island was colonized by the Greeks, but they regarded "the Cypriots as an alien people." Thomas Ehrlich, *Cyprus 1958–1967* (New York: Oxford University Press, 1974), p. 9.

3. For the earlier history of Cyprus see: Sir George Francis Hill, *A History of Cyprus*, 4 vols. (Cambridge: Cambridge University Press, 1940–1952); H. D. Purcell, *Cyprus* (New York: Praeger, 1968); Doros Alastos, *Cyprus In History; A Survey of 5,000 Years* (London: Zeno, 1955).

4. Robert Blake, *Disraeli* (New York: St. Martin's Press, 1967), pp. 644–654.

5. Following the Treaty of Brest-Litovsk in 1918 between Turkey and Russia, the Turks hoped to recover Cyprus after being given Ardahan, Kars, and Batum by Russia. Great Britain continued administering the island, since Turkey had lost World War I, along with the Central Powers. J. C. Hurewitz, *Diplomacy in the Near and Middle East—A Documentary Record: 1914–1956*, vol. 2 (Princeton: D. Van Nostrand, 1956), 31–33.

6. As quoted in Sir Harry Luke, *Cyprus: A Portrait and an Appreciation* (London: George G. Harrap, 1957), pp. 172–173.

7. As quoted in *History Speaks: A Documentary Survey* (Nicosia: Turkish Communal Chamber, 1964), pp. 39–40.

8. C. Spyridakis, *A Brief History of Cyprus*, 3rd ed. (Nicosia: Zavallis Press, 1964), p. 64.

9. Great Britain. Colonial Office. *Franco-British Convention of 23 December* 1920 (Cmnd. 1195. London: Her Majesty's Stationery Office, 1921).

10. For the full text of the Treaty of Lausanne see Fred L. Israel, ed., *Major Peace Treaties of Modern History 1648–1967* (New York: McGraw-Hill, 1967), pp. 2301–2367.

11. Great Britain. Colonial Office. *Cyprus: Memorial from the Greek Elected Members of the Legislative Council* (Cmnd. 3477. London: Her Majesty's Stationery Office, 1930), p. 3.

12. *Cyprus Demands Self-Determination* (Washington: Royal Greek Embassy Information Service, 1954), pp. 21–22.

13. Anthony Eden, *Full Circle* (London: Cassell, 1960), p. 414.

14. Ibid., p. 403.

15. *Turkish Views on Cyprus* (New York: Turkish Information Office, [n.d.]), pp. 15–22.

16. Ferenc A. Vali, *Bridge Across the Bosporus* (Baltimore: The Johns Hopkins Press, 1971), p. 236.

17. Walter F. Weiker, *The Turkish Revolution 1960–1961* (Washington: The Brookings Institution, 1963), pp. 33–34.

18. For the full text of the Radcliffe proposals see Great Britain. Colonial Office, *Constitutional Proposals for Cyprus: Report Submitted to the Secretary of State for the Colonies*

by the Right Hon. Lord Radcliffe, G. B. E. (London: Her Majesty's Stationery Office, 1956), Cmnd. 42, pp. 5–44.

19. Sir Hugh Foot, *A Start in Freedom* (New York: Harper and Row, 1964), p. 159.

20. Stephen G. Xydis, *Cyprus: Conflict and Conciliation 1954–1958* (Columbus: Ohio State University Press, 1967), p. 514.

21. For an in-depth study of the making of the Cyprus state, see Great Britain. Colonial Office. *Constitutional Proposals For Cyprus: Report Submitted to the Secretary of state for the Colonies by the Right Hon. Lord* Radcliffe, C.B.E. (Cmnd. 42. London: Her Majesty's Stationery Office, 1956); Great Britain. Colonial Office. *Cyprus Report for the Year 1959* (London: Her Majesty's Stationery Office, 1961); Great Britain. Colonial Office. *Cyprus* (Cmnd. 1093. London: Her Majesty's Stationery Office, 1960).

22. Royal Institute of International Affairs, *Cyprus: The Dispute and the Settlement* (London: Chatham House, June 1959), pp. 57–61; see appendix C for the full text of the Zurich Agreements.

23. Stanley Kyriakides, *Cyprus: Constitutionalism and Crisis Government* (Philadelphia: University of Pennsylvania Press, 1968), pp. 72–73.

24. James M. Boyd, "Cyprus: Episode in Peacekeeping," *International Organization* 20, no. 1 (Winter 1966):3.

25. Harry J. Psomiades, "The Cyprus Dispute," *Current History* 48, no. 285 (May 1965): 271–272.

26. *Manchester Guardian Weekly*, March 5, 1959, as quoted by Roy P. Fairfield, "Cyprus: Revolution and Resolution," *Middle East Journal* 13, no. 3 (Summer 1959): 235–248.

27. Since his election on October 18, 1950, as archbishop of the Greek Orthodox Church on Cyprus, Makarios III has always favored enosis, as did his predecessors. See *Cyprus Demands Self-Determination* (Washington, D.C.: Royal Greek Embassy Information Service, 1954), pp. 21–22. As quoted by *New York Times*, November 22, 1964, p. 7, Makarios stated: "I have been and will always be in favor of enosis. But enosis must be achieved without strings or conditions and only after removal of all foreign bases and the last foreign soldier." Grivas in his memoirs claims that he had an agreement with Makarios never to depart from the enosis aim. Charles Foley, ed., *The Memoirs of General Grivas* (London: Longmans, Green, 1964); see also, Great Britain. Colonial Office. *Terrorism in Cyprus; The Captured* Documents (London: Her Majesty's Stationery Office, 1956); Charles Foley, *Legacy of Strife: Cyprus from Rebellion to Civil War* (Baltimore: Penguin, 1964).

28. Interview of the president of the House of Representatives, Glafkos Clerides, to the "Voice of Germany." Public Information Office of the Republic of Cyprus, press release, October 27, 1971.

CHAPTER 2

1. See appendix D, Treaty of Guarantee, Article II.

2. The separation of municipalities was a Greek idea originally. But it came to be regarded by the Greeks as a first step toward partition. Robert Stephens, *Cyprus: A Place of Arms* (London: Pall Mall, 1966), p. 176. Separate Greek and Turkish mu-

nicipalities in the five major towns has been considered by some observers to be impracticable. *Economist*, January 4, 1964, p. 10.

3. A private interview with Zafer Ali Zihni, the director of the Turkish Cypriot Information Office in Nicosia, July 30, 1970, and June 3, 1972.

4. Purcell, p. 315.

5. A private interview with Rauf R. Denktaş, the president of the Turkish Cypriot Communal Chamber, May 28, 1972.

6. A private interview with Osman Örek in Nicosia, July 28, 1970.

7. Ambassador Ümit Halûk Bayülken, former foreign minister of Turkey from December 11, 1971 to January 26, 1974, mentions President Makarios' official visit to Turkey in 1962, and the Turkish forewarning to the Greek Cypriot leader not to tamper with the Cyprus Constitution, which might be contrary to the Zurich-London accords. He writes that Makarios was told by the Turkish leaders at the presidential palace in Ankara that "every new state and its government may encounter some practical difficulties in the administration of a newly independent country, and that such difficulties could be overcome through consultations and good-will among the members of the two communities in the Government and Parliament. The President of Cyprus should act after the independence of the country not merely as the leader of the Greek Community but as a unifying factor for both the Turkish and Greek Cypriots. The Turkish Government would gladly be ready if necessary to use its best influence with the Turkish Community so that practical difficulties could be solved by consultation between the two communities. The Turkish leaders emphasized on the other hand, their strong conviction that any inclination by the Greek Cypriot leadership to amend the Constitution which had been in effect for a very short period only could seriously jeopardize relations between the two communities and thereby involve Turkey and Greece." Halûk Bayülken, "Cyprus Question and the United Nations," *Foreign Policy* (a quarterly review published in Turkey) 4, no. 2–3 (February 1975): 131.

8. For a detailed account of the proposals see *Facts About Cyprus* (Nicosia: Cyprus Chamber of Commerce and Industry, January 10, 1964). See also Halil Ibrahim Salih, *Cyprus: An Analysis of Cypriot Political Discord* (New York: Theo. Gaus, Sons, 1968), pp. 99–100; for the full text see appendix F.

9. The Greeks were prepared to act with force to any Turkish negative reaction to the thirteen-point plan. EOKA members were being armed with government weapons and were ready for the hostilities. With the approval of Makarios, a contingency plan was also prepared by the enosists. The plan was to amend the Cyprus Constitution, abrogate the international agreements, initiate the idea of self-determination, and bring about enosis by means of a plebiscite. The Greeks were to permit no Turkish justification for intervention in Cyprus. When the Turks refused to accept the proposed amendments to the Cyprus Constitution, Makarios put his plan into effect, and the Greek attack began in December, 1963. The Greek contingency plan was published by a pro-Grivas Cyprus newspaper, *Patris*, on April 21, 1967, and Makarios has never refuted it. See also Purcell, pp. 322–323.

10. International agreements are made between states or organizations of states creating rights and obligations, governed by international law. A unilateral denunciation of an international agreement by a state is illegal and is contrary to *pacta sunt servanda*. It is an important principle of international law that no power can change or abrogate a treaty unless all the contracting powers peacefully reach agreement.

Charles G. Fenwick, *International Law* (New York: Appleton-Century-Crofts, 1962), pp. 450–453; J. L. Brierly, *The Law of Nations* (New York: Oxford University Press, 1963), p. 339; Gerhard von Glahn, *Law Among Nations* (New York: The Macmillan, 1965), pp. 445–447. According to Lord McNair a treaty is not rendered *ipso facto* void, or nullified by one of the parties, "by reason of the fact that such party was coerced by the other party in concluding it, whether that coerced by the other the time of signature or of ratification or at both times." Arnold Duncan McNair, *The Law of Treaties: British Practice and Opinions* (Oxford: Clarendon Press, 1961), p. 208.

11. A private interview with Glafkos Clerides, May 26, 1972. Clerides was reluctant to grant me an interview because of my Turkish-Cypriot background. However, after a telephone call to him by Denktaş to his residence and assurance of the scholarly intentions of my research, he did agree to give me an audience in his office in the Cypriot parliament. During my interview, Clerides was very cautious with the words he used and the information he disclosed to me. My attempts to obtain an audience with President Makarios were a failure, although I presented a series of interview questions to Clerides to forward to the presidential palace.

12. Public Information Office, The Republic of Cyprus, press release, October 29, 1971. Statement by H. B. the President of the Republic, Archbishop Makarios, on the internal situations in Cyprus.

CHAPTER 3

1. "The traditional hostility between Greece and Turkey, to a great extent instigated by religious differences, has dug deep roots in the island." *Daily Star* (Beirut), March 25, 1971.

2. "Bi-communal differences were strengthened during the British rule in Cyprus from 1878 to 1960. The British colonial administration did not encourage communal cooperation. Indeed, the British, from the very beginning, accentuated bi-communalism when they placed the administration of education under bi-communal authorities. The Greek-Orthodox Church directed the schools of the Greek Cypriot community and thus enhanced Greco-Byzantine tradition. The Turkish Cypriots controlled their own school system and thereby strengthened their Turkish national tradition. Thus education served as a non-integrating factor. Moreover, it tended to fortify the historical and cultural bonds of the two Cypriot communities with their respective 'mother countries,' Greece and Turkey." Kyriakides, pp. 163–164.

3. Stephens, p. 213.

4. Because of the proximity of the island of Cyprus to Turkey, which is only 40 miles away, security considerations play an important role in the minds of the Turkish authorities. In case of war, maritime traffic to two principal ports of Turkey, Istanbul and Izmir, might be dominated by an enemy power; therefore, sea traffic would have to be directed to Iskenderun and Mersin, which are at the far eastern corner of Asia Minor's Mediterranean coast. The use of Iskenderun and Mersin harbors will only be possible if Cyprus was under the control of a friendly state. Vali, *Bridge Across the Bosporus*, pp. 47 and 242–243.

5. *Bozkurt*, July 30, 1970. Prime Minister of Turkey, Süleyman Demirel, told the correspondent of the Athens newspaper *Acropolis* that "enosis was quite unthinkable

. . . the Greek and Turkish Cypriots should accomplish a peaceful coexistence in the island."

6. Public Information Office of the Republic of Cyprus, press release, October 31, 1971. Interview of Makarios by the German newspaper *Die Welt* of Hamburg.

7. Turkish Cypriot constitutional rights have been largely obliterated. Turks are now relegated to the position of second-class citizens with no political participation in the Cyprus government. George Lenczowskie, ed., *United States Interests in the Middle East* (Washington, D.C.: American Enterprise Institute, 1968), p. 109.

8. C. L. Sulzberger, "Greece under the Colonels," *Foreign Affairs*, January, 1970, pp. 300–311.

9. Turkish Foreign Minister İhsan Sabri Cağlayangil stated that Turkey would not hesitate to intervene if an attempt were made to overthrow Makarios and impose a unilateral solution (enosis). *Christian Science Monitor*, April 22, 1970.

Under the Treaty of Alliance between Cyprus, Greece, and Turkey, the latter two powers are permitted to station 950 men and 650 men respectively on the island. Great Britain. Colonial office, *Cyprus* (Cmnd. 1093, London: Her Majesty's Stationery Office, 1960), pp. 88–90. Since December, 1963, the two countries have surreptitiously increased the number of their troops.

10. This idea was stressed by Vice-President Dr. Fazıl Küçük in a private interview in Nicosia at his official residence, July 23, 1970. See also Turkish Communal Chamber (Cyprus) *Special News Bulletin*, February 21, 1968.

CHAPTER 4

1. The Greek national contingent has since returned to camp, but the Turkish national contingent continues to remain encamped around Aghırda, Orta Keuy, and Geunyeli on the Nicosia-Kyrenia road.

2. In September, 1964, two Swedish officers were caught by the Cyprus government smuggling arms for the Turkish Cypriots between Kokkina and Lefka. Purcell, p. 351. A number of British soldiers were court-martialed by the British government for trafficking arms to the Turkish Cypriots for monetary gain. Michael Harbottle, *The Impartial Soldier* (London: Oxford University Press, 1970), p. 189.

3. Philip E. Jacob, Alexine L. Atherton, Arthur M. Wallenstein, *The Dynamics of International Organization* (Homewood, Ill.: Dorsey Press, 1972), p. 207.

4. U.S. *Department of State Bulletin* vol. 50, No. 1287 (February 24, 1964): 283.

5. Ibid., p. 284.

6. Philip Windsor, *NATO and the Cyprus Crisis*, Adelphi Paper No. 14 (London: Institute for Strategic Studies, November, 1964), p. 6.

7. *New York Times*, March 1, 1964.

8. Thomas Williams Adams, *AKEL: The Communist Party of Cyprus* (California: Hoover Institution Press, 1971), pp. 87–88.

9. *New York Times*, December 29, 1963, p. 1.

10. U.S. *Department of State Bulletin* 50, no. 1282 (January 20, 1964): 90.

11. Adams, *AKEL*, p. 2

12. For the bases used by Great Britain, between 1960 and 1965, the Cyprus government was paid £12 million ($31 million). The bases employ 12,000 Cypriots and

channel about £18 million ($47 million) annually into the local economy. *Christian Science Monitor*, May 24, 1972. In May, 1974, Labour party Defense Minister Roy Mason made a statement favoring abandonment of the military bases of Great Britain on Cyprus and Malta and saving $125 million. On Cyprus, Great Britain has about 7,000 men, whose function is to be the guardian of NATO's southern flank. Prime Minister Harold Wilson will be hard-pressed to convince his NATO allies that Great Britain is justified in abandoning its bases on Cyprus. Due to expansion of the Soviet naval fleet in the western Mediterranean and with the reopening of the Suez Canal, the British bases on the two islands have additional strategic importance. *New York Times*, April 25, 1974.

13. United Nations. Security Council. *Verbatim Record of the One Thousand and Ninety-Fifth Meeting*. S/PV. 1095, 18 February 1964, par. 58. Also pars. 41 and 63.

14. United Nations. Security Council. *Verbatim Record of the One Thousand and Ninety-sixth Meeting*. S/PV. 1096, 19 February 1964, par. 74.

15. United Nations. Security Council. *Letter dated 25 February 1964 from the Permanent Representative of Turkey Addressed to the Security Council*. S/5561, 25 February 1964.

16. In an open motorboat from Turkey, Denktaş, accompanied by two Turkish Cypriot colleagues, attempted to enter Cyprus clandestinely near Famagusta on October 31, 1967, but they were apprehended shortly after landing. After a short detention by the Cyprus government, Denktaş and his companions were flown to Turkey. United Nations. Security Council. *Report by the Secretary-General on the United Nations Operation in Cyprus* (For the period 13 June to 8 December 1967). S/8286, 8 December 1967.

17. United Nations. Security Council. *Message dated 8 February 1964 from Mr. N.S. Khrushchev Addressed to the Prime Minister of the United Kingdom, the President of the United States, the President of France, the Prime Minister of Turkey and the Prime Minister of Greece, Concerning the Question of Cyprus*. S/5534, 8 February 1964.

18. United Nations. Security Council. *Bolivia, Brazil, Ivory Coast, Morocco and Norway Draft Resolution*. S/5571, 2 March 1964.

19. United Nations. Security Council. *Resolution as Proposed by 5 Powers (S/5571) Adopted Unanimously by the Security Council on 4 March 1964*. S/5575, 4 March 1964.

20. United Nations. Security Council. *Resolution Proposed by 5 Powers (S/5601), Adopted Unanimously by Council*. S/5603, 13 March 1964.

21. The Greek Cypriot leaders justified their unilateral nullification of the treaty on the basis that the circumstances had changed radically—*rebus sic stantibus*—according to law of nations. Furthermore, the Turkish government had violated the essential provisions of the Treaty of Alliance. The violations cited by the Greek Cypriots against Turkey are (1) the unauthorized move of the Turkish contingents from their camps to positions on Nicosia-Kyrenia road, where they have remained; (2) the Turkish air force attack against Cyprus in August, 1964. Criton G. Tornaritis, *The Treaty of Alliance* (Nicosia: Printing Office of the Republic of Cyprus, [n.d.]). The Treaty of Alliance does not state where the Greek and Turkish contingents are to be stationed; however, a supplementary agreement concluded provides that "the Hellenic and Turkish Forces shall be garrisoned in the same area as near each other as possible and within a radius of five miles. . . . " The Turkish troops met those conditions. Agreement Between the Kingdom of Greece, the Republic of Turkey and the Republic of Cyprus for the Application of the Treaty of Alliance, August 16, 1960, Article XV.

22. As quoted in *New York Times*, March 1, 1964.

23. United Nations. Security Council. *Report by the Secretary-General on the United Nations Operation in Cyprus* (For the period 13 December to 10 March 1965). S/6228, 11 March, par. 274.

24. United Nations. Security Council. *Report by the Secretary-General, dated 29 April 1964, on the Operations of the UNFICYP*. S/5671, 29 April 1964.

25. *Economist*, July 4, 1964, p. 28.

26. Stephens states that Great Britain opposed Makarios' plans for unilateral abrogation of the Treaties of Alliance and Guarantee on January 1, 1964, because the British sovereignty over the two base areas on the island would also be abrogated by such an action. The NATO allies of Great Britain, including the United States, strongly supported the British position because of the strategic importance of the British bases. Stephens, pp. 185–186. The Treaty of Establishment was reached between Cyprus and Great Britain covering an area of 99 square miles for two sovereign British military bases at Akrotiri and Dhekelia.

27. For the full text see appendix G. The letter was published in *Hürriyet* (Turkey) on January 13, 1966, but the Turkish government confiscated the whole publication. The letter was made public by the White House on January 15, at the request of Ankara.

28. Since the 1963 Cyprus crisis, Turkey's relations with the Western powers has not been good and there exists an anti-Western feeling. Kemal H. Karpat, ed., *Political and Social Thought in the Contemporary Middle East* (New York: Praeger, 1970), p. 12.

29. In early June, 1964, Turkey was prepared to invade Cyprus on the claim that the UN forces were unable to preserve the peace. The American ambassador was informed of the impending military action against Cyprus, and this elicited the letter by President Johnson to Prime Minister İnönü. Robert E. Riggs, *Foreign Policy and US/UN International Organization* (New York: Appleton-Century-Crofts, 1971), p. 129.

30. Robert McNamara, secretary of defense, had expressed his conviction that in a war Turkey would be victorious against Greece. Edward Weintal and Charles Bartlett, *Facing the Brink* (New York: Scribners, 1967), p. 30.

31. *New York Times*, June 24, 1964. Professor Nihat Erim, prime minister of Turkey from March, 1971, until April, 1972, gives an excellent account of Prime Minister İnönü's visit in 1964 to Washington, D.C., and the American proposals that were presented to Turkey. Professor Erim accompanied Prime Minister İnönü to the United States and was an active participant in the talks concerning Cyprus, both in the United States and Geneva. Nihat Erim, "Reminiscenses on Cyprus," *Foreign Affairs* (a quarterly review published in Turkey) 4, no. 2-3 (February 1975): 156–163.

32. The document in respect to the Geneva talks was sent to the writer by the Turkish embassy in Washington, D.C. The Turkish document was translated by the writer into English. The full account of the Geneva talks has never appeared in any other book.

33. The Cyprus issue and the Geneva conference were summarized in a speech, "Cyprus: The Anatomy of the Problem," delivered by Dean Acheson before the Chicago Bar Association, March 24, 1965.

34. Ibid.

35. Ibid.

36. United Nations. Security Council. *Verbatim Record of the Eleven Hundred and Forty-Third Meeting*. S/PV. 1143, 9 August 1964.

37. United Nations. Security Council. *Verbatim Record of the Eleven Hundred and Forty-Second Meeting.* S/PV. 1142, 8 August 1964. Turkey's use of unilateral military action in 1964 was justified under Article IV of the Treaty of Guarantee and was consistent with the UN Charter. Greece and Cyprus argued that Turkey had violated both the sovereign equality accorded the island under Article 2, sections 2, 3, and 4 (reinforced by Article 33) of the UN Charter, which asserts a commitment on the part of member states to settle disputes peacefully and to "refrain in their international relations from the threat or use of force against the territorial integrity or political independence of any state, or in any other manner inconsistent with the Purpose of the Nations." Cyprus and Greece strengthened their argument by maintaining that Article 37, of the International Law Commission's draft Law of Treaties, provided that "a treaty is void if it conflicts with a peremptory norm of general international law from which no derogation is permitted." United Nations. General Assembly. *International Law Commission,* Draft Law of Treaties, Article 36. No. A/5509, 1963.

38. United Nations. Security Council. *Resolution Proposed by 5 Powers (S/5603), (S/5578).* S/5868, 9 August 1964.

39. *Report of the United Nations Mediator on Cyprus to the Secretary-General* (Nicosia: Public Information Office, [n.d.], pp. 23–28; see also Stephens, pp. 202–203; Linda B. Miller, *Cyprus: The Law and Politics of Civil Strife,* (Cambridge, Mass.: Harvard University Press, 1968), pp. 57–58.

40. A new mediator was not appointed to replace Plaza because of the opposition of the governments of Cyprus and Turkey. Harbottle, p. 56.

41. During this time, General Grivas conducted his own intelligence investigation of the National Guard on Cyprus and a conclusive evidence was uncovered that a conspiracy did exist. The suspected Greek Army officers were apprehended and sent back to Athens for a court-martial. Adams, *AKEL,* p. 177.

42. *New York Times,* July 18, July 31, 1966.

43. *New York Times,* July 17, 18, and 22, 1965.

44. Ibid., March 26, 27, 1966.

45. Miller, p. 59. Also *New York Times,* May 15, 1966.

46. *New York Times,* May 29, 1966.

47. *The Soviet Union and the Middle East: A Summary Record,* 23rd Annual Conference of the Middle East Institute, Washington, D.C., October 10–11, 1969, pp. 23–24.

48. United Nations. Security Council. *Provisional Verbatim Record of the Thirteen Hundred and Eighty-Third Meeting.* S/PV/1383, 24 November 1967.

49. United Nations. Security Council. *Letter dated 27 November 1967 from the Permanent Representative of the Soviet Union Addressed to the Security Council.* S/8268, 27 November 1967.

50. Ibid.

51. Quoted in *New York Times,* September 11, 1967.

52. *Turkish Digest* (Washington, D.C.: Office of the Press Counselor, Turkish Embassy) 6, no. 3 (March 1970): 5.

53. *Times* (London), November 29, 1967. General Grivas's attack was approved by the Greek government with the objective of putting the Turkish Cypriots in their place, or, as *Economist* (London), December 2, 1967, reported, "show who is the top dog."

54. United Nations. Security Council. *Special Report by the Secretary-General on Developments in Cyprus*. S/8248, 16 November 1967.

55. The UNFICYP estimated that 6,000–7,000 Greek National Army troops were sent to Cyprus. The exact number of men withdrawn between December 8 and January 16, 1968, by Greece cannot be assessed since the withdrawals were not supervised. Harbottle, pp. 165–166.

56. United Nations. Security Council. *Special Report by the Secretary-General On Recent Developments Regarding Cyprus* (S/8323), 3 January 1968. This writer was informed by the director of the Cyprus Turkish Information Center, Zafer Ali Zihni, on June 3, 1972, that the "Turkish Cypriot Provisional Administration" was changed to the "Cyprus Turkish Administration" in the middle of 1971. See also United Nations, Security Council. *Report by the Secretary-General on the United Nations Operation in Cyprus* (For the period 1 December 1971 to 26 May 1972). (S/10664), 26 May 1972. For the full text of the Basic Provisions, see appendix H.

57. Salih, p. 157.

58. United Nations. Security Council. *Report by the Secretary-General on the United Nations Operation in Cyprus* (For the period 8 June to 2 December 1968). S/8914, 4 December 1968.

59. United Nations. Security Council. *Report by the Secretary-General on the United Nations Operation in Cyprus* (For the period 3 June to 1 December 1969). S/9521, 3 December 1969.

60. Ibid.

61. *Cyprus Mail*, March 9, 1970.

62. *Time*, March 23, 1970.

63. *Cyprus Mail*, March 13 and 28, 1970.

64. Ibid., April 16, 1970.

65. *Christian Science Monitor*, March 19, 1970.

66. *Cyprus Mail*, April 16, 1970.

67. Ibid., July 23, 1970.

68. *Christian Science Monitor*, March 18, 1970; *Cyprus Mail*, March 13, 1970.

69. *Cyprus Mail*, March 13, 1970.

70. *Cyprus Mail*, March 14, 1970.

71. *Ibid.*, November 22, 1970; see also United Nations. Security Council. *Report by the Secretary-General on the United Nations Operation in Cyprus* (For the period 2 June 1970 to 1 December 1970). S/10005. 2 December 1970.

72. Ibid., July 17, 1970.

73. *Daily Star* (Beirut), April 5, 1971.

74. Public Information Office of the Republic of Cyprus, press release, September 21, 1971. Interview of Makarios by Robert Southgate of the Independent Television News London. To a question in respect to enosis, Makarios said: "I am in favour of Enosis."

75. *Christian Science Monitor*, September 8, 1971.

76. *Christian Science Monitor*, September 16, 1971.

77. The prime minister of Turkey, Nihat Erim, on September 10, 1971, warned the prime minister of Greece, George Papadopoulos, that if Grivas's presence led to attacks on the Turkish Cypriots, Ankara would take "strong action." *Christian Science Monitor*, September 15, 1971.

78. *Cyprus Mail*, October 27, 1971.

79. *Christian Science Monitor,* February 6, 1973.

80. Public Information Office of the Republic of Cyprus, press release, April 27, 1972. Interview of President Makarios by the Athens newspaper *Eleftheros Cosmos.*

81. *Alithia* (weekly, Nicosia), June 5, 1972, wrote that Grivas demanded the resignation of Makarios within two months when they met in March, 1972. Grivas had also demanded the resignation of three ministers—interior, foreign, and education —so that they could be replaced by persons to prepare the public for a struggle for self-determination and enosis. Makarios' response to Grivas's demands was negative.

82. *Cyprus Mail,* February 5, 1973.

83. *Elevtheria* (Nicosia), July 13, 1971.

84. *Daily Star* (Beirut), March 3, 1972.

85. *Cyprus Mail,* June 2, 1972.

86. Ibid., June 11, 1972.

87. Ibid., March 7, 1973.

88. Ibid., March 9, 1973.

89. The Greek Cypriot papers that have supported enosis and Grivas have been *Ethniki, Messemvrini, Gnomi,* and *Patris. Makhi* expresses the enosists' ideas, and its editor is Nicos Sampson, who was active in the struggle for the independence of Cyprus.

90. The regime of George Papadopoulos was overthrown by a new military junta lead by Brigadier General Dimitri Ioannides on November 25, 1973.

91. *Christian Science Monitor,* February 6, 1973.

92. Ibid., February 10, 1973.

93. Ibid., May 24, 1972.

94. United Nations. Security Council. *Report by the Secretary-General on the United Nations Operation in Cyprus* (For the period 20 May to 30 November 1971). S/10401, 30 November 1971.

95. Ibid.

CHAPTER 5

1. A private interview with Dr. Neçdet Ünel, president of the House of Representatives of the Turkish Cypriot Administration, in Nicosia, June 10, 1972.

2. *United Nations General Assembly, Official Records,* Nineteenth Session, 1964-1965 Annexes, vol. 1. (New York: United Nations, 1966), pp. 11–13; United Nations. Security Council. *Report by the Secretary-General dated 10 September 1964 on the United Nations Operations in Cyprus.* S/5950 and Add. 1, 2-, 10 September 1964; United Nations. Security Council. *Report by the Secretary-General on the United Nations Operations in Cyprus.* S/6102, 12 December 1964; James A. Stegenga, *The United Nations's Force in Cyprus* (Columbus, Ohio: Ohio State University Press, 1968), pp. 142–149; Vali, p. 255.

3. The foreign assets of the Cyprus government increased from $105,320,000 in 1963 to $209,910,000 at the end of 1969. The increase is due to: (1) Foreign military expenditures in Cyprus annually: $61,460,000; (2) Turkish government assistance to the Turkish Cypriots: approximately $20,000,000 annually; (3) tourism: $14,460,000 annually. Turkish Communal Chamber (Cyprus) *Special News Bulletin,* June 18, 1970. Annually, Greece spends about $20,400,000 on its military forces in Cyprus. Purcell, p. 378.

4. The Greek Cypriots are the major benefactors of the tourist trade, because of bad publicity given the tourists by the Greeks concerning the Turkish Cypriot sectors and the limited availability of hotels and entertainment facilities. Tourism in 1972 earned Cyprus about $48 million from 228,300 foreign visitors. *Los Angeles Times,* February 25, 1973. As stated earlier, President Makarios prohibited the supply of building materials to the Turkish sectors from 1964 until March 7, 1968. Since then, the Turkish sectors have been able to construct new hotels and other facilities to attract tourists.

5. United Nations. Security Council. *Report by the Secretary-General on the United Nations Operation in Cyprus* (For the period 1 December 1971 to 26 May 1972). S/ 10664, 26 May 1972. The report makes a reference to the decision of the Turkish Cypriot leadership to establish a "provisional Cyprus Turkish administration." Thereafter, the use of the term "Turkish Cypriot Administration" became a common practice among the Turkish Cypriots.

6. United Nations Force in Cyprus. U.N. Information Office, press release UNC 292.4, January, 1968.

7. *Bozkurt,* July 7, 1970; *Cyprus Mail,* July 8, 1970. The thirty Turkish Cypriot Legislative Assembly members include seven lawyers, five medical doctors, three holding B.A. degrees in political science, four journalists, one dentist, one veterinary surgeon, and nine members of the civil service, army, and business. The average age is between forty and forty-five. The oldest member is sixty and the youngest is thirty years of age. Turkish Communal Chamber (Cyprus) *Special News Bulletin,* No. 1882, July 11, 1970.

8. Turkish Communal Chamber (Cyprus) *Special News Bulletin,* No. 1884, July 15, 1970.

9. Ibid.

10. *Bozkurt* and *Halkın Sesi,* February 17, 1973.

11. *Special News Bulletin,* February 17, 1973.

12. Ibid., February 22, 1973.

13. In reality the Turkish Cypriot defense force is under the leadership and command of an officer from Turkey, with the rank of colonel, whose official title is *bayraktar* ("standard-bearer"), and the person who is second in command is known as *sancaktar* ("flag-bearer"). These two individuals, in conjunction with the commander of the Turkish contingents in Cyprus, have the supreme authority in most civil as well as military matters in the Turkish Cypriot sectors, and for their actions they are answerable to Ankara.

14. United Nations. Security Council. *Report by the Secretary-General on the United Nations Operation in Cyprus* (For the period 2 December 1969 to 1 June 1970). S/9814, 1 June 1970.

15. Turkish Communal Chamber (Cyprus) *Special News Bulletin,* No. 1293, February 21, 1968.

CHAPTER 6

1. *Cyprus Mail,* July 18, 1970.

2. Rauf R. Denktaş, "Cyprus: On the Threshold of New Talks," *Foreign Policy* (a quarterly review published in Ankara, Turkey) 2, no. 2 (January, 1972): 64.

3. *Cyprus Mail*, March 30, 1971.

4. Ibid., June 17, 1971.

5. Denktaş, p. 60.

6. *The Cyprus Problem: A Brief Review* (Nicosia: Cyprus Turkish Information Centre, February, 1970), pp. 17–19.

7. United Nations. Security Council. *Report by the Secretary-General on the United Nations Operation in Cyprus* (For the period 2 December 1969 to 1 June 1970). S/9814, 1 June 1970.

8. United Nations. Security Council. *Report by the Secretary-General on the United Nations Operation in Cyprus* (For the period 1 December 1971 to 26 May 1972). S/10664, 26 May 1972.

9. *Cyprus Mail*, June 9, 1972.

10. Ibid., June 10, 1972.

11. Ibid., June 1, 1972.

12. In March, 1973, the supporters of Makarios, as a reprisal against the Grivas sympathizers' raids on police stations, exploded bombs on their properties. No life was lost and property damage was minor, but the wave of violence between the Makarios and Grivas collaborators may escalate. *Christian Science Monitor*, March 19, 1973.

CHAPTER 7

Note: A part of this study was presented at the annual meeting of the Southwestern Political Science Association at San Antonio, Texas, March 27, 29, 1975.

1. According to an article in *Milliyet* on Nikos G. Sampson, it was the consensus of the enosists to declare the union of Cyprus with Greece on July 22, 1974, after the overthrow of President Makarios. However, because of the lack of support for the plan by the Greek officers from the mainland, the planned military move was never executed. The plan called for the declaration of enosis after the invasion of Cyprus by Turkey, and Greece was to launch an attack against the Turkish forces on the mainland of Turkey and on Cyprus. *Milliyet*, July 19, 1975.

2. About 400 to 450 Greek Cypriots were killed during the coup d'état. *Cyprus Mail*, April 25, 1975.

3. On July 21, 1974, a Turkish jet by mistake attacked and sank the 3,500-ton Turkish destroyer *Kocatepe* (ex-U.S.S. *Harwood*) off the coast of Paphos. The Turkish destroyer was mistaken for a Greek warship. An Israeli vessel had rescued 42 survivors on life rafts and about 40 to 80 crew members were dead and 110 missing. *New York Times*, July 23, 1974.

4. Retired Vice Admiral Petros Arapakis, on January 9, 1975, said that he had opposed the military junta's July, 1974, threat to declare war against Turkey, and that he was opposed to sending the Greek fleet to Cyprus without air cover. *Facts on File* 35, no. 1784 (January 18, 1975): 30.

5. Since 1964 the Turkish government has been very discreet concerning its economic, financial, political, and military alignment with the West. The American diplomatic pressure and arms embargo applied on Turkey since 1974 has forced the Turks to reevaluate their foreign policy commitments. Turkey has implemented a

policy of reconciliation with its communist neighbors in the areas of economics, finance, technology, and arms trade. On July 9, 1975, Turkey and the Soviet Union signed a $700 million credit agreement. The Soviets undertook to supply Turkey with machinery to build an iron and steel mill, an aluminum plant, and two thermal power stations. The Soviet aid to Turkey is more than $1 billion since 1967. Premier Alexei N. Kosygin attended the new steel mill complex opening on December 27, 1975, in Iskenderun. The four-day visit of Premier Kosygin is a sign of continued development of new political ties between Moscow and Ankara. There are speculations that in the very near future the two countries will sign a nonaggression pact and that there will be more arms sales to Turkey. *Cyprus Mail*, February 8, and July 10, 1975. See also *New York Times* and *Christian Science Monitor*, December 22, 28, and 30, 1975.

6. At the conclusion of the four-day visit of Libyan Prime Minister Abdel Salem Jallud to Turkey, on January 6, 1975, a general agreement on political, economic, and technical relations was signed which provided: (1) Libya would provide Turkey with 3 million tons of crude oil and 250,000 tons of fuel oil annually at "special" low prices; (2) a Libyan grant for the building of an oil refinery in Turkey; (3) the construction of a cement factory and of all highways in Libya by the Turkish Highways Department; (4) transference of skilled and unskilled Turkish workers (about 100,000) to Libya to meet most of Libya's labor needs; 3,000 Turkish technicians and skilled workers are already working in Libya; (5) Turkey would provide Libya with unspecified small arms; (6) Turkey declared itself in favor of a "complete and unconditional withdrawal of Israeli troops from the occupied Arab territories"; and (7) Libya expressed its support for Turkey on the Cyprus conflict. *Cumhuriyet*, January 6, 1975. See also *Middle East Intelligence Survey* (Tel Aviv: Middle East Information Media Ltd.) 2, no. 20 (January 15, 1975): 160., and *Facts on File 35*, no. 1784 (January 18, 1975): 30. In 1975 Libya gave Turkey seven F-5 A warplanes as part of $33 million of military aid. *Brief* (an Israeli fortnightly publication on Middle East Affairs) 1-5, no. 117 (November, 1975).

7. On July 21, 1974, President Zulfikar Ali Bhutto of Pakistan offered to send volunteers to fight with Turkish soldiers in Cyprus. *Hürriyet*, July 22, 1974.

8. By the use of the term *national interest*, the author is stressing a foreign policy by which the entire Turkish peoples will benefit. The Turkish national interest is whatever the majority of the people say it is. Turkey's action in Cyprus was to protect its national interest versus that of Greece. Whatever strengthens national security and protects the way of life of the people is in the national interest.

9. See two informative articles on the opium question: James W. Spain, "The United States, Turkey and the Poppy," *Middle East Journal* 29, no. 3 (Summer, 1975):295–309; Yüksel Söylemez, "The Question of Narcotic Drugs and Turkey," *Foreign Policy* (Turkey) 4, no. 4 (June, 1975):144–155.

10. On February 5, 1975, Prime Minister Sadı Irmak said that Turkey would review all its military commitments to the U.S. and NATO. Turkey is considering shutting down the twenty powerful early-warning installations that the U.S. uses to monitor Soviet military movements and missile activity. The U.S. major radar and tracking stations in Turkey are located at Sinop, Diyarbakır, and Incirlik. *Christian Science Monitor*, February 6, 1975. See also *Newsweek*, February 24, 1975, p. 36. On June 17, 1975, a day after the meeting of the National Security Council of Turkey, a note was delivered to the American ambassador, William B. Macomber, Jr., in

Ankara asking the U.S. to start negotiations on the future of the American military installations within the thirty days. The note stated that if "action is not taken to initiate the talks" the twenty-five American military installations will be subjected "to a new situation." The NATO bases will not be affected by the Turkish action; furthermore, Turkey's commitment to the western defense system was unchanged. The Turkish government holds the opinion that the bilateral agreements between the two states was unilaterally relegated to a piece of paper by the U.S. congressional action. Turkey cannot even buy the arms it needs on commercial terms, and the weapons it had ordered and paid for before the congressional arms embargo cannot be delivered, forcing the Turks to pay for storage. Applying the embargo to arms already paid for is an unprecedented action against an ally of the U.S. *Hürriyet* June 16, 17, 18, 1975. See also *New York Times* and *Christian Science Monitor*, June 17, 18, 1975.

The Turkish takeover of key American electronic intelligence-gathering stations has cost the United States about 25 percent of its ability to monitor Soviet missile launches. At the European Security and Cooperation Conference in Helsinki, Finland, Prime Minister Demirel refused the offer of $50 million in military aid to Turkey by President Ford to induce the Turks to reopen the American bases. *New York Times*, August 1, 1975. Turkey has demanded an annual payment of about $500 million from the U.S. as one of its conditions for reopening the American bases. The money demanded is to indemnify Turkey against the risk of nuclear attack from the Soviet Union. *Christian Science Monitor*, November 12, 1975.

11. On July 20, the U.S. Army placed an 800-man paratroop batallion on alert in Italy in case it was needed to evacuate American citizens from Cyprus. Rumors state that the American force might have been used to destroy the U.S. intelligence radio installations on the island in order to prevent them from falling into the hands of the Greek communist party members. On September 8, the U.S. Defense Department disclosed that a Marine detachment was on alert to remove atomic weapons stockpiled in Greece and Turkey in the event of war between the two states. *Facts on File*, 34, no. 1767 (September 21, 1974): 765.

12. Ibid., no. 1759 (July 27, 1974): 590.

13. Unsubstantiated rumors state that on July 25–26 Greece landed 1,500–3,000 troops at night at the port of Karavostasi in the northwest. Furthermore, Greece had brought reinforcements to Cyprus in fourteen Greek transport planes that landed in Nicosia airport.

The former navy commander Admiral Kemal Kayacan stated that Turkey was ready to strike against Greece in 1974 if Greece had attacked Turkey because of the Cyprus invasion. *Hürriyet*, July 21, 1975.

14. The U.S. Embassy in Athens on August 21 released a statement that during the Greco-Turkish crises in 1974, arms in an American depot at Soudhas Bay, in western Crete, worth about $5 million were stolen by the Greek military command. *New York Times*, August 22, 1975.

15. It is estimated that there are about 2,000 to 3,000 EOKA-B members. *Cyprus Mail*, April 8, 1975.

16. A Turkish writer analyzes the pro-Greek sentiment of the British as follows: "several sentimental factors have also affected the British attitude towards Greece and Cypriot Greeks. . . . the close Greek relations with Britain all through its history ever since Greece became independent. On the other hand, only fifty years ago Tur-

key had fought against a common British-Greek front. Religious factors are also significant. The Christian-Moslem distinction still carries an influence, at least subconsciously, in the assessment of contemporary international problems. The deep influences of ancient Greek civilization on the Western world may be another factor in forming the attitudes towards international problems involving Greece. . . . the fear that a new Cyprus adventure might bring a repetition of the dreadful difficulties with which EOKA action in Cyprus had confronted the British colonial administration in the 1950's." Ömer Kürkçüoğlu, "British Policy During 1974 Cyprus Crisis," *Foreign Policy* (a quarterly review published in Turkey) 4, no. 2–3 (February, 1975): 185.

17. U.S. Department of State, Bureau of Public Affairs, September 23, 1974, news release.

18. According to reports, Secretary of State Henry Kissinger knew in advance that Turkey planned to invade Cyprus in July, 1974, and rejected the suggestion of U.S. Ambassador to Greece Henry Tasca that the Sixth Fleet be used to block them. Kissinger was opposed to the American involvement in the crisis, pledging to Athens that the U.S. would "get the Turks out of Cyprus." *Washington Post*, November 21, 1974.

19. The new U.S. Ambassador to Cyprus is William R. Crawford, who was ambassador to Yemen. Crawford was former deputy chief of mission in Nicosia.

20. On August 22, Prime Minister Bülent Ecevit hinted that Turkey might provide port facilities for the U.S. Sixth Fleet if Greece withdrew its facilities. *New York Times*, August 23, 1974.

21. On April 27, 1975, Athens announced that the United States will: (1) Close its air base adjoining Hellenikon airport at Athens; (2) Stop the use of Elefsis, 17 miles west of Athens, as a home port for six destroyers and 1,700 crewmen as well as for 1,100 dependents who live on the mainland. By September, 1975, the American use of Elefsis is to terminate and the dependents are expected to be out. (3) The remaining U.S. bases in Greece will come under control of the Greek commanders. *Christian Science Monitor*, May 1, 1975 see also *Time*, May 12, 1975.

22. On NBC TV "Today" show, on February 6, 1975, U.S. Secretary of Defense James Schlesinger said that the U.S. military aid cutoff to Turkey was not in the best interest of NATO and that the Turks had been singled out and punished by Congress for their use of American weapons to invade Cyprus. He went on to say that other U.S. allies had used weapons supplied by America to suppress fighters for independence, which was a violation of the provisions of the foreign military aid bill of 1961.

The suspension of arms assistance and sales to Turkey in 1975 involved about $200 million, including $90 million in sales, $80 million in grants, and $10 million for supply service. The ban also applied to the $230 million contract in tank equipment for the modernization of Turkey's M-48 tanks, which was to resume in 1977. *Time*, February 17, 1975, p. 55. See also *Facts on File* 35, no. 1784 (January 18, 1975): 30.

23. The Turkish government increased its military budget for 1975 to $1.85 billion, a 50 percent increase over the 1974 budget. Since the Cyprus invasion, Turkey has emphasized development of self-sufficiency in weaponry.

24. Between October 29, 1974, and January 27, 1975, Turkey withdrew 6,000 soldiers from Cyprus as a good-will gesture to pacify the members of the U.S. Congress. The war has been very costly to both the Greeks and the Turks, financially,

militarily, and in human terms. Turkey is selling "peace operation" bonds to pay for its Cyprus invasion. Turkey's military operations in Cyprus have cost the Turks $2.5 billion, 500 dead, and 6,000 wounded. The Greek war dead are estimated to be about 6,000. *Cyprus Mail*, April 25, 1975.

25. Secretary of State Kissinger reiterated the administration's opposition to the "cutoff of aid to Turkey, regardless of what progress may be made in the negotiations." U.S. Department of State, Secretary of State, press conference, Bureau of Public Affairs, January 28, 1975. The U.S. policy in respect to Cyprus was further clarified in a statement released by the Department of State in March, 1975. "We (the U.S.) believe that the Cyprus question can only be resolved through a fair and freely negotiated settlement which preserves the sovereignty, territorial integrity, and independence of Cyprus, alleviates human suffering on the island, and enables Cypriots to live in peace and security. We have sought to discourage unilateral actions by either side that would complicate efforts to achieve a peaceful settlement. We will do all we can to support political negotiations between the two communities on the island, and to play an active role in assisting them to reconcile their differences and to achieve a peace of conciliation." U.S. Department of State, Bureau of Public Affairs, March, 1975, news release.

26. *Foreign Assistance Act of 1961, Statute at Large* 75, section 505 (1961); *United States Code Congressional and Administrative News, 87th Congress—First Session, 1961,* Vol. 1, *Laws, Messages, Executive Orders, Proclamations, etc.* (St. Paul, Minn.: West Publishing, 1961), p. 483 The Foreign Assistance Act of 1961, section 505, states that "military assistance to any country shall be furnished solely for internal security, for legitimate self-defense, to permit the recipient country to participate in regional or collective arrangements or measures consistent with the Charter of the United Nations, or otherwise to permit the recipient country to participate in collective measures requested by the United Nations for the purpose of maintaining or restoring international peace and security."

The Turkish action was also judged to be contrary to the United Nations Charter, Article 2 (4), which stipulates that all members are to "settle their international disputes by peaceful means in such a manner that international peace and security, and justice, are not endangered."

27. *Foreign Military Sales Act, Statutes at Large* 82, Section 4 (1968); *United States Code Congressional and Administrative News, 90th Congress—Second Session, 1968,* Vol. 1, *Laws* (St. Paul, Minn.: West Publishing, 1968), pp. 1544–1545. The Foreign Military Sales Act of 1968, section 4, states: "Defense articles and defense services shall be sold by the United States Government under this Act to friendly countries solely for·internal security, for legitimate self-defense, to permit the recipient country to participate in regional or collective arrangements or measures consistent with the Charter of the United Nations, or otherwise to permit the recipient country to participate in collective measures requested by the United Nations for the purpose of maintaining or restoring international peace and security. . . . "

28. There are about 2.8 million Greek-Americans in the United States.

29. President Gerald R. Ford in his speech on the state of the world before a joint session of Congress in April, 1975, reaffirmed his conviction that Congress should lift the arms embargo against Turkey. He continued, saying: " . . . I earnestly ask Congress to weigh the broader considerations and consequences of its past actions on the complex Greek and Turkish dispute over Cyprus. Our foreign policy cannot

be simply a collection of special economic or ethnic or ideological interests. There must be a deep concern for the overall design of our international actions. . . . United States military assistance to an old and faithful ally—Turkey—has been cut off by action of the Congress. This has imposed an embargo on military purchases by Turkey, extending even to items already paid for—an unprecedented act against a friend. These moves, I know, were sincerely intended to influence Turkey in the Cyprus negotiations. . . . We are continuing our earnest efforts to find equitable solutions to the problems which exist between Greece and Turkey. But the results of the congressional action have been to block progress toward reconciliation, thereby prolonging the suffering on Cyprus; to complicate our ability to promote successful negotiations; to increase the danger of a broader conflict. . . . Our longstanding relationship with Turkey is not simply a favor to Turkey; it is a clear and essential mutual interest. Turkey lies on the rim of the Soviet Union and at the gates of the Middle East. It is vital to the security of the eastern Mediterranean, the southern flank of Western Europe, and the collective security of the Western alliance. Our U.S. military bases in Turkey are critical to our own security as they are to the defense of NATO." U.S. Department of State, Bureau of Public Affairs, April 10, 1975, news release.

The House of Representatives voted on October 3 to partially end the eight-month military arms embargo against Turkey. The Congress agreed to permit Turkey to have the $185 million in arms already purchased, because of the Turkish elections on October 12. The refusal to ease the embargo would have forced Premier Demirel to take further action against the American bases in Turkey before the Turkish elections. Furthermore, the U.S. did not wish to jeopardize Demirel's position since he was more favorable to the American presence in Turkey than his opposition. President Ford was asked to report back to Congress within 60 days on the progress made to reach a Cyprus settlement and on the issue of opium. By this congressional action, Turkey was permitted to buy arms in the U.S. through commercial channels, but not through the American government. *New York Times*, October 3 and 7, 1975. The U.S. Senate Foreign Relations Committee on February 7 approved a bill providing $155 million in military aid to Turkey, which was $50 million less than requested by President Ford. It made the aid contingent on progress toward a Cyprus settlement, a requirement the Turks find unacceptable. *New York Times*, February 8, 1976.

30. When Secretary of State Kissinger attended the CENTO meeting in Ankara in May, 1975, he failed to persuade Bülent Eçevit to agree to any concessions to be made by Premier Demirel to Prime Minister Caramanlis when they met in Brussels during the NATO conference. In the absence of a truce between the Justice party and the Republican Peoples party, whose head is Eçevit, Premier Demirel cannot make any concessions on Cyprus.

31. The militarization campaign includes the islands of Chios, Samos, Lesbos, Nikaria, and Rhodes. *Cyprus Mail*, April 11, 1975. The militarization of the Aegean Islands by Greece is contrary to the Italian Peace Treaty signed in Paris on February 10, 1947. Section V, Article 14, of the treaty states that the Dodecanese Islands, namely Stampalia (Astropalia), Rhodes (Rhodos), Calki (Kharki), Scarpanto, Casos (Casso), Piscopis (Tilos), Misiros (Nisyros), Calminos (Kalymnos), Leros, Patmos, Lipsos (Lipso), Simi (Symi), Cos (Kos), and Castellorizo "shall be and shall remain demilitarized." Fred L. Israel, ed., *Major Peace Treaties of Modern History 1648–1967* (New York: McGraw-Hill, 1967), p. 2429.

32. *Cyprus Mail,* October 19, 1974.

33. Information released by the Department of State in March, 1975, states that "an international relief effort, coordinated by the UN High Commissioner for Refugees, was organized to meet the immediate needs of the Greek and Turkish Cypriot refugees. From July 1974 to February 1975 the total international relief effort amounted to $45 million. Of this total, the U.S. contributed $14.1 million in cash and supplies." U.S. Department of State, Bureau of Public Affairs, March, 1975, news release.

34. *New York Times,* August 2 and 4, 1975.

35. In an interview, Turkish Foreign Minister Melih Esenbel said "that Greek concessions on Cyprus could not be traded for Turkish concessions or Turkish rights on Turkey's continental shelf in the Aegean." Turkey considers them to be two separate issues and is unwilling to discuss a package deal. *Christian Science Monitor,* January 20, 1975. Turkey boycotted the NATO exercises in February-March because of Greek restrictions on flights over the Aegean Sea.

Since the Turkish invasion of Cyprus, Athens has placed military installations on the Dodecanese Islands in the Aegean Sea, which Turkey considers to be in violation of the 1947 Treaty of Paris, which stipulated that they will remain demilitarized. *Facts on File* 35, no. 1797 (April 19, 1975): 263.

36. *New York Times,* June 1, 1975.

37. At the first United Nations International Conference on the Law of the Sea Conference held in Caracas, Venezuela, in 1974, a decision was reached permitting coastal countries to extend their territorial waters from 3 miles to 12 miles. It was also agreed to allow countries to lay claim to economic zones stretching 200 miles from their shores. At the fourth session of the Law of the Sea Conference held in New York in March, 1976, Turkey informed the participants in a memorandum that it will emphatically oppose any decision to extend Greece's territorial waters to 12 miles, thus giving Greek islands along the Turkish coast control over the continental shelf. Foreign Minister Ihsan Sabri Caglayangıl said: "Everybody now knows the possible political and military consequences of extending territorial waters in the Aegean to twelve miles." Turkey wishes to settle the issue in a fair manner through a bilateral Greek-Turkish agreement; otherwise, Greece's attempt to enforce the 12-mile limit will lead to a Greco-Turkish military confrontation. *Christian Science Monitor,* March 17, 1976.

38. *Facts on File* 35, no. 1803 (May 31, 1975): 373. The Nicosia international airport as of March 15, 1976, was not yet in operation due to the inability of the two ethnic groups to reach a consensus over the joint jurisdiction.

39. *New York Times,* December 4, 1974.

40. During his five-day visit to Cyprus on January 2, 1975, the former Turkish premier Bülent Ecevit told the Turkish Cypriots that Turkey would not retreat from the situation brought about by the Turkish invasion and that Turkey does not recognize Makarios as president of Cyprus. *Halkın Sesi,* January 3, 1975.

41. *Facts on File* 34, no. 1778 (December 7, 1974): 97.

42. *Bozkurt,* February 14, 1975. *Cumhuriyet,* February 14, 1975. See also *Time,* February 24, 1975, pp. 32–33. *Christian Science Monitor,* February 18, 1975. *New York Times,* February 18, 1975.

43. *Cyprus Mail,* February 20, 1975. *Halkın Sesi and Bozkurt,* February 19, 20, and 21, 1975. See also *Facts on File* 35, no. 1805 (June 14, 1975). For the complete text

of the Turkish Cypriot federal state constitution see appendix I. The Turkish Cypriots postponed the referendum from May 18 to June 8 because of political pressure applied on Turkey by the U.S., Great Britain, and Greece.

44. On January 13, 1976, Glafkos Clerides submitted his resignation to Makarios as the Greek Cypriot negotiator because of a conflict of opinion over the issue of the bizonal federation as demanded by the Turks. Clerides had made statements to the effect that he would consider some parts of the Turkish proposals acceptable. Later he withdrew his resignation after a plea from Prime Minister Karamanlis. *Cyprus Mail*, January 14, 15, and 16, 1976. The communal talks between Clerides and Denktaş in New York in September, 1975, and in Vienna in February, 1976, under the auspices of Secretary General Kurt Waldheim made no progress.

45. On August 27,1974, newspapers reported that a Greek Cypriot Liberation Army had been formed and was undergoing training in the Troodos mountains. It included members from EOKA-B and the National Guard. A new Greek Cypriot movement whose goal is to unite Greeks "in the struggle for survival and the liberation of the island" has been organized in Nicosia and held its first meeting on May 25, 1975. According to a newspaper report in *Phileleftheros* on May 26, the members of the movement were linked to the coup d'etat against President Makarios in July, 1974.

46. Following the compulsory retirement of Brigadier General Ioannides on August 25, 1974, Premier Karamanlis forced sixteen other brigadier generals into retirement the following day, along with hundreds of lower-ranking officers who were supporters of the junta. On October 23, George Papadopoulos and four ex-junta members were arrested and exiled to the Aegean island of Kea, sixty miles southwest of Athens. Papadopoulos' four aides were Michael Roufogalis, former chief of the Greek intelligence service; Ioannis Ladas, former head of the military police; and two former cabinet ministers, Stylianos Patakos and Nikolaos Makarezos. On December 30 another twelve ex-junta members including Brigadier General Dimitri Ioannides were arrested, and on January 20, 1975, were charged with insurrection and high treason against the nation-state. On August 23, George Papadopoulos, Nikolaos Makarezos, and Stylianos Patakos were sentenced to die in front of the firing squad, but two days later the death sentences were commuted to life imprisonment by the Greek Cabinet. The same month, Brigadier General Dimitri Ioannides was sentenced to life imprisonment. By January 11, 1976, Ioannides had been given two terms of life imprisonment and an additional sentence of eight years on two separate charges. He was given five years for ordering the destruction of the files of the EAT-ESA interrogation camp run by the special investigation branch of the military police, and three years for being instigator of the torture of two members of parliament. The files contained 3,027 documents relating to interrogation of the political prisoners. The documents were destroyed after the collapse of his eight-month-old dictatorship. *New York Times*, August 24, 1975, and January 11, 1976. *Facts on File* 36, no. 1838 (January 31, 1976): 73. On March 16, 1976, Ioannides was given an additional fourteen years of imprisonment for instigating a military coup against the civilian Greek government in February, 1975. He was accused, along with former colonel Demetrios Papapostolou, who was sentenced to ten years in prison, for giving directions for a conspiracy to junior military officers who visited them in prison. *New York Times*, March 17, 1976. Despina, wife of Papadopoulos, was charged on September 4, 1974, with collecting a government salary during her husband's administration

without working. *Christian Science Monitor*, January 20, 1975. On November 18, 1975, she was indicted on charges of fraud against the government. She was alleged to have received salaries totaling $25,000 from the Greek intelligence service from April, 1967, through November, 1973, though she rendered no services. *Facts on File* 35, no. 1829 (November 29, 1975): 894.

47. On February 24, 1975, Karamanlis' government announced that it had foiled an attempted coup to restore the ousted military junta. The military officers that were involved in the coup planning were stationed in the environs of Athens, and in northern Greece. The officers involved in the coup were dissatisfied with Prime Minister Karamanlis' policies over Cyprus, the purges of the pro-junta elements from the armed forces, and the political freedoms restored to the communist party members. *New York Times*, February 25, 1975. In a later development, on March 5 twenty generals were forced into retirement by the Greek government. On March 15, Athens retired 140 army, navy, and air force officers as part of its purge of officers sympathetic to the junta. They were also charged to have been involved in the February coup attempt against the government of Premier Karamanlis. *New York Times*, March 16, 1975.

CHAPTER 8

1. On March 19, 1975, Great Britain, in a white paper, strongly committed itself to cutting its defense expenditures in the next ten years. Britain will withdraw most of its forces from east of the Suez Canal by April, 1976. Britain will concentrate its forces in NATO's central region, the Eastern Atlantic and English Channel areas. The cutback is designed to ease the strains on the British economy. *Cyprus Mail*, March 20, 1975.

2. The United States Central Intelligence Agency operates similar monitoring stations in Hong Kong, London, Nigeria, Okinawa, Vienna, Puerto Rico, and other places. They monitor worldwide radio and television broadcasts. The Foreign Broadcast Information Service (FBIS) monitoring station at Karavas, Kyrenia, was closed by the Turkish Cypriot administration in July, 1975. *New York Times*, July 27, 1975.

APPENDIX: G

1. Following the assassination of President John Fitzgerald Kennedy on November 22, 1963, Vice-President Lyndon Baines Johnson succeeded him as President. From November 22, 1963, until January 20, 1965, the United States was without a Vice-President because at that time there was no constitutional provision for filling a vacancy in the Vice-Presidency; therefore, President Johnson felt that he should not travel outside the United States during that time since there was no one who could perform his state duties in his absence or replace him immediately in the event that he was unable to perform his duties. On January 20, 1965, following national elections in November, 1964, Lyndon B. Johnson was sworn in as President with Hubert Horatio Humphrey as his Vice-President. The Presidential succession was clarified by the 25th Amendment to the Constitution in 1967.

BIBLIOGRAPHY

Adams, Thomas Williams. *AKEL: The Communist Party of Cyprus*. California: Hoover Institution Press, 1971.

―――. "Cyprus: A Possible Prototype For Terminating the Colonial Status of a Strategically Located Territory." Ph.D. dissertation. University of Oklahoma, 1962. (Microfilm.)

―――. *U.S. Army Area Handbook for Cyprus*. Washington, D.C.: Government Printing Office, 1964.

Adams, Thomas Williams, and Alvin J. Cottrell. *Cyprus Between East and West*. Baltimore: The Johns Hopkins Press, 1968.

Aimilianides, Achilleus K. *Hellenic Cyprus*. Nicosia: Ethnarchic Council of Cyprus, 1946.

Alastos, Doros. *Cyprus Guerrilla: Grivas, Makarios, and the British*. London: Heinemann, 1960.

―――. *Cyprus in History: A Survey of 5,000 Years*. London: Zeno, 1955.

―――. *Cyprus: Past and Future*. London: Committee for Cyprus Affairs, 1943

Andriopoulos, Angelo. "The United Nations Peacekeeping Force in Cyprus and the Changing Greek Regimes." Ph.D. dissertation, Fordham University, 1970. (Microfilm.)

Anthem, Thomas. *The Greeks Have a Word for It: Enosis*. London: St. Clemens Press, [n.d.].

Armaoğlu, Fahir H. *Kıbrıs Meselesi, 1954–1959: Türk Hükümeti ve Kamu Oyunun Davranışları*. Ankara: Sevinc Matbaası, 1963.

Arnold, Percy. *Cyprus Challenge*. London: Hogarth Press, 1956.

Barker, Dudley. *Grivas: Portrait of a Terrorist*. London: Camelot Press, 1959.

Bartlett, Charles. *Facing the Brink*. New York: Scribners, 1967.

Bedevi, Vergi H. *Cyprus Has Never Been a Greek Island*. Third ed. Nicosia: Halkın Sesi Press, 1964.

Bilgi, A. Suat. *Le Conflict De Chypre et Les Cypriotes Turcs*. Ankara: Ajans-Türk Matbaası, 1961.

Bilgi, A. Suat, et al. *Cyprus: Past/Present/Future*. Ankara: Ajans-Türk Matbaası, [n.d.].

Boyd, James M. *United Nations Peace-Keeping Operations: A Military and Political Appraisal*. New York: Praeger, 1971.

Brierly, J. L. *The Law of Nations*. New York: Oxford University Press, 1963.

Brown, Neville. *Strategic Mobility*. New York: Praeger, 1964.

Chacalli, George. *Cyprus Under British Rule*. Nicosia: Phoni Tis Kyprou, 1902.

Christodoulou, D. *Cyprus Certificate Geographies*. London: Longmans, Green. 1954.

Communism in Cyprus. Nicosia: Government Printing Office, [n.d.].

Couloumbis, Theodore A. *Greek Political Reaction to American and N.A.T.O. Influences*. New Haven: Yale University Press, 1966.

Cyprus Demands Self-Determination. Washington, D.C.: Royal Greek Embassy Information Service, 1954.

Cyprus: The Background. London: Royal Institute of International Affairs, 1959. (Chatham House Memoranda.)

Cyprus: The Dispute and the Settlement. London: Oxford University Press, 1969. (Chatham House Memoranda.)

The Cyprus Problem Before the United Nations. Nicosia: Public Information Office, 1965.

Cyprus: Touchstone for Democracy. Athens: Constantinidis and Michalas, 1958.

Cyprus: Turkish Reply to Archbishop Makarios' Proposals. [n.p.] Turkish Aid Society of New York, Inc., [n.d.].

Dentkaş, Rauf R. "Cyprus: On the Threshold of New Talks," *Foreign Policy* (Ankara) 2, no. 2 (January, 1972): 64.

Dixon, Hepworth W. *British Cyprus*. London: Chapman and Hall, 1879.

Durrell, Lawrence. *Bitter Lemons*. New York: Dutton, 1957.

Eden, Anthony. *Full Circle*. London: Cassell, 1960.

Ehrlich, Thomas. *Cyprus 1958–1967*. New York: Oxford University Press, 1974.

Facts About Cyprus. Nicosia: The Cyprus Chamber of Commerce and Industry, 10th January, 1964.

Fenwick, Charles G. *International Law*. New York: Appleton-Century-Crofts, 1962.

Flinn, Henry William. *Cyprus: A Brief Survey of its History and Development*. Nicosia: W. J. Archer, 1924.

Foley, Charles. *Legacy of Strife: Cyprus From Rebellion to Civil War*. 2nd ed. Baltimore: Penguin Books, 1964.

————, ed. *The Memoirs of General Grivas*. London: Longmans, Green, 1964.

Foot, Hugh. *A Start in Freedom*. New York: Harper and Row, 1964.

Foot, Sylvia. *Emergency Exit*. London: Chatto and Windus, 1960.

Gazioğlu, Ahmet. *İngiliz İdaresinde Kıbrıs*. Istanbul: Erkin Basımevi, 1960.

Gibbons, H. Scott. *Peace Without Honour*. Ankara: ADA Publishing House, 1969.

Glahn, Gerhard von. *Law Among Nations*. New York: Macmillan, 1965.

Great Britain. Colonial Office. *Conference on Cyprus: Documents Signed and Initialled at Lancaster House on February 19, 1959*. Cmnd, 679. London: Her Majesty's Stationery Office, 1959.

————. *Constitutional Proposals for Cyprus: Report Submitted to the Secretary of State for the Colonies by the Right Hon. Lord Radcliffe, C.B.E.* Cmnd, 42. London: Her Majesty's Stationery Office, 1956.

————. *Cyprus*. Cmnd, 1093. London: Her Majesty's Stationery Office, 1960.

————. *Cyprus: Correspondence Exchanged Between the Governor and Archbishop Makarios*. Cmnd, 9708. London: Her Majesty's Stationery Office, 1956.

————. *Cyprus: Statement of Policy*. Cmnd, 455. London: Her Majesty's Stationery Office, 1958.

————. *Terrorism in Cyprus: The Captured Documents*. London: Her Majesty's Stationery Office, 1956.

————. *The Tripartite Conference on the Eastern Mediterranean*. Cmnd, 9594. London: Her Majesty's Stationery Office, 1955.

Gudek, Bahadir, et al. *Kıbrıs*. Ankara: Ajans-Türk Matbaası, 1964.

Gunnis, Rupert. *Historic Cyprus: A Guide to its Towns and Villages Monasteries and Castles*. 2nd ed. London: Methuen, 1956.

Gürsoy, Cevat et al. *Kıbrıs ve Türkler*. Ankara: Ayyılıdız Matbaası, 1964.

Harbottle, Michael. *The Impartial Soldier*. London: Oxford University Press, 1970.

Hill, Sir George Francis. *A History of Cyprus*. 4 vols. Cambridge: Cambridge University Press, 1940–1952.

History Speaks: A Documentary Survey. Nicosia: Turkish Communal Chamber, 1964.

Home, Gordon C. *Cyprus: Then and Now*. London: J. M. Dent, 1960.

Ilgaz, Hesene. *Kıbrıs Notları*. Istanbul: Doğan Kardeş Yayınları, 1949.

Information Services. *Cyprus Today*. London: Her Majesty's Stationery Office, 1955.

James, Allan. *The Politics of Peace-Keeping*. London: Praeger, 1969.

Jeffery, George. *A Description of the Historic Monuments of Cyprus*. Nicosia: William James Archer, 1918.

Jones, W. Byford. *Grivas and the Story of EOKA*. London: Robert Hale, 1959.

Karagil, Nevzat, comp. *Kıbrıs Meselesi Üzerinde Son Konuşmalar Ve Yazılar*. Istanbul: Anıl Matbaası, 1964.

Karayiannis, George. *The Cyprus Problem, December 1963–August 1964*. Nicosia: Pan Publishing House, 1967.

Karpat, Kemal H., ed. *Political and Social Thought in the Contemporary Middle East*. New York: Praeger, 1970.

Kaye, Mary Margaret. *Death Walked in Cyprus*. London: Staples Press, 1956.

Keefe, Eugene K., et al. *Area Handbook for Cyprus*. Washington D.C.: Government Printing Office, 1971.

Keshishian, Kevork K. *Romantic Cyprus*. London: Mark and Moody, 1960.

Kıbrıs Cumhuriyeti Anayasası. Lefkoşa: Kıbrıs Hükümet Matbaasında Basılmıştır, 1960.

Kocagüney, Vehbi. *Elli Bin Türk Şehidinin Yatağı Kıbrıs*. Istanbul: Ülkü Kitap Yurdu, 1953.

Kökdemir, Naci. *Kıbrıs: Dünkü–Bugünkü*. Ankara: Istiklâl Matbaası, 1956.

Koslin, Adamantia Pollis. *The Megali Idea—A Study of Greek Nationalism*. Ph.D. dissertation, The Johns Hopkins University, 1958. (Microfilm.)

Kouchouk, M. Fazıl. *The Cyprus Question: A Permanent Solution*. Nicosia: Halkın Sesi Press, 1957.

———. *The Voice of Cyprus*. Nicosia: Bozkurt Press, 1956.

Kyrou, Alexis A. *Elliniki Exoteriki Politik*. Athens: Zombola Press, 1955.

Kyriakides, Stanley. *Cyprus: Constitutionalism and Crisis Governemnt*. Philadelphia: University of Pennsylvania Press, 1968.

Lee, Dwight E. *Great Britain and the Cyprus Convention Policy of 1878*. Cambridge: Harvard University Press, 1934.

Lenczowski, George, ed. *United States Interests in the Middle East*. Washington, D.C.: American Enterprise Institute, 1968.

Loher, Franz Vond, and A. Batson Joyner. *Cyprus: Historical and Descriptive*. New York: J. J. Little, 1878.

Luard, Evan, ed. *The International Regulation of Civil Wars*. New York: New York University Press, 1972.

Luke, Sir Harry. *Cyprus: A Portrait and an Appreciation*. London: George G. Harrap, 1957.

Maier, Franz George. *Cyprus: From Earliest Time to Present Day*. London: Eleck Books, 1968.

Mayes, Stanley. *Cyprus and Makarios*. London: Putnam, 1960.

McKinnon, Campbell. *Turkey and Greece: Closer Unity—Now!* New York: Vantage Press, 1968.

McNair, Arnold Duncan. *The Law of Treaties: British Practice and Opinions*. Oxford: Clarendon Press, 1961.

Metin, Hüseyin. *Kıbrıs Tarihine Toplu Bir Bakış*. Nicosia: Halkın Sesi Basımevi, 1959.

Meyer, A. J., and Simos Vassiliou. *The Economy of Cyprus*. Cambridge: Harvard University Press, 1962.

Miller, Linda B. *Cyprus: The Law and Politics of Civil Strife*. Cambridge, Mass.: Harvard University Press, Center for International Affairs, 1968.

Newman, Philip. *A Short History of Cyprus*. London: Green, 1953.

Orr, C. W. J. *Cyprus Under British Rule*. London: Robert Scott, 1918.

Paris, Peter. *The Impartial Knife*. New York: David McKay, 1962.

Planned Massacre of Turks in Cyprus. Ankara: Turkey at Ajans-Türk Press, [n.d.].

Purcell, H. D. *Cyprus*. New York: Praeger, 1968.

Riggs, Robert E. *Foreign Policy and US/UN International Organization*. New York: Appleton-Century-Crofts, 1971.

Riza, Halit Ali. *The House of Representatives—The Separate Majority Right*. Nicosia: Halkın Sesi Press, 1963.

Rossidis, Zeno G. *The Island of Cyprus and Union With Greece*. 3rd ed. Athens: [n.p.], 1954.

Royal Institute of International Affairs. *Cyprus: The Dispute and the Settlement*. London: Chatham House, 1959.

Salih, H. İbrahim. *Cyprus: An Analysis of Cypriot Political Discord*. New York: Theo. Gaus, Sons, 1968.

Seligman, Adrian. *The Turkish People of Cyprus*. London: Press Attache's Office, Turkish Embassy, 1956.

Soviet Union and the Middle East: A Summary Record. The 23rd Annual Conference of the Middle East Institute, Washington, D. C., October 10–11, 1969.

Spears, Sir Edward. *The Orthodox Church in Cyprus*. London: Turkish Press Attache's Office, [n.d.].

Spyridakis, C. *A Brief History of Cyprus*. 3rd ed. Nicosia: Zavallis Press, 1964.

———. *A Brief History of the Cyprus Question* Nicosia: Cyprus Ethnarchy Office, 1954.

Stegenga, James A. *The United Nations Force In Cyprus*. Columbus, Ohio: The Ohio State University Press, 1968.

Stephens, Robert H. *Cyprus: A Place of Arms*. New York: Pall Mall, 1966.

Storrs, Sir Ronald. *A Chronology of Cyprus*. Nicosia: Government Printing Office, 1930.

———. *The Memoirs of Sir Ronald Storrs*. New York: G. P. Putnam's Sons, 1937.

———. *Orientation*. London: Nicholson and Watson, 1943.

Storrs, Sir Ronald, and Bryan Justin O'Brien. *The Handbook of Cyprus*. 9th ed. London: Christophers, 1930.

Tevetoğlu, Fehti. *Kıbrıs ve Kommunism*. Ankara: Ajans-Türk Matbaası, 1966.

Thorp, Willard L. *Cyprus: Suggestions for a Development Programme; Prepared for the Government of the Republic of Cyprus*. New York: United Nations, 1961.

Tornaritis, Criton G. *The Treaty of Alliance*. Nicosia: Printing Office of the Republic of Cyprus [n.d.].

Torun, Şükrü. *Türkiye, İngiltere ve Yunanistan Arasında Kıbrısın Politik Durumu*. Istanbul: Gazateciler Matbaası, 1956.

Tremayne, Penelope. *Below the Tide*. London: Hutchinson of London, 1958.

Turkey and Cyprus; A Survey of the Cyprus Question with Official Statements of the Turkish Viewpoint. London: Press Attache's Office, Turkish Embassy, 1956.

Türkiye Milli Gençlik Teşkilatı. *Kıbrıs Meselesi ve Türkiye*. Istanbul: Anıl Matbaası, 1954.

Vali, Ferenc A. *Bridge Across the Bosporus*. Baltimore: The Johns Hopkins Press, 1971.
————. *The Turkish Straits and NATO*. Stanford: Hoover Institute Press, 1971.
Weir, W. W. *Education in Cyprus*. Larnaca: American Academy, 1952.
Windsor, Philip. *NATO and the Cyprus Crisis*. Adelphi Paper No. 14. London: Institute for Strategic Studies, November 1964.
Woodhouse, C. M. *Apple of Discord: A Survey of Recent Greek Politics in their International Setting*. London: Hutchison, 1948.
Xydis, Stephen G. *Cyprus: Conflict and Conciliation 1954–1958*. Columbus: The Ohio State University Press, 1967.
————. *Cyprus: Reluctant Republic*. The Hague: Mouton, 1973.
Yanacopoulou, Ellen Antoinette. *The Cypriot Nationalist Movement*. M.A. thesis, Georgetown University, 1958.
Yasın, Özker. *Kanlı Kıbrıs; Bir Şahlanışın Destanı*. Istanbul: Varlık Yayınevi, 1964.

INDEX

196

CYPRUS: THE IMPACT OF DIVERSE NATIONALISM ON A
STATE
was composed in VIP Janson, Display in Souvenir by Chapman's Photo-
typesetting, Fullerton, California, printed by McNaughton & Gunn, Inc.,
Ann Arbor, Michigan, and bound by Kingsport Press, Kingsport, Tennessee.
Project Editor: James R. Travis
Production: Paul R. Kennedy
Book & Jacket design: Anna F. Jacobs